Bill 'Swampy' Marsh is an award-winning writer/performer of stories, songs and plays. He spent most of his youth in rural south-western New South Wales. Bill was forced to give up any idea he had of a 'career' as a cricketer when a stint at agricultural college was curtailed due to illness, and so began his hobby of writing. After backpacking through three continents and working in the wine industry, his writing hobby blossomed into a career.

His first collection of short stories, *Beckom (Pop. 64)* was published in 1988; his second, *Old Yanconian Daze*, in 1995, and his third, *Looking for Dad*, in 1998. During 1999, Bill released *Australia*, a CD of his songs and stories. That was followed in 2002 by *A Drover's Wife* and *Glory, Glory: A Tribute to the Royal Flying Doctor Service* in 2008 and *Open Roads: The Songs and Stories of Bill Swampy Marsh* in 2017. He has written soundtrack songs and music for the television documentaries *The Last Mail from Birdsville: The Story of Tom Kruse, Source to Sea: The Story of the Murray Riverboats* and the German travel documentaries *Traumzeit auf dem Stuart Highway, Clinic Flights (Tilpa & Marble Bar), Traumzeit in dem Kimberleys* and *Einsatz von Port Hedland nach Marble Bar*.

Bill has won and judged many nationwide short story and song-writing competitions and short film awards as well as running writing workshops throughout Australia. He has performed his songs and stories in outback places such as Mount Dare (pop. 10), down the Birdsville Track as part of the Great Australian Cattle Drive, on The Ghan as part of Great Southern Rail's Anzac Tribute Journey and at the Transport Hall of Fame gala dinner in Alice Springs as a support act to Slim Dusty.

More Great Australian Outback Towns and Pubs Stories is part of Bill's very successful series of Great Australian Stories including: *More Great Australian Outback Yarns* and *Great Australian Ambos Stories* (2022), *Great Australian Outback Yarns Volume I* and *Great Australian Volunteer Firies Stories* (2021), *Great Australian Outback Trucking Stories* (2019), *Great Australian Bush Funeral Stories* (2018), *Great Australian Outback Nurses Stories* (2017), *Great Australian Outback Teaching Stories* (2016), *Great Australian Outback Police Stories* (2015), *Amazing Grace: Stories of Faith and Friendship from Outback Australia* (2014) (later published as *Great Australian Bush Priest Stories*), *The Complete Book of Australian Flying Doctor Stories* and *Great Australian Outback School Stories* (2013), *Great Australian CWA Stories* (2011), *New Great Australian Flying Doctor Stories* and *The ABC Book of Great Aussie Stories for Young People* (2010), *Great Australian Stories: Outback Towns and Pubs* (2009), *More Great Australian Flying Doctor Stories* (2007), *Great Australian Railway Stories* (2005), *Great Australian Droving Stories* (2003), *Great Australian Shearing Stories* (2001) and *Great Australian Flying Doctor Stories* (1999). Bill's biography *Goldie: Adventures in a Vanishing Australia* was published in 2008 and his semi-autobiographical collection *Swampy: Tall Tales and True from Boyhood and Beyond* was published in 2012.

More information about the author can be found at:
www.billswampymarsh.com
Facebook – Bill 'Swampy' Marsh

MORE GREAT AUSTRALIAN OUTBACK TOWNS AND PUBS STORIES

BILL 'SWAMPY' MARSH

ABC
BOOKS

The ABC 'Wave' device is a trademark of the
Australian Broadcasting Corporation and is used
under licence by HarperCollins*Publishers* Australia.

HarperCollins*Publishers*
Australia • Brazil • Canada • France • Germany • Holland • India
Italy • Japan • Mexico • New Zealand • Poland • Spain • Sweden
Switzerland • United Kingdom • United States of America

HarperCollins acknowledges the Traditional Custodians
of the land upon which we live and work, and pays respect
to Elders past and present.

First published in Australia in 2023
by HarperCollins*Publishers* Australia Pty Limited
Gadigal Country
Level 13, 201 Elizabeth Street, Sydney NSW 2000
ABN 36 009 913 517
harpercollins.com.au

A catalogue record for this book is available from the National Library of Australia

ISBN 978 0 7333 4293 6 (paperback)
ISBN 978 1 4607 1587 1 (ebook)

Cover design by HarperCollins Design Studio
Cover image: Horse drinking beer at Tooth's brewery, 10 August 1942, by N. Herfort courtesy
Mitchell Library, State Library of New South Wales (FL19117759)
Author photograph by Chris Carter
Typeset in Bookman ITC Std by Kelli Lonergan
Printed and bound in Australia by McPherson's Printing Group

Dedicated to those wonderful people I've met and interviewed
along the way, and who have since passed ...
your stories will live on forever.

Warning:

This book may contain the names of Aboriginal and Torres Strait Islander people now deceased.

The stories in this compilation are derived from interviews. In order to preserve the authenticity of these oral accounts, the language used and the views expressed are faithful to the original storytelling. In doing so, some stories may cause offence.

The stories in this compilation contain material that some readers may find distressing. If you need help, please contact:

- Lifeline on 13 11 14
- Beyond Blue on 1300 224 636
- MensLine Australia on 1300 78 99 78

Publisher's note:

The publisher does not necessarily endorse the views expressed or the language used in any of the stories.

Due to the sensitivity of some of these stories, a number of place names, locations and people's names have been changed.

Special thanks to Publishing Director, Brigitta Doyle, editors Lachlan McLaine and Julia Cain, Rights and Contracts Associate Nicolette Houben, along with Head of Business Development Guy Bensaul, Royalties Manager ANZ Brendon Redmond and the promotions and sales staff at ABC Books-HarperCollins Australia, without whose support these stories may never have seen the light of day; and to my precious support crew of Chris Carter, Marguerite Hann-Syme and Margaret Worth.

Contents

Contributors

The stories contained in this book are written from interviews recorded by Bill 'Swampy' Marsh. The contributors are:

Bernard Arrantash
Richard Astbury
Tanya Battel
Ross & Helen Beckhouse
Alan 'Bronco' Brett
Andrew Cameron OAM
Chris Carter
Jane Clemson
Sue Colwill
Ray Cook
Lew Couper
Rick Darling
Les & Norma Davey
Maude Ellis
Cheryl Fontaine
John Forbes
David Freeman
Norman 'Pickles' Fulmer
Ted Gade
Bruce Gallagher
Jack 'Goldie' Goldsmith
Bob & Pat Greenhill
Bernadette Greensill
Marguerite Hann-Syme
Alfred 'Alf' Harris
David & Christine Harris
Marion Harrington
Dr Hans-Ullrich Henschel
 MD OAM
Elizabeth Hutchins

Elsie Jackson
Dean 'Lightning' Jamieson
Robyn Jessiman
Wayne Kennedy
David Kerr
Michael 'Mick' Lanagan
Angela & Daniel Lo-Faro
Jock MacDonald
Jeanette & Garry Mann
Victoria Grace 'Vicky' Marsh
Michael McInerney
Mavis Mincherton
Edna Monaghan
Mick 'The Mad Irishman'
 Monaghan
Roy Moore
Gaynor Moran
Kevin O'Brien
Paula & Tim O'Connor
Brian 'Dinga' & Justine
 Outtram
Ian Parkes
Frank & Marie Partington
John Price
Ron and Krys Pawlowski
Garry 'Gazza' Purcell
Peter 'Simpy' Simpfendorfer
John Thomas
Margaret Worth
Gary & Helen Zanardi
... and many, many more

Introduction

I've been writing the Great Australian Story series now for over twenty years. In doing so I usually spend two to three months out on the road, travelling around various parts of Australia, interviewing people. These face-to-face interviews are the ones I most enjoy because I get to sit down and chat with the people, within their own environment, more as a friend would.

Of course, I can't drive over all of Australia for each book. That'd be impractical. So I have to record a number of interviews over the phone. Unfortunately, for the past couple of years, due to COVID, my travels have been severely restricted. So, for *More Great Australian Outback Towns and Pubs Stories*, I decided to ring some of my favourite storyteller-friends, those I'd already visited over the years, in search of a yarn or two. That's when I discovered that a number of them had passed on. So, in respect to them, and in appreciation of the pleasure I've had meeting and chatting with them – sharing a few laughs and the occasional tear – I've adapted some of their original stories in this book so that, while they may have passed, their wonderful stories will continue to be read.

Little Town

For each of the books I write, I also write and record a song to go with the particular theme. For the Ambos book, it was 'Band of the Lord', a song in appreciation of the ambo-paramedics from CareFlight, Northern Territory, Helicopter Unit, and others, who helped save my life after a near-death tumble from Gunlom Falls in Kakadu National Park. For the Firies it was 'A Bush Fire', an adaptation of Henry Lawson's poem 'The Fire at Ross' Farm'. For the Trucking book, it was 'When the Mailman Comes', a song for legendary mailman-trucker Tom Kruse, who delivered mail and supplies along the Birdsville Track back in the 1930s–50s; from which John Heyer's award-winning film-documentary *The Back of Beyond* is still included in *100 Greatest Films of Australian Cinema*. For the Bush Funerals it was 'Tall Man – an Ode to Henry Lawson'. And so it goes on back through the many books I've written.

For *More Great Australian Outback Towns and Pubs* I've penned the song 'Little Town'. The inspiration or instigation most probably came from my childhood, when I lived in a little town in the south-west of New South Wales: Beckom, pop.64. In Beckom, as in most of the small places I've since visited, whenever times got tough, we all pitched in and helped each other out. And like Beckom, over the years, with the advent of modern technology and communications, better and faster transport and roads, many of those little towns have suffered. The banks leave, the railway stations get passed by, shops close and people drift off elsewhere in search of work. Yet, these small places remain a precious memory to those who have lived there. They've been an integral part of someone's life, someone's upbringing, and thus have shaped who those people are today.

As with the other songs I've included in my many collections, they're better listened to on the audio recordings we make of the books. Which is, of course, a blatant plug to go out and buy the audio recording as well.

Verse 1 – *Little town, country people, just like you and I*
Wake each day to the beauty of a clear blue sky
Working hard at their labours as in years gone by
Farming soil, helping neighbours in their trying times

....

Chorus – *But now the trains don't come*
And the banks they've gone
And the silo's lying dry
And my old man, he can't understand
Why the highway's passed him by

....

Verse 2 – *Generations gone forever*
Trying to survive
Doesn't matter what the weather
It leaves you high and dry

....

Chorus – *But now the trains don't come*
And the banks they've gone
And the silo's lying dry
And my old man, he can't understand
Why the highway's passed him by

....

Bridge/
Chorus – *Little town, country people, just like you and I*
         Working hard at our labours trying to survive
         But now the trains don't come
         And the banks they've gone
         And the silo's lying dry
         And my old man, he can't understand
         Why the highway's passed him by
         Why the highway's passed him by

        ....

Little town country people. Little town, country people
Little town country people. Little town ... country people.

Ballidu – WA

Now, where do I start? Well, Ballidu is a couple of hundred kilometres north of Perth, and thirty or so kilometres north of Wongan Hills. It's out in what's called the Wheatbelt Country. I've always been an avid supporter and member of the CWA – Country Women's Association – and the only time I've had a break was for a couple of years when I had a run-in with our then local president and I thought, Well, I'm not going to be in it with her. So that's how that worked out. Then, after she left, I rejoined and I'm still a member. In fact, in January 2020, I was awarded an Honour Badge by the CWA of Western Australia in recognition of seventy-six years of service. So how about that!

During my time with the CWA, I've taken on many roles. At one stage, I was our divisional secretary. I enjoyed doing that because you get out and about and you meet lots of people and that sort of thing. It was a wonderful experience. We're like a big family. At present, I'm branch secretary; though, in saying that, I'm trying very hard to get out of the position because I reckon my use-by date is well past.

Over the years, I've had a lot of humorous experiences. Different ones always say to me, 'Tell us about Mrs Barrett.' Mrs Barrett was a real character. To many people, she was a very sort of posh and uppity woman. She lived just near me, in Ballidu, at the back of the shop. This was when my boys had upgraded their business to bigger trucks and they were carting a lot of sheep. So they'd arrive home at all times of the day and night and say, 'Mum, can you fuel the truck up while I grab a bite to eat?' That sort of thing, so I was very involved.

In those days, there wasn't a truck mechanic in Ballidu and one of my boys was keen on fixing the trucks. So if something had gone wrong, he'd get the truck manual out and he'd start pulling the blessed thing to bits. And it'd be, 'Mum, will you please come and help me', or 'Mum, hang onto the torch will you and shine the light in here' or 'Please pass me the spanner or the spark plug' or 'Please do this, that or the other'.

At that time, Mrs Barrett was our divisional president. She was a funny woman, really. She took the job on and, oh, she just loved it – revelled in it actually. As different ones said, 'She only did it because she liked to be at the forefront of operations.' Of course, being divisional president, she'd be invited to all the little CWA branches away out in the sticks; places like Jibberding and Kalannie. At that time, she had a small Volkswagen and, with what little experience I'd had helping my sons on the trucks, she thought I knew everything there was to know about vehicles, and so I became her 'chief mechanic'.

'Oh, Mavis,' she'd say, 'I've got to go to Calingiri, can you come with me?'

When I'd say, 'Yes', she'd say, 'Well, that's good because if anything goes wrong with my car you'll know how to fix it.' And I'm thinking, Well, I very much hope that nothing goes wrong with your car then.

But oh, she was a dreadful driver. She just whizzed around the place as if she didn't have a care in the world. Off we'd go and she'd be looking out into the paddocks to see what was going on and, before you'd know it, she'd just about be off the road and into a blooming paddock. And, as she got to a corner, she'd change down into a lower gear. Then once we got around the corner, she'd plant her foot down on the accelerator and off we'd go, and I'd often have to say to her, 'Mrs Barrett, don't you think you'd better change up a gear or two?'

All that sort of thing, and oh, she'd sing. And poorly I might add. Worse still, she just loved to sing when she was driving.

It'd drive me crackers, it would. And she'd get so carried away with the singing that she'd start pumping the accelerator up and down in rhythm with the song and we'd be going along the blessed road in leaps and bounds, like a kangaroo. Oh, I tell you; and one day she took her cousin with us. We were going to Piawaning for some function or other. Both Mrs Barrett and her cousin were very large women, and I'm not terribly big. This was in the middle of winter, it'd been pouring with rain and the road between Ballidu and Piawaning was terrible; awfully slippery. Anyhow, as usual, I'd been invited along as chief mechanic and Mrs Barrett's husband had told her that it'd be better if she went up around Miling and came back down to Piawaning on the better road.

Okay, so I'm in the back seat of the little Volksie and away we go – full throttle. But her husband hadn't realised that the Main Roads people had decided to dig up a lot of the Miling–Piawaning road and resurface it, had he? So when we got to this muddy chopped up section, I said, 'You'd better slow down, Mrs Barrett.'

But no, not her. She didn't worry about that. She didn't slow down. She just went flat out into it and the whole car got absolutely covered in mud. Of course, now she couldn't see out the windscreen properly, could she, and so we soon came to a dead stop. So there we sat, Mrs Barrett and her cousin and me, looking into this muddy windscreen. Then, after a minute or two, she passed me over a cloth. 'Mavis,' she said, 'could you get out and wipe the windscreen please?'

So I had to clamber out from the back seat between these two large women and into about eighteen inches of deep mud to wipe the blessed windscreen. And even after that she wouldn't slow down – no, not her – and, of course, with all this mud going everywhere, it wasn't long before she couldn't see properly again. So she said, 'Mavis, hang your head out the window and tell me if I'm in the middle of the road, will you?'

Oh, I tell you. You can almost picture it can't you? But she's dead now, Mrs Barrett. Actually, they've both gone – her and her husband. But oh, some of the things that went on during those old days, you just wouldn't believe.

And great memories too. Great, great memories. Anyway, those sorts of things happen in the bush, don't they? It's what makes the bush, really, isn't it? You've just got to go along with it all and try not to get too upset.

Footnote – Ballidu is in the centre of the Wheatbelt region of Western Australia, a touch over two hundred kilometres north of Perth, and has a population of between fifty and sixty. The name 'Ballidu' comes from a Noongar Aboriginal word meaning 'on this side' or 'in this direction' and 'Duli' relating to a nearby rock-hole.

Surveyor General John Septimus Roe first travelled through the district in the mid-1830s – seven years after the founding of the Swan River Colony. However, for the following sixty years, the only white people to pass through were the Benedictine monks from New Norcia, shepherding their flocks of sheep, and the sandalwood cutters. The town site was gazetted in 1914. A primary school opened in 1922 and was moved to its current premises in 1924. At its peak, the school boasted a hundred students but, by the mid-2010s, enrolment had fallen to just four.

Ballidu's motto is 'Where friendship is never out of date' and it prides itself on its good wholesome country living, clean air, lack of traffic, low crime and vandalism, and a caring community. There aren't many facilities in town but there is a town hall, an art gallery and a general store that supplies basic needs. The Ballidu Tavern was built in 1922, as the Ballidu Hotel, and reportedly serves nice cold beer and a pretty mean pizza. A post office opened in 1928. The bulk wheat bins opened in 1940. As for special events, the Contemporary Arts Society still holds regular exhibitions of local and well-known Australian artists. The region is known for its extremely diverse flowering plants, with more than 1400 species.

Barmedman – NSW

This story has been adapted from a collection of Roy Moore's 'memories-in-progress'.

Roy here again, mate, the bloke from Barmedman that you interviewed a few years back for your truckies' book. We both went to Yanco Agricultural High School, remember? I would've been in Fifth Year at about the time you started. Then the last time I saw you, you were about fourteen. You were sitting outside the Barmedman Hotel waiting for your dad. No doubt, with your dad being the manager of the Commercial Bank over in Beckom, he'd come over to catch up with the manager feller here and they'd popped into the pub for one or three and a yarn with some of their clients.

Anyhow, for a while now I've been jotting down some memories of my time in Barmedman, from the '50s through to the '70s. Though Barmedman's a virtual ghost town these days, back in those days it was still a pretty thriving place. Even though the Royal Hotel had shut down by then, there were still two pubs: the Queensland and the Barmedman. The Queensland was where the more wealthy farmers and businessmen drank, and the only time they went over to the Barmedman was to employ a labourer. As to its layout, the Queensland had the main bar area with a small room opposite, which had a fireplace – that's where we'd play cards in the winter, in front of the open fire. It still had the old stables out the back. They were from the 1940s, when two locals used to deliver the mail out to the farms by horse and sulky.

Pubs back then were for men patrons only, and the only time a woman went inside was to drag her hubby out. I remember one time, being in the main bar, when a woman burst in through the back door. 'Where is he? Where is he?' We didn't have a clue who she was after. But eighty-year-old Freddy Fielgert certainly did. Like a shot, he went into hiding behind the bar. And so, when Fred's wife got to the bar area and couldn't find him, it was, 'I know the so-and-so's in here somewhere. So tell him he'll get it, when he comes home,' and she left in a huff, leaving old Freddy quaking in his boots.

See, it wasn't till the mid-1970s that women were allowed into the pub and even then they'd have to go out to a larger ladies' lounge area, well away from earshot of the main bar. Also, unless you'd travelled twenty miles, legally, all the pubs in New South Wales were supposed to be closed to locals on Sundays. But that didn't stop us. Each Sunday after church, while the women got together at someone's house for morning tea, us men would sneak in through the back door of the Queensland for a session. Another time, I was in the Queensland. It was a Saturday afternoon and Clive, the bank teller, was in the ladies' lounge chatting up a nurse from West Wyalong. She was a real dish and, by the looks of it, they were getting along really well. So well in fact that Clive thought he was onto a sure thing. Next thing he came over to me. 'Roy,' he said, with a sly wink, 'I'm gonna take this bird out 'n show her the sights of Barmedman. Can yer look after her for a tick while I zip home 'n clean myself up a bit?'

'Okay,' I said, so I moved into the ladies' lounge to make sure no one else made a move on her. Anyhow, we got chatting and one thing led to another and by the time Clive arrived back at the pub, all spruced up and ready to go, me and the nurse had already gone. I won't tell you where to or what happened between us other than to say that's how I got the nickname, 'Horny'.

Like I said, winter Friday nights we'd play cards in the small room with the fire. Mostly it was euchre or poker, with maybe four tables of four blokes. Then, when it got late, the publican would say, 'Fellers, I'm done. I'm off ter bed. Serve yerselves. Here's the keys. Lock up when yer leave,' and we'd keep on playing till early morning, serving ourselves beer and leaving our money on the till. As you might gather, we were serious about our cards. So much so that one night the local copper was there in his civvies, playing with us. Around midnight he got into a heated argument with one of the fellers he was playing against. Anyhow, the copper up and he stormed off home, put on his uniform, then came back and arrested the feller and put him in jail overnight. I mean, what an arsehole of an act that was.

Now, up till the late '50s, the draught beer came in wooden eighteen-gallon kegs that were lowered down into the hotel's cellar, from trapdoors up on the outside footpath. It wasn't till the early '60s that stainless steel kegs came in. We drank Reschs. It was known as the working man's beer and most of us drank from the smaller seven-ounce glasses. That's because neither of the pubs had air conditioning or cool rooms so, if you drank from larger glasses, the beer got too warm. It wasn't till after 1968, when the pubs were getting cool rooms and water air conditioners, that we moved up to drinking out of ten-ounce middy glasses. Two brands of bottled beers were sold – longnecks of DA and KB – and, during winter, to warm themselves up, some of the older generation drank hot Bonox with a dash of rum in it. But oh, everybody smoked back in those days so, when the smoke got down below head level and you couldn't see who you were talking to, the publican would turn on the exhaust fan.

The Barmedman Hotel was across the road from the Queensland. It was patronised more by the working class; people like shearers, fettlers and labourers. It had a smaller bar area and it also had a small room across the hall, which was used later by the women, when they were allowed into the pub. One night I was in the Barmedman when a farmer burst in, 'Come outside! Yer gotta see this!' When we did, there was this massive mob of flying foxes flying overhead, heading west to the irrigation area of Griffith. 'What sort are they?' someone asked. 'Don't know,' said someone else. So two blokes dashed over to their vehicles and grabbed their shotguns. *Boom! Boom!* They shot a few down in the main street. When we took a closer look, they turned out to be what's called Little Red Bats; the ones that eat insects and pollinate eucalyptus trees. Mind you, they also eat fruit, which was probably why they were heading to Griffith.

On Friday nights, both the pubs would be chockers and on weeknights, they'd be pretty bare. And back then it was an unwritten law that nobody touched anybody else's money – ever. So, if you were going out to the toilet, you'd leave all your change on the bar. And if you ran out of cash, you'd ask the publican if you could go on the 'tab'. If that was okay, he'd write your name in a book and you'd pay him back the next time you were in town. Oh, and when a friend came into the pub and you wanted him to join you for a beer and a yarn, you'd call out 'Your shout!' And after each shearing shed had cut-out, the publican would cash in the shearers' cheques, which meant he'd have to have anywhere up to $10,000 cash lying around in his safe to pay them out.

Then, like I said, the Royal Hotel wasn't operating by the 1960s. That was more back in Dad's time. The Royal used to be next to Canberra Hall; a dance hall whose floor was sprinkled with sawdust when a ball or a dance was on.

Canberra Hall had a supper room with a kitchen. Both a ladies' and men's toilet were down the back, though, most times, us blokes would just wander out into the dark for a pee. Apparently, the Royal was the first two-storey brick building in Barmedman. It opened in about 1908 and, like I said, by the 1960s it was no longer operating. Dad once told me how the publican at the Royal was a real cunning bastard. See, every now and then the Sergeant of Police used to pop in to each pub in town and scab a free beer, and he always reckoned the Royal had the worst beer of them all.

What'd happen is this: the publican at the Royal would keep a half-full glass of old flat beer behind the bar and, when he saw the Sergeant walk in, he'd just top it up with fresh beer to give it a bit of a head. 'Here yer go, mate,' he'd say, nice and friendly, and pass the glass over to the copper. Oh, and something else that may be of interest is that, in all Australian hotels, the spill-tray – the slops tray – had to have a purple dye added to it, just in case a dodgy publican might dish it up to his patrons. And believe you me I've come across some pretty dodgy publicans in my time. Too right I have!

Anyhow, one of my greatest regrets was never getting to have a beer with my dad. That's because he'd just died in 1964, when I reached the legal drinking age of eighteen. In fact, my first legal beer was at my father's wake. Before then I'd have a few on the sly. But after I was given Dad's car, I was able to drive to town. And that was great because, before then, I had to ride my pushbike the six miles into town and back, and I found it a lot easier to drive home drunk than it was to ride a pushbike drunk, where I'd be forever falling off the bloody thing.

When I became legal, a seven-ounce beer used to cost the equivalent of seven or eight cents and a middy – a ten-ounce – was around twelve cents. 750-millilitre DA and KB longnecks were our only takeaway beers and they were around thirty-six cents each. Back then, twist-top bottle caps and stubbies weren't around as yet, so we just used the car's steel bumper bar to knock the top off the longnecks. 375-millilitre steel beer cans were around. They were about eighteen cents but, because we never had any ice to keep them cold, we hardly ever drunk them. Then, before ring-pull cans arrived in the late 1960s, we used to have to use a can opener, which punched a 'V' hole in their lid.

But oh, a lot of different stuff went on back then. Whenever Des Morton and I came home from the pub, we'd always drive side by side. There were two main reasons for that: 1) with the roads being so crook and gravelly, neither of us would get a broken windscreen and 2) we didn't have to travel in the other's dust. Then, when we got to the intersection at Moore's Road, we'd stop and knock the top off a longneck and down it before it was, 'See yer later,' and Des'd head off home to Wargin.

Other than the beer and the friendships, another thing I liked about the pubs back then was that they were places where you'd meet all sorts of different characters and learn about life in the bush. Like, I always tried to have a yarn with the swaggies and drifters who were passing through town. They were a colourful lot. Most of them had little to no money and some would come into the pub and call out, 'Empty an ashtray into a glass, cigarette butts and all!' Then we'd all pay for a nip of spirit to be put in the glass, and they'd drink it. It must've had a God-awful taste. But the swaggie got a strong, free drink out of it, which was what he wanted.

Others would come into the pub with all sorts of musical instruments. Bottle tops nailed to a broomstick was one. Another was a broomstick, with a wire attached to it and then to an empty tea chest, and they'd either bow or pluck the wire. That gave a nice bass sound. Gum leaves played with their mouth was another one. Even carrots, with a mouthpiece routered out of them, were played like a flute. But my favourite was a wood handsaw that was played with a violin bow; it had a real eerie, haunting sound to it. Most of them would just play for drinks and, of course, they'd sing along with their instrument. So it made for a great night. Us locals would have a good sing-along and the swaggie would get a belly full of grog, without having to pay a cent.

Then there were the drifters who'd pass through in horse-drawn or camel-drawn covered wagons – like gypsy wagons. None of them seemed to be in any real hurry. They just went from town to town, wandering the backroads, picking up work here and there. I remember one of the cameleers setting up camp down at the oval and making a bit of money by charging kids ten cents a ride on his camel. Then there were the drovers. They were down-to-earth bushies. I really enjoyed yarning with them. I'd shout them a beer and listen to their stories about places I'd never been to and only dreamed about going to; and of their everyday life experiences, sleeping out under the stars by a campfire, and droving sheep or cattle through sunshine, hail and floods, drought and dust storms. It would've been a tough life, but one I really longed to experience.

I also enjoyed yarning with the older farmers; hearing about what it was like in the old horse-team days, how they always started sowing wheat on April 1, whether it'd rained or not. That was because it'd take them so long to sow a three-hundred-acre crop with just the one team of horses. And also how they got by without electricity and not having refrigeration, so they'd salt their meat or keep it in a salt brine. And how they'd ride a horse twenty miles to a dance somewhere and have to be home before sunrise to feed their draughthorses with chaff. See, back then, every farmer had to cut up to fifty acres of hay to provide their horses with feed, twice a day. Then, just in case of a drought, those who had sheep or cattle had to cut extra hay. See, I don't think the kids of today fully realise just how hard times were back then. Many an old farmer told me how, even after the harvest cheque had come through, they'd barely have enough left over to feed their family. So the women had to make and mend all the family's clothes and they'd have small vegie gardens which, because it was so dry, they'd water from the washing up waste or from the occasional bath.

Another old timer I loved having a beer and yarn with was an old stockman called Paddy. Paddy was quite a bit older than me and he worked on a farm about twenty mile out of town. He only came to town on the weekends. He'd arrive early on the Saturday, in either a horse and sulky or just on horseback, and he'd set himself up in the pub and drink all day. Then, before the pub shut, he'd buy a dozen longnecks to see him through the night. Sunday morning he'd start up in the pub again. He had lots of stories about the old times and, the more beers I shouted him, the more stories he seemed to have. Then on the Sunday night, he'd struggle back onto his horse and it'd take him back home. The horse had done the trip so often that it knew its way. And just as well too, because Paddy'd be sound asleep by the time they'd got to the end of the street.

But by gee we used to get up to some larks. There was the time somebody let a snake out of a bag in the front bar. Cleaned the place out in seconds it did. That's till we worked out that it was a non-poisonous carpet snake. So we all had a good laugh about it and we wandered back in off the street, and continued on drinking, snake and all. Of course, there was the occasional barney. Like when one of the patrons king-hit a fellow drinker, and so she was on. Everyone joined in. And when the news got around that there was a fight going on in the pub, blokes came from everywhere, wanting to join in. Luckily a mate closed the main bar doors out onto the street, which stopped the mob from getting into the bar and joining in. Then there was my mate, John. No joke, John could down a jug of beer in four and a half seconds – a jug being equal to six middies. So, after a footy game, we'd bet the opposition that John could down a jug in under six seconds. 'Bullshit,' they'd say. So we'd lay bets and, when John downed the jug within the six seconds, we'd split our winnings with him.

I mean, thank God there were no breathalysers back then because, by closing time, we'd be well and truly stonkered. And if it was an away game of footy, we might have a hundred miles to travel home. Like, if we'd played at Leeton, after the game we'd down a few beers in the pub there. On our way home, we'd stop off at Ardlethan to have a few more. Then we'd grab a few longnecks for the last leg. So by the time I got back to the farm, I'd just about fall out of my car. Other times I wouldn't even bother. Another time we were in the Euabalong pub and an Aboriginal fella came along and started scraping his bare feet on the metal foot scraper just outside the front door. You know those grate things that you scrape the mud off your boots on. Problem being, there was no mud. This's strange, we thought. Why the hell would someone want to scrape their bare feet on a metal door scraper? Turned out that he was scraping the catheads – thorny jacks and/or three-cornered jacks and/or bindi-eyes – out of the soles of his feet. I mean, the soles of his feet must've been like bloody leather because, if I trod on just one cathead, the pain nearly killed me!

Then, in about 1977, disaster struck! There was a beer strike in Victoria and New South Wales, and the only beer we could get was a brand called Courage. And bloody hell, it had such a bitter vile taste that we reckoned it took courage to drink it. Mate, it was so crook that men who'd never drunk spirits or wine in their entire lives started drinking either or both. So it was a great relief when the strike was over and our Reschs draught beer came back on tap, and we were able to buy KB and DA longnecks to take away. Oh, and that's right: I've got to tell you this one. Another night in the Barmedman, the publican served up plates of what he called 'bush oysters'. Little did they know that me and a mate had been marking lambs all day and we thought it'd be a great joke to feed their testicles to the clientele. So the publican done them up to look like oysters, added a bit of Worcestershire sauce, and everyone loved them. 'Just beautiful.' Best thing they'd ever tasted. That's till we told them what they were!

Footnote – Barmedman is in the Riverina sheep and wheatbelt region of New South Wales, approximately four hundred and fifty kilometres west of Sydney. One interpretation of the town's name is that it's a Wiradjuri word meaning 'long water'. Another is that it's named after nearby Barmedman

Station, which, in turn, was named after a small village in Scotland, which, in turn, no longer exists.

John Oxley explored the area in 1817 and, although he described the Wiradjuri people as being 'strong and healthy', he was a little less glowing in his appraisal of the environment, describing its open plains as being 'desolate areas (that) would never again be visited by civilised man'. In 1827 Surveyor General Thomas Mitchell passed by and, due to its flatness, named the area 'The Levels'. In the 1830s, as the first European settlers moved in, bitter conflict broke out between them and the Wiradjuri people. By 1849, the Barmedman pastoral run covered thirty-six thousand acres. Gold was first discovered in 1872 and, although larger amounts weren't found until 1882, by 1903, due to the high cost of pumping water from the mines, mining was discontinued.

In 1878, a public house opened in what was then known as 'Barmedman Reefs'. A store opened soon after, as did a blacksmith and a wheelwright. The first public house and store was burnt down in 1881. By early 1882, two hotels were operating – the West Coast of New Zealand and the Barmedman. By the end of 1882, a third hotel – the Melbourne Club Hotel – had opened. In 1894, Barmedman's population stood at around four hundred and its public school had an attendance of one hundred.

The town's main attraction is its Mineral Swimming Pool, which is rumoured to be the largest mineral pool in the world. Because of its high mineral content, some believe it has therapeutic healing properties.

Broken Hill – NSW

This story has been adapted from a collection of 'written life-memories' by Peter 'Simpy' Simpfendorfer.

I met my wife Norma when she was nursing at Fairfield Hospital, Sydney, and we married in November 1968. Norma was originally a 'banana bender' – a Queenslander. We moved to Dubbo, New South Wales, at the end of our honeymoon, myself as senior clerk within the Public Works Department, and, before our first son was born, Norma nursed at Dubbo Base Hospital.

In 1975, I obtained a position based in Dubbo as senior administrative co-ordinator, Community Health, Orana Far West Region. Across the state, there were eight such positions with the Orana Far West being, geographically, the largest of the lot. It took in Walgett, Coonamble, Gilgandra, Dunedoo, Mudgee, Gulgong, Wellington, Dubbo, Narromine, Nyngan, Bourke, Brewarrina, Cobar, Wilcannia and Broken Hill, plus all points west to the South Australian border and north to the Queensland border. I now forget the exact area but the term 'tyranny of distance' was commonly used. Though, mind you, the people in head office didn't see it that way. They'd glance at a map and say, 'Go here. Go there. It's not far. It's only half an inch on the map,' without a clue that half an inch on the map might equate to a hundred-kilometre drive.

You'll note that I mentioned Broken Hill – or The Hill as it's more commonly known – in the description of my region. We mostly drove there and back. We'd leave Dubbo at about 7 a.m. and arrive in The Hill at around 4 p.m. – with a toilet stop or two

– making it a nine-hour journey. Now, to give you some idea as to this 'tyranny of distance' business, just the one-way drive was over seven hundred and fifty kilometres, with the legs: Dubbo to Nyngan, one hundred and eighty-two kilometres, or a two-hour drive. Nyngan to Cobar, one hundred and thirty-one kilometres, or a one-hour-twenty-minute drive. Cobar to Wilcannia, two hundred and sixty-one kilometres, or a two-and-a-half-hour drive, and Wilcannia to Broken Hill, one hundred and ninety-six kilometres, with a driving time of two hours. So it was a long day in the 'saddle', and that was just to get there.

Part of my responsibilities covered bush nursing centres in the likes of Collarenebri, Enngonia, Quambone and Wanaaring, where my team oversaw around one hundred and fifty personnel and over a hundred motor vehicles. Because of their remoteness, these bush community nurses were in fact 'de facto doctors'. Shortly after I commenced duty, I was told to investigate a female worker from Broken Hill who'd run up a $1300 phone bill in just three months. After a bit of sleuthing, it became obvious that many of them were private in nature. So I drove to The Hill and interviewed the woman, who admitted that around $900 were private, including an hour-long conversation to a boyfriend in Cowra.

The Hill was, and still is, an interesting and unique outback centre. In those days, the Barrier Industrial Council was all-powerful and, because we were often asked to show proof of our union membership ... or else, we always carried our cards. We mostly stayed at Mario's Palace Hotel, since made famous in movies such as *Priscilla Queen of the Desert* and the *New Royal Flying Doctor Service* television show. Mario's was central. It was comfortable, we always received friendly service and it had the best sausages and eggs breakfast in town. I remember one time Mario coming up to us during a breakfast and humbly apologising for how he'd soon have to raise our bed and breakfast accommodation from $9 to $9.50 per night, to which we didn't argue.

With The Hill being The Hill, there were numerous pubs in town. But we mainly restricted ourselves to either Mario's or the Muso's – Broken Hill Musicians Club – or the Demo – Barrier Social Democratic Club – or the Black Lion Hotel or the Pig and Whistle, or sometimes all five in the one night. Early one morning, a mate and I were still kicking on in the Pig when the police turned up. 'Hey,' they said, 'you two haven't been working a mine's shift so leave immediately.' Apparently, only mine-shift workers were allowed to drink at that hour of the morning and, as we were still in our short-sleeve business shirts, shorts and socks, it was obvious we weren't in that category.

A visit to the nearby small historic mining town of Silverton was mandatory. Silverton Hotel's been featured in several movies – *Mad Max* for one – and in many advertising commercials. In the late 1970s, the publican was a woman called Innes McLeod. Like me, Innes was a member of the Australian Beer Can Collectors Association and so had a large collection on display. A couple of other things are worth mentioning. More often than not, an alcoholic horse would be blocking your entry through the pub's swinging front doors, with its head hanging inside, hopeful of cadging a free beer. The second is where a funnel was stuck down the front of a first-time visitor's pants and a twenty-cent coin placed on their forehead. The trick was, if they could drop the twenty cents into the funnel, without using their hands, they got free beer. Problem was, to start with, their forehead would be facing the ceiling and, while they were figuring out how to get the twenty cents into the funnel, someone would pour a beer down the funnel, wetting their pants. All good clean fun and most people took it well, although one boss kicked up such a stink when his trousers got soaked that we thought 'serves the bastard right'.

In saying that we 'mostly drove', when there were enough of us with business to do in The Hill, we'd sometimes charter a flight direct from Dubbo or we'd jump on a commercial flight via Sydney. I remember the time ten of us took a charter flight from Dubbo to The Hill. We'd planned to be in town for three days and two nights. Mid-morning on day three, a weather warning came through about an approaching storm front, with winds strong enough to close the airport. So we decided to get out of the place asap. We managed to contact all involved, except one – the bloody pilot. Being a pilot, we knew he wouldn't be in a pub so we rushed around town until we found him and we eventually took off moments before they closed the airport. We were in a small twin-engine plane and, while we were over Wilcannia, an updraft hit us and, in the blink of an eye, we rocketed up about 1200 feet. In turn, a number of the passengers lost their breakfast. So, when we finally reached Dubbo, a wretched line of people trotted off the tarmac carrying sick bags.

Another not-so-memorable return trip from The Hill occurred after I'd organised a catch-up with an old mate. So I drove the work car to our meeting place – the Southern Cross Hotel-Motel – where we began our catch-up drinking session. And we inadvertently kept on drinking, without anything to eat, until I don't remember when. Because next thing, I woke up with a doozey of a hangover, in my room at Mario's Hotel. I then decided to walk back to the Southern Cross to rescue my work car. But when I stepped out the front door of Mario's, lo-n-behold, there it was, parked right outside, and I still have no idea how it got there. To make matters worse, after I'd showered and packed the car, the darn thing had a flat battery and wouldn't start. Anyhow, the NRMA finally came to my rescue with that one. But then, to make matters even worse, I'd somehow been hit with a serious case of gastro! So the drive back to Dubbo took quite a few hours longer than usual due to me having to visit every porcelain stop along the way. Suffice to say, by the time I got home, my rectum was wrecked!

But back to this 'tyranny of distance': I once worked out that, if I followed departmental guidelines with regard to speed regulations and required rest stops, I couldn't legally drive to The Hill in the allotted time. After I mentioned this in dispatches, one of my bosses flew out from Sydney to check out this 'tyranny of distance' rubbish. Along with four staff – two men and two women – he decided to tour the region in a brand new departmental XB Falcon sedan. Anyhow, while the boss was driving between Bourke and Brewarrina, he rolled the thing and wrote it off.

See, what used to happen on those dirt roads was, because they were so corrugated, if it hadn't been raining, you'd drive in the smoother table drain beside the road. Then, when you came to a cattle-grid, you'd just zip back up onto the road, go over the cattle-grid, then go back down into the table drain. The thing was, when the boss got near a cattle-grid and tried to get up on the road, he flipped the car. Fortunately, there were no serious injuries, but everyone ended up hanging upside down in their seat belts, with the two females dangling there with their skirts around their heads. But being so far from anywhere, it was more than thirty minutes before a vehicle came along and offered to take the two ladies back to Bourke. Then it wasn't until several hours later that a tow truck arrived to pick up the vehicle and the males. The twist there was that, even though this was before mobile phones, by that stage the staff in head office, Sydney, were already having a good laugh about it. So news travels, ay!

Another time, when I was relieving as an assistant hospitals inspector, Broken Hill Base Hospital had a serious fire. From memory, the hospital was three storeys. On the second floor was a horse-haired padded cell. It turned out that the inmate in the padded cell had a bit of 'form' in as much as he'd lost most of his arm trying to blow up a police station over in Western Australia. Then, apparently, after some kind soul had given him a cigarette and a box of matches, he'd pulled out some of the padding and set it alight, and the fire spread rapidly, causing a lot of damage. I can't recall if anyone actually died, but the authorities had to call in Mines Rescue to help evacuate the hospital because the town fire brigade's ladders couldn't reach high enough up into the building.

So now I'll come to my final Broken Hill or bust saga. By this stage I was with the Housing Commission in Wagga Wagga. Now, Wagga Airport was prone to fog, particularly in winter, which resulted in many a delayed flight. One winter's evening, I made my way to Wagga Airport to fly to Sydney's Mascot Airport. I was to overnight then catch the following morning's flight to Broken Hill. I had my work papers packed in with my clothes. Anyhow, the departing flight from Wagga was delayed due to fog and was eventually cancelled due to mechanical trouble. The Wagga mob then rebooked me on the next morning's early flight out of Wagga. Good, so I'd still be able to connect with my Broken Hill flight. Before I went back home for the night, I asked the Wagga mob to hold my luggage and book it through on my new flight. The thing was, when I returned to Wagga Airport at 'sparrow fart' the next morning they'd already sent my luggage through to Sydney the previous evening and it was waiting for me in the transit lounge at Mascot. Okay, I could handle that. Though, as it turned out, my early morning flight from Wagga was also delayed, which now made my connection to The Hill extremely tight, time wise. So when we got into the air, I told the cabin crew of my situation and they said they'd ring forward and hold the Broken Hill flight for me.

When we arrived at Mascot, I was first off the plane. Then, over the intercom, came the message, 'Would passenger Simpf-eh! Simpfen-eh! Oh, Peter whatever-your-name-is, recently arrived from Wagga Wagga, your Broken Hill flight is awaiting departure. Please proceed to Gate 3, immediately.' I mean, fancy getting a personalised message, even if they couldn't pronounce my name! Then I remembered that my luggage, including all my work papers, was waiting for me in the transit lounge. So I hot-footed it down there and explained the situation to the customer service officer. He said he'd try to get it on my Broken Hill flight but, if he couldn't, it'd arrive in The Hill, via Adelaide, that evening. So I sprinted as best I could to Gate 3 and I was met by a flight attendant who escorted me onto the plane, where all the other passengers were waiting patiently. My newfound fame must've proceeded me because, while some of them gave me a loud cheer, the remainder rolled their eyes, sighed and groaned.

However, that was not the end of the saga. The flight crew then couldn't secure the hatch-door. So they had to call an engineer, and we eventually departed Mascot an hour later. Now, although the flight itself was uneventful, the dramas weren't yet over. See, if there was a headwind, the plane often arrived late in The Hill. And if it was a tailwind, the flight would arrive early. Which is why the District Officer would wait in his office until he heard the plane pass overhead, before driving out to the airport. Trouble was, this time, due to the unusual weather conditions, the plane didn't fly in over the town. It approached the airport from a different direction.

So when I alighted, not only was my luggage not on the flight, but, to top it off, there was no sign of the District Officer. With no mobile phones in those days, I then had to wait for him to arrive. Which he didn't, because he hadn't heard the plane fly over his office. Anyhow, in the end, I found a public telephone box and rang him and he eventually came out to pick me up. Then, that evening, we had to go back out to the airport to collect my luggage, which had arrived in The Hill, via Wagga Wagga, via Sydney, via Adelaide. So that was one of my more memorable trips to The Hill.

Footnote – Broken Hill, population around seventeen thousand, is a mining city in the far-west of New South Wales, near the South Australian border. The nearest major city, Adelaide, is over five hundred kilometres to its south-west and Sydney is over a thousand kilometres to its east. The earliest human settlers are believed to have been the Wilyakali people who, due to the lack of a permanent water source, only lived in the area intermittently. Broken Hill was given its name due to the number of hills that appeared to have a break in them. Due to mining, those hills no longer exist.

The first European to visit the area was Major Thomas Mitchell, the then Surveyor General of New South Wales, in 1841. Three years later, explorer Charles Sturt passed by in search of an inland sea. In 1860–61, the ill-fated Burke and Wills expedition set up a base camp at nearby Menindee. Pastoralists began moving into the area during the 1850s, with the main trade route being along the Darling River. In 1883, boundary rider Charles Rasp discovered what he thought was tin, though it later proved to be silver and lead. The orebody from which it came turned out to be the largest and richest of its kind in the world. Rasp and six associates founded Broken Hill Propriety Company – BHP – in 1885. BHP ceased operations at Broken Hill in February 1939, but mining has continued at the southern and northern ends of the Line of Lode.

Broken Hill has played an integral part in the history of the Australian labour movement. Some of its bitterest industrial disputes were in 1892, 1909 and 1919, leading to the 1923 formation of the Barrier Industrial Council. Despite slowing economic conditions, Broken Hill remains Australia's longest running mining town and was added to the National Heritage List in 2015. Broken Hill's solar plant, completed in 2015, is one of the largest in the Southern Hemisphere.

In its heyday, Broken Hill boasted more than seventy hotels. Although there are only twenty or so remaining, all are worth checking out for their unique charm and ambience, their friendly outback characters, their cold beer and good, solid, tucker. For that special gourmet surprise, don't forget to order a side serve of Broken Hill's original signature dish, 'cheese-slaw'.

Broken Hill has been the inspiration for many artists including Brushmen of the Bush members, Pro Hart and Jack Absalom; and writers such as Arthur Upfield and Ion Idriess wrote of the area. The Hill and its environs has featured in many films including the 1971 adaptation of Kenneth Cook's 1961 novel *Wake in Fright*. More recently, Max Barry's 2013 novel *Lexicon* was set in Broken Hill. Over the years, author Bill 'Swampy' Marsh has conducted many writing workshops and author performances, and has been a Writer in Residence in 'The Silver City'.

Camooweal – Qld

In memory of Maude Ellis.

When I was very young, our family moved to Camooweal – right over near the Northern Territory border. Dad was working on properties around the area, so he only came into town to visit us when he could. Later on he got a poisoned ear and, when he was just about to get out of hospital, he died of a heart attack.

The house we lived in was made of corrugated iron and bush timber and it had a dirt floor. A little verandah was out the front and we had a big rainwater tank. This was before the water was laid on in town so, if we run out of water, we had to cart some in. There was also no electricity so there was no electric washing machines. All we had was washtubs and washing boards and coppers to boil up the water for the washing. For a bath, we had a big tub – so it was basically all of us in together. There was no fridges of course. All we had was one of them old Coolgardie safes. It was a big, square, galvanised box thing with charcoal and mesh wire around it and we'd put wet bags over it to keep things cool.

In them days, Camooweal was a big droving place. Other than a few houses and the hotel, it had a shire hall, and it was a real big thing for us kids to go down there and watch the monthly dances. An old feller played the piano and someone else was on the drums, and they polished the floor with sawdust so that everyone could glide around on it. Yeah, just glide around. The CWA ladies used to do the catering and they'd boil up water in cleaned-out kerosene tins for the tea. But oh, they really dressed up for those occasions. They really did. The women wore some of the most beautiful long evening dresses you're ever likely to see.

We didn't have a vegie garden but there was a Chinese gardener in town, Ah Wing. We called him Ah Bah, which meant 'father'. He was married to a lady from Burketown, Dora, and they had four or five kids. My sister later married one of their older boys, Charlie Ah Wing. But Ah Bah had everything in his garden; pumpkins, potatoes, everything you could name. He drew water up from a well with his old horse going round and round. And the horse was rigged up in such a way that buckets of water would come up and they'd get tipped into a trough, then the water would run from there, out along handmade drains into his garden. No hoses or anything. Ah Bah had it so well laid out that he sold vegies to a lot of people in the town as well as the outlying station people. If you saw Camooweal now, you wouldn't think it could be done. He even had fruit trees.

A lot of Aboriginal families once lived in Camooweal. That came about after the Aboriginal workers out on Lake Nash Station went on strike for equal wages. Then when the white station owners were forced to pay award wages to all their workers, they couldn't afford to pay everyone, so that's when a lot of Aboriginal stockmen and their families, similar to ours, drifted into Camooweal. But now, since they've been given some of that land back, a lot of the Aboriginal people have moved back out there and set up their own community.

I was about six when I started school at Camooweal. That would've been in about 1935. Because it got so hot, they built the school off the ground on big poles so that a good airflow could get underneath. We used to play games under there as well. We even ate our lunch there. I guess it's like what schools call a 'wet area' these days – a place where the kids can go when it's raining. Though mind you, it didn't rain too much out at Camooweal. Hardly ever. Of course, the King of England and the Commonwealth was still alive and kicking back then so, when the bell rang, we all stood in line. After the boys raised the flag, we sang 'God Save the King', then we'd march up the steps and into the school to a marching tune. I can't remember what the tune was just now but if I heard it I would.

Those days, Camooweal only went up to Grade 7. We had two teachers. A lady taught the lower grades and a man, who was the headmaster, taught the higher grades. The teachers were all right. The man married one of the local Riley girls and the woman teacher was pretty good too. But I used to get the cane quite a bit. It wasn't that I was naughty. Not really. It's just that I wrote with my left hand when I was supposed to write with my right hand. See, back then, all the tools and things was made for right-handers, so I guess they figured that's the way everyone should go. But even when I'd try to write with my right hand, I'd still end up getting the cane because my work was so messy. Then if I pulled my hand away before I was hit with the cane, I'd get a few more.

So I was forced to write with my right hand. And even to this day, I still write with my right hand, but do everything else with my left hand. I iron and I cut things up with my left hand and I taught myself to knit upside down. And because it was war time, we knitted squares to be made into blankets and we knitted socks and gloves – all to be sent off to our soldiers. A lot of my family, like my grandchildren and my great-grandchildren, they're left-handed too, just like me. But the poor old hands have got arthritis these days. Still, we soldier on, don't we?

In our first years at school, we'd write on a slate with chalk. Then after we'd learnt how to write properly on the slate, we was given a lead pencil and we learnt to write with that on paper. And if you made a mistake, you rubbed it out with a rubber. Though you dare not call them 'rubbers' these days do you? After that, we started writing with pens that had ink nibs, and each morning the boys would mix up the ink powder with some water and that'd be our daily supply of ink. We sat in pairs at iron-framed wooden desks, and the inkwell was up the top, in the middle, and we had blotting paper, to blot up any splotches we made. And I made lots of blots.

We played games like all-rounders – that's like softball. Another game we played was like netball. Then there was always our big end-of-year sports day. Oh, that was such a big thing. We had running races and three-legged races and egg and spoon races. But the biggest thing we had was the billy goat races. A lot of the boys trained their own goats specially for the race, and they'd put reins on them, then they'd sit on their backs and away they'd go. No saddles. It was all bareback.

I don't know if you've ever seen the book *The Border and Beyond*, written by Lilian Ada Miller. Well, in it there's a picture of half a dozen boys all dressed up with braces, shirts, shorts, socks and boots, with some of them wearing straw hats, all sitting on their goats, with their halters, bare-back, ready to take off, and they'd race for about a hundred yards. Actually, Lilian Ada Miller was originally Ada Freckleton. The Freckletons used to own the main grocery store in town. Ada's brother, Joe, was the only one of the family that remained living in Camooweal, and he run the shop right up till his death.

But we all had goats. Everyone in Camooweal had goats. Because goats just ate weeds and rubbish, they cost nothing to feed. In return, they gave us milk and, when times was bad, they were our meat. You could also make butter and cheese from their milk. We didn't, but you could and you could also use their skins as floor rugs or blankets. Some people even used goats for carting wood and water. Oh, you can't beat a goat. In Ada's book it says, 'There are those of us who believe that there should be a monument to the goat in Camooweal, so great was the peoples' dependence on the animal in the early struggling pioneering days.'

And I agree with that. Before I'd even go to school, I'd help Mum milk the goats of a morning. Then she'd let them out of the yard and off they'd go, off to the town common. And when it was time for their afternoon milking, me and a couple of my girlfriends, we'd go out and meet the goats as they was wandering back in and we'd put them in the yard and we'd milk them. So if you had a few goats and some vegies and you had a few chooks, you were just about right in a place like Camooweal.

Actually, back in 1993, they had the Camooweal school centenary reunion. I went back for that, and I got a centenary cup and a cookery book and my sister gave me Ada Miller-Freckleton's book. And we all signed the school roll book and we had our photos taken and we planted a tree each and things like that. But I don't know if the trees would still be alive now. It's too dry out in Camooweal and, when the school holidays are on, there's no kids about the place to water them. But I haven't been back there since the school centenary reunion. These days I have to travel to places by bus so, if I'm heading through that way, say over to Brisbane or back home to Darwin, the bus just sort of shoots straight through town and out the other side, and I stay on it.

Footnote – Camooweal is in the far north-western corner of Queensland, near on 1500 kilometres from Darwin, 2000 kilometres from Brisbane and 12 kilometres from the Northern Territory border. The original inhabitants, the Indjilandji people, cared for and lived on the land for thousands of years before white settlement.

In search of the lost explorers Burke and Wills, William Landsborough passed through the area in the early 1860s. Soon after Landsborough, George Sutherland arrived with eight thousand sheep to take up a lease at Lake Mary, on the nearby Georgina River. It's said that, at the shock of seeing eight thousand sheep descending upon them, the Indjilandji fled in fear. But due to ongoing friction, stock losses to dingos and wedge-tailed eagles, lack of water and isolation, Sutherland was soon forced to abandon his lease.

Where the town got its name from is uncertain. One theory is that it comes from George Telford Weale, who surveyed the area on camel in the early 1880s. Another is that surveyor Henry Stuart Russell named it after the 'cam wheel' of his measuring apparatus. A third, and more plausible theory, is that it's derived from an Aboriginal word meaning 'strong wind'.

The initial settlement was at nearby Lake Francis and, in 1885, was moved to its current site. As well as being a colonial customs post with the then South Australian controlled Northern Territory border, Camooweal became an outpost for transporters and drovers. A post office opened in 1885 and by year's end, it boasted two hotels, two butchers, a boarding house, a smithy, a saddler, a Chinese garden, several houses and a police barracks. What later became known as 'Freckleton's Store' was also built in 1885.

Camooweal Provisional School opened in 1893 and by 1909 was state run. The town's bore was drilled in 1897. By 1926 Camooweal had a population of a hundred and was the northern terminus of the newly established Queensland and Northern Territory Aerial Services – QANTAS – route across western Queensland. The road through Camooweal – now the Barkly Highway – was the inland defence route during World War Two, taking over one thousand vehicles a day. The town was electrified in 1952.

The Drovers Camp Museum celebrates past drovers and, as well as regular gymkhanas and horseracing events, there's an annual Drover's Camp Festival. In 1971, Australian country music icon Slim Dusty recorded the song 'Camooweal', which was written by David Kirkpatrick and Alex 'Mack' Cormack. Author Bill 'Swampy' Marsh has stayed at the Post Office Hotel and says that its chicken parma with chips and salad is a winner.

Coen – Qld

Swampy, your first book on outback towns and pubs certainly struck a chord, especially the story about Coen. If you remember, I'm the feller who wrote the book *Policing 'The Coen' 1885–2011*. On my part, it was an attempt to record some of the historical events, up in Cape York Peninsula, around the Coen area. As an example: in the late 1800s there was a lot of friction between the newly arriving pastoralists and the Aboriginals. This was largely due to the various clans spearing cattle and horses for their own consumption. Of course, in the humid heat, the freshly killed meat would only last for a couple of days, so they'd eat what they could and leave the rest to rot.

In an attempt to stop the practice, the police ran supervised bullock killings at selected locations around Cape York. Word would go out that this was to happen on a given full moon, and the Aboriginals were welcome to come and partake in a feast of fresh meat. And it worked well; the spearings reduced and it also helped to appease the Indigenous folks' attempts to thwart the spread of grazing throughout those outlying areas. Now, as to why these events took place on a full moon: while the Aborigines didn't have the know-how nor the means of telling the date and the time, they were well aware of when the full moon was going to be.

So that's just one example of what's in my book. A more personal incident was set around the Stolen Generation. As we all know, a good many Stolen Generation stories relate to Indigenous families being torn apart. And that's truly tragic. But there was also some good that came out of it, and this is a classic instance. Back in the early 1960s, when I was a policeman at Coen, there was a half-caste woman. She was married to an Indigenous man and they had a big family. My wife and I knew them well. In fact, the woman, in particular, was a very good friend of ours.

When I was gathering information for my book, I came across the case of an eighteen-year-old white boy who'd had sex with a young sixteen-year-old half-caste girl and she'd got pregnant. This happened in 1937 when the *Aboriginal Protection Act* prohibited any form of sexual relations between Aboriginals – which included half-castes – and white people. For some reason the case fascinated me and I began to wonder what had happened to the sixteen-year-old girl. Where was she these days? How did things turn out? So I started to do a bit of digging. As you may appreciate, due to marriage et cetera, a sixteen-year-old girl in 1937 would most probably have a different surname by the early 1960s. Still, I began at the beginning and I followed the girl through two different surnames. When I got to the third, much to my surprise, it turned out to be the woman that my wife and I were friends with.

Her father had been a white mining prospector, around the Coen area. Anyhow, this white prospector had sex with a full-blood Aboriginal woman and the half-caste girl – our friend – was the result. After the white prospector had moved on, the Aboriginal mother then took up with a full-blood Aboriginal. He was a half-wild nomadic Murri – which is what the Aboriginals are known as up that way – and he'd neglected the young girl quite badly. With the mother being subject to the lore and thus rule of her Murri husband, she could do little about the welfare of the little girl. Then, when the young girl was about nine, a police patrol discovered her in such a poor state that they decided she needed a better chance in life. So they brought her into Coen where she was placed with a white grazing family who headquartered – lived – in town. This family then brought the girl up as one of their own. She lived in the house with them. She ate with them. In fact, when the boss was out in the mustering camps, she slept in the same room as the missus. She even took on their surname.

When the girl was sixteen, she met a young eighteen-year-old white fellow. The two families had gardens down the back of their adjoining properties' houses. The girl used to water her boss' garden and the young white fellow used to water his boss' garden. That's where they met, and one day they said, 'Let's get to know each other better. How about we meet behind the cow yard tonight at 7 o'clock?' Which they did, and unfortunately the girl became pregnant. As a result, the police were notified and, when they investigated the matter, the girl admitted having sex with the young white fellow. The police then got an admission from the lad and he was charged under the *Aboriginal Protection Act* for having sex with an Indigenous woman. He was convicted and fined something like five pounds and he soon moved on. On the other hand, the girl remained with the grazing family. Then, when she was old enough, she and her child moved out of the home and, now being well adapted to town life, they stayed in Coen.

By the time my wife and I arrived in Coen, the woman had married an Indigenous man. They were a good, solid, respectable family and, although I never broached the subject about her getting pregnant to the young white fellow, we did talk about her being brought to Coen as a young nine-year-old and placed into protection. When I inquired as to her feelings on the matter, she told me she was forever grateful that she wasn't left to suffer out in the wilds, as part of a 'nomadic group', so to speak. In fact, she said that being placed with the white grazing family was, and I quote, 'The best thing that ever happened to me. They treated me well.' So that's just one story that's had a great effect on me.

A very different incident occurred back in 1964. This white fellow had been employed as a waiter in a restaurant down in

Melbourne. Being well trusted by his boss, he was given the responsibility of driving the other staff home, in his boss' car, after work each night. Which he did very reliably, until the night he didn't return with his boss' car. There was a police investigation, but they couldn't find hide nor hair of the fellow nor the car. Of course, with Coen and Melbourne being at virtual opposite ends of Australia, we'd heard nothing about all this. Then one day, one of the Murris arrived in town and he come up to me. 'Sarge,' he said, 'I just got a lift up from Musgrave.' Musgrave's about a hundred miles south of Coen and, mind you, it's over some of the most shocking roads you could ever imagine. He said, 'It was with a white bloke in a Hillman Minx, would you believe it?'

Now a Hillman Minx in that sort of country just didn't make sense. Those days you'd barely get a four-wheel-drive vehicle up the track. Anyhow, this white fellow had apparently hit a rock and holed the sump and he'd asked the man to walk into town to get some help. As the Murri described the situation, 'Sarge,' he said, 'this bloke, 'e's out there all broke down to bits.'

I then got in touch with a local who was a bit of a mechanic and I asked him to go out and find the fellow, fix his sump and bring him and his vehicle into town. Which he did. But I thought, Gee, this's a bit strange, driving around the wilds of Cape York in a tiny Hillman Minx. So we decided to do a police check on the man and the vehicle. At the best of times, communications were never that good on the overland telegraph line, but we eventually got through to Cairns. Cairns then passed our request on to Brisbane. Brisbane passed our request on to Sydney. Sydney passed our request on to Melbourne and Melbourne replied, 'Yes, the Hillman Minx is the very same Hillman Minx that'd disappeared.' So this fellow had driven from Melbourne, all the way through Victoria, then all the way through New South Wales, into Queensland and right up into Cape York Peninsula and he'd ended up 'broke down to bits' just short of Coen.

When we got word about the vehicle being stolen, the fellow fessed-up straight away. 'Yes,' he said, 'I stole the car. I wanted to go to Thursday Island and see the sights but I came to grief down the track a bit.'

Anyhow, we arrested him and we took possession of the car. But then we had to arrange for an escort to fly up from Cairns and take the fellow back down there for the court case. Of course, living in such a remote place as Coen, to arrange all that from our end took some time. Then it took Cairns another fair while to organise a plane to come up to Coen and get the fellow. So we had him with us for a good couple of weeks. Back then, the Coen lock-up was just a tiny cell in the backyard of the police station. And because it got as hot as Hades in there during the day, it would've been cruel to have had him locked up from dawn to dusk. So I decided to let him out after he'd had his breakfast. Sometimes we'd get him to do a bit of work around the place. Other times he was free to wander around the police complex. And on a hot afternoon, we'd take him to the swimming hole, about two miles out of town, where we'd have a barbecue and a bit of a splash around. Come night-time, we'd lock him back up in the cell.

And we got on well – he and I. Really well, in fact. I'll always remember him as being a different but decent sort of fellow. In fact, I'd love to catch up with him one of these days as I'm sure he'd have some very fond memories of his time in Coen. Of course, he realised, if he tried to shoot through, he'd have to find his way through a hell of a lot of rugged terrain before he reached civilisation. So I don't think he ever entertained the idea of escaping and, of course, we did look after him very well. So much so that, by the time he was escorted onto the plane to go down to Cairns for his trial, he was in tears with having to leave us.

Footnote – Coen is five hundred and sixty kilometres north of Cairns and five hundred kilometres south of the tip of Cape York Peninsula. Kaanju – or Kandju – is the regional Aboriginal language. In 1623, Jan Carstensz, navigator of the ship *Pera*, named a local river Jan Pieterszoon Coen, after the Governor-General of the Dutch East India Company. It's now named the Archer River, of which the Coen River is a tributary.

Gold discoveries during the mid-1870s were short-lived and the small settlement struggled until the Great Northern Mine boom in the late 1890s. A post office opened in 1893. Gold mining was in decline in the 1930s but, by then, pastoralists were moving in and Coen became more established. Today the population is around four hundred. It has an airstrip, a public library, a guesthouse, two general stores with fuel, a hospital, post office, police station, primary school, a ranger base and a hotel.

In the mid-1970s, a group of plumbers, armed with the letter 'S', turned the signage on Coen's hundred-year-old Exchange Hotel into the Sexchange Hotel. The hotel offers good 'old-fashioned hospitality', with 'comfortable rooms, a caravan park, dongas and a camping area where you can sleep under the stars'.

Coonamble – NSW

Dear Swampy, when you were in Coonamble last time you mentioned how you were taken by the number of nickname caricatures that were on display along our streets. And so, as we are known as the 'nickname town of Australia', I have gathered together a much longer list of names, with their nicknames, of people in and around Coonamble. I hope you are well and that you can come back and visit us again soon and perhaps do another performance and maybe even run another writing workshop.

Anyhow, I'll read them out in alphabetical order. So here we go: there's Albert 'Dead-Eye' Allan. Ayoub 'Arab' Joseph is from an Afghan family. Noel 'Horsey' Bacigalupo is named so because he's always on a horse. There's Stephen 'Diesel' Baker, John 'Softly-Softly' Brien and Anne 'Roonie' Brydon. There's the Canhams: Joe is known as 'Maggot' and Raymond is called 'Icy'. There's Gwyn 'Gin and Tonic' Connick, Brendon 'Gumpy' Crawford, Kevin 'Boof' Cullen and Bob 'Black Rat' Day. Bert 'Wingy' Doyle is so named because he only has one arm. Cecil 'Shanghi Rooster' Fitzgerald is one of our great Aboriginal characters and Norman 'Pickles' Fulmer is someone you've previously interviewed for stories.

There's the Hamilton family where Anthony is called 'Pampy', Clinton 'Juicy', Danny 'Boon', Harry 'Moosey' and Rodney is known as 'One Tit' – though I'm not exactly sure where that one came from – and there's John 'Wombat' Hayword. As for the Head family: Alma is nicknamed 'Tiny', Bradley is 'Bassett', Colin is 'Monkey', Johnny is 'Long Pocket', Mervyn is either 'Mickie' or 'Big Wegs', Neville is 'Nummie' and Norman's nickname is 'Bull'.

In the Hodgson family, Barry's called 'Dick', Cecil 'Boof', Ernest 'Foxey', Frank 'Irish', Jamie 'Freck', Neville 'Sausage', Noel 'Wingnut', Phillip 'Woodheap' and Robert is known as 'Dirk'. As you can see, they're quite a large family. Then there's the Horan family where Brian is also called 'Wingnut', Eamon 'Oogey', Terry 'Taggert' and Reg is called 'The Yank'.

The two Hunts are Gordon 'Half-Pint' and Kenneth 'Skel'. Tony Iffland is known as 'Sparrow'. Penny Jordan is known as 'Bubbles', Noel Kennedy is 'Nakka' and James Killen is 'Needs', as in 'needs killing'. I love that one. Then Frank Lane is 'Singer', named so after Frankie Lane the singer, James Maher is 'Pluck' and Raymond Mathes is known as 'Cornbag'. As for the McKeown family, Arthur is called 'Bluey', Bruce 'The Ghost', Eric 'Jughead', Geoff 'Wet Eye' and Kenneth, the son of Eric, is known to one and all as 'Jughead Junior'. Then there's Michael 'Wooleybah' McMahon. Within the Mulholland family, Kevin is nicknamed 'Sox', Mervyn is known as 'Sparks', Robert as 'Choot' and Wayne is called 'Whip'.

The Nicol family is another large one with Alan being called 'Hawk-eye', Dave is 'Nicco', Gadstone is 'Joe', Kevin is 'Cork', Mervyn is 'Ecco', Raymond is 'Abbie', Reg is 'Black Ant' and Ted is 'Date'. John Page is known as 'Dumpling' and Peter Pennel is nicknamed 'Whacky'. Our undertaker, Raymond Pickering, is known as 'Bones' and Russell Pickering as 'Boorie'. Then there's Michael 'Agg' Quilkey and Christian 'Stinky' Ramien. In the Robertson family there's Arthur 'Top-Deck', Henry 'Tracker' – whose plaque is in the street – Tom is known as 'Puss' and Tony as 'Deckie'. Then there's Barry 'Shiner' Ryan. Bert Sharp answers to both 'Sparrow' and/or 'The Ferret' – depending on the day and the time of day. As for the Smiths; Geoff is known as 'Frog' and Lorraine as 'Sarge'. Then there's Rodney 'Cockroach' Vallett. As for the Whiteheads, Gordon is called 'Nugget' and Les answers to 'Pudden'.

Frank Wooding is known as 'Fluffy'. Within the Wrigleys, Dennis is known as 'Fixer' and James as 'Zippa'. Finally there's Kevin 'Cock Sparrow' Yeo and Stephen 'Birdman' Zawada. And that's just to name a few of us.

So good luck, and all the best with the book and, like I said, you're welcome to pop by any time.

Footnote – Coonamble is on the Castlereagh River, in the central-western plains of New South Wales, near on four hundred and fifty kilometres north-west of Sydney. It's known as 'the gateway to the north-west'. There is some conjecture as to the town's naming: some say it's taken from the Gamilaraay word *guna* meaning 'faeces' and *-bul* meaning 'having much'. Another is that its name has been derived from the Aboriginal word *gunambil* which is believed to mean 'full of bullock's dung'; though the last local full-blood Gamilaraay believed it was more to do with 'full of dirt'.

Prior to European settlement, the Coonamble area was inhabited and cared for by the Kamilaroi, Kawambarai and Weilwan Aboriginal groups. When, in 1818, John Oxley and party passed through just north of where the town stands today he wrote, 'Aboriginal bark huts were to be seen in every direction along the Castlereagh River.' In 1840, James Walker established the first pastoral run in the area, and by 1855 land on the Castlereagh River was set aside for the town site. The site was surveyed in 1859 and a post office established. The town was officially gazetted in 1861, with a courthouse and jail being built the following year.

In 1865, John Dunn, the only surviving member of Ben Hall's bushranging gang, was shot, captured, then hanged a year later for murder. Coonamble's first public school opened in 1869 and a police station and stables were built by 1870. By 1871, Coonamble's population reached two hundred. A new courthouse was opened in 1877, as was a new police station. The statue that stands in front of the police station is that of Constable John Mitchell, who was shot in 1885 while trying to prevent two prisoners from escaping.

A new post office opened in 1881, a bridge was completed over the Castlereagh River in 1883 and Irish Brigidine nuns set up a school in that same year. The school was later dismantled and relocated to Pokolbin, six hundred kilometres away. The first bore in the Coonamble district was drilled in 1894 and the railway arrived from Dubbo in 1903. In early 1929, a devastating fire destroyed thirty-eight buildings in the main street – Castlereagh Street.

These days, Coonamble's annual rodeo draws around a thousand competitors and four thousand spectators and it hosts an annual across-the-arts Moorambilla Festival. The town's main street features old pubs, interesting murals, amusing nickname caricatures and a number of Art Deco buildings.

The Commercial Hotel was first built in 1876, and, after being destroyed by a fire, was rebuilt in 1912. Today the upstairs verandah offers excellent views, particularly from its featured Cobb & Co lookout tower.

The Terminus Hotel was built in 1903 and has since undergone renovations. Situated near the old railway station, it's advertised as a 'family friendly hotel'. Don't miss out on the Lions Club meat raffles.

The Bucking Bull Hotel – the oldest original surviving hotel in Coonamble – was built as a single storey establishment in the 1880s, with a second storey being added in 1924. To add to its intrigue, there have been two suspicious deaths in the hotel and some say it's haunted. The Bucking Bull serves a variety of meals, including their well-renowned 9-inch and 12-inch Raging Bull pizza, and beers, highlighted by their own special 'Bull Piss'.

Sons of the Soil Hotel was originally built in 1879 as the Hibernian, later to be renamed the Occidental and, in 1889, Tattersalls. It was burnt down in the 1929 fires and was rebuilt and renamed as the Sons of the Soil Hotel in 1984. At the time of writing, the hotel is under new management, and is starting to run different and unique events. One Facebook posting announced a Lingerie Waitress Night where Ellie, the lovely lingerie waitress, would be gracing the bar during the 5.30 to 9.00 p.m. pool competition! The lovely Ellie would also be on deck for Friday morning's $5 breakfast.

Cue – WA

I was at the University of Queensland, doing a Master of Tropical Health, when I met a female German medical student. We just ran into each other. So yeah, one thing led to another then, as you do, we got married and we had two children. My wife was ten years younger than me, but she got terribly homesick and eventually decided to return to Germany with our two children. Because I didn't go, I became a bit lost. So when I saw a job going at a solo nursing post, over at Cue, Western Australia, I thought I'd throw my hat into the ring. I got the job and so Cue's where I went to next. That was back in the early 2000s.

Cue's an old gold-mining town in the mid-west of Western Australia. By the time I got there, all the big mines had closed. It was virtually a ghost town. But it was a lovely place to work. It had great community spirit and I made friends quickly. I well remember many a unique happening that occurred while I was there. One being when the Catholic nun – Sister Gerri Boylan of the Good Samaritans – arrived from nearby Mount Magnet one Sunday morning to conduct the weekly service. By that stage, the population of Cue had fallen to below two hundred.

At 10 a.m. Sister Boylan and I met on the steps of St Patricks, and there we sat, waiting in the hopes that some more parishioners may appear. When none did, both of us went inside the church and Gerri made a start. Considering the sparse congregation that was sat before her, Gerri was doing a pretty good job of the service: that's until she reached the part where she needed someone to stand at the lectern for the second reading of the Mass. At that point, Gerri looked over the assembled congregation of just one lonely soul – me – and announced, 'Would anyone like to come up and read today's verse?'

At that point, I looked to my left. I looked to my right. Then I turned around and looked toward the back of the church. Still no one and, so, with no other volunteers, I called out, 'Well, Sister, if no one else is prepared to read today's verse, I'm willing to give it a go.' So I got up and walked out front to the lectern, where I read the selected passage from the Good Book to the many ghosts of the distant past, who were occupying the empty pews. So that's what Cue was like in the early 2000s, when, back in the 1900s at the height of the gold rush, there were about ten thousand people in and around Cue – including one young shire engineer, Herbert Hoover, who later became President of the United States of America.

In my time, a lot of the old buildings from Cue's glory days were still standing. Actually, in many ways, the whole town resembled a movie set from some Wild West town in Arizona or Nevada, with its ornate shop-fronts and overhanging verandahs. Even a couple of the building frontages had retained the old hitching rails for horses. At that time, I was living just along the road from an historic French-designed building that wouldn't have been out of place on the outskirts of Paris ... oh, apart from it being clad in corrugated iron, that is. Then, the current mayor and his wife, who became a shire councillor, ran the hardware and grocery shop, Bell's Emporium. That's another wonderful building, which also looks as if it hasn't changed in the last hundred years or so.

But with being the town's one and only nurse, I obviously became very involved in everyone's lives. In doing so, I dealt with the whole spectrum; from those who were mildly ill, to those who were a bit down and needed a chat, to those who'd been involved in major traumas such as heart attacks and car or motor bike accidents. I well recall when a bikie hobbled into the clinic very much the worse for wear. 'I've had a bit of a tumble off me Harley Davidson,' he announced.

'What happened?' I asked.

'Hit a bloody roo,' he said.

'Where?' I asked.

'Smack-bang in its bloody chest,' he said.

I was thinking he might've been having a lend of me, but I wasn't sure. 'No,' I responded, 'I mean whereabouts was the accident?'

'Oh,' he said, 'about twenty k's north of here. So I pushed me Harley int'a the scrub, so no one'd pinch it. 'N I left a pile of rocks on the roadside so I could find it later.'

I thought, Crikey, being as precious as a Harley Davidson is, even that's not safe. I said, 'Mate, it'll get nicked for sure.' So I rang the owners of Nallan Station, near where the bikie had come off his Harley. After I'd had a chat to them, I said to the bikie, 'Look, I've just rung the owner and his son, and they said they'd pick up your bike and keep it safe. Then after your rehabilitation in Perth, you can come back and fetch it off them.'

'Thanks,' he said. 'Good idea.'

And that's what did happen. But not only did the owner and his son go and pick up this bikie's precious Harley, they also did some running repairs on it and got it going. And once they got it going, they reckoned they had great fun zipping around Nallan Station, on this hulking great machine, mustering cattle. 'Oh,' they said, 'it worked like magic. As soon as the cattle hear the humongous noise of the thing, they soon take notice.' I mean, imagine going out mustering on a Harley Davidson!

Another incident also stands out. At about two o'clock one morning I got a knock on my door. 'Andrew, there's been an accident.'

Anyhow, there was this poor man – a little chap of only about fifty kilos – he'd had a bit to drink and he was walking across the road in the dead of the night when he got hit by a car.

Just the impact from that broke both of his legs. But then, when he got tossed up into the air, he went straight through the car's windscreen. And then, when the driver slammed on his brakes, the chap went flying back out the window. Oh, he was in a hell of a bad way, a real mess. I thought, Surely he's dead? Anyhow, I did the basic ABC – airway, breathing and circulation – and sure enough, he was still alive. So a friend came and helped me put him in the back of my car and we drove him up to the clinic.

When I checked him out at the clinic, he almost had no blood pressure and, other than his broken legs, he'd not only smashed his shoulder but the skin on his head had been ripped off – degloved, as they say – from going through the windscreen, twice. Now, I don't know if it was due to the amount of alcohol he'd consumed or what, but he didn't seem to be in too much pain. I had IV drips going in and, because his pelvis had also been smashed, I put a firm sling around him. Then, after I'd straightened his legs, I got a neighbour to come over and hold his head at a tilt to help drain the blood that was pouring out. When I rang the Royal Flying Doctor Service (RFDS) and told them what'd happened, they couldn't believe he was still alive. I said, 'Well, he is and so you'd better come out and get him. But make it quick!'

Then, because of our distance from Perth, I had to wait a couple of hours for the plane to come and pick him up and take him away. And that's the last I thought I'd ever see of him. But no, against all odds, six months later, the chap limped back into the clinic and thanked me for saving his life.

As for some of the characters in town: other than the afore-mentioned current mayor and his shire councillor wife, my next-door neighbour was the then mayor. I remember how he'd often invite me to council meetings when they were in need of input into various health issues. He lived in a caravan on a kind of industrial block. I was always welcome over there and we had some great yarns. Then my neighbours on the other side – a married couple – owned a prospecting claim out near Lake Austin, which is a salt lake about twenty kilometres south of Cue. I'd sometimes go out there on a weekend with them and poke around the old tailings. One evening, after about six months of getting to know them, they said, 'I think we know you well enough to trust you by now, Andrew.' With a consenting nod the wife reached into the pantry and, from behind some biscuit tins, she lifted out a tall glass jar. 'Have a look at this,' she said, and there before my very eyes shone the largest nugget of alluvial gold I've ever seen in my life. And that's true! It must've been close to a kilogram. They'd apparently found it, just six inches below the surface and with the use of a simple metal detector. I mean, wow!

Across the road from me was another couple, who'd lived in Cue almost forever. Lovely people. Just lovely. The husband often popped in to the clinic under the guise of having his blood pressure checked. Though, in reality, he just wanted a yarn and a cup of tea, which was totally fine by me. One of his passions was woodworking; a pursuit he was a master craftsman at.

As for some of the others: a few years before I got there, six Italian gentlemen from Perth had bought the local Bank of New South Wales in Cue's main street. It's another classic, solid stone building. They'd paid peanuts for it and had turned it into a getaway retreat from their wives – or so they said. I met them on several occasions when they'd drive up to Cue to collect a trailer-load of live baby kid-goats, which were destined for the pot or roasting oven back home. They'd often invite me around to their backyard campfire barbecues and urge their homemade red wine onto me. Though, with being on call for my medical work 24/7, I couldn't take up their offer. More's the pity.

Another great character was a Vietnam veteran whom I'll just call Jack. Jack suffered from PTSD. On Anzac Day I'd be asked to cook the breakfast for the few old diggers who lived in and around Cue. Jack lived with his young family in the abandoned Lutheran stone church. They'd also bought it for peanuts and had turned it into a sort of home. By describing it as 'sort of a home', it wasn't high-end living by any stretch of the imagination. Though, being stacked to the hilt with curios they'd salvaged from the old dump, it certainly wasn't boring. I visited them quite often and sat and listened to the vast wealth of stories Jack had gleaned from the area's past. Then sometimes he'd say, 'How about we go fossicking around an old dump?'

'Okay,' I'd say and, when we did, we'd find hundred-year-old pieces of crockery and odds and sods from the old gold-mining days. And he'd take me out on excursions to visit places of interest, such as Australia's oldest known mine, Wilgie Mia, which is in the Weld Range. For over 40,000 years, Aboriginal people have revered the spot for the astonishingly bright red ochre pigment that they use for ceremonial purposes.

Then sometimes Jack'd say, 'Hey, I'm taking the family out for a swim. Want'a come along?' And we'd end up out at some abandoned mine site for a midsummer swim in its man-made lakes. Even the 'Strictly no Entry' signs on the gateways didn't faze Jack. Not at all. Anyhow, where else could you go and cool off when it was 45 degrees in the shade and the nearest legal swimming pool was at least a couple of hundred kilometres away. But I distinctly remember that one of Jack's very special spots was a certain tree, just out of town. As I said, he suffered from PTSD, and that's where he'd go when things got difficult and he'd just sit there and contemplate; thinking about whatever he'd think about. I never asked.

Anyhow, while I was at Cue, the Australian Nurse of the Year awards people started sending out flyers to all the hospitals and clinics asking for nominations. Now, I don't know who was behind it – like, who put in the nomination – but about three months later I got a call saying that I'd been selected to represent Western Australia as their Nurse of the Year. That was in 2004, and so they flew me over to Melbourne where we had a big cocktail evening and all that sort of hoopla. It was a good night – a great night actually. At that stage, Tony Abbott was Minister for Health and he gave out the awards. When I got mine for being the West Australian Nurse of the Year, I said, 'Thank you very much,' and I went back and sat down at my table. Then they announced, 'Now, for the overall Nurse of the Year. Stand up Andrew Cameron.' For a second there, I was looking around to see who this other Andrew Cameron might be. When he didn't stand up, I realised that it was me. I was completely blown away. So yes, I have many fond memories of the township of Cue and of its people.

Footnote – Cue is in the mid-west of Western Australia, near on six hundred and fifty kilometres north-east of Perth. Prior to European settlement, the Watjarri Aboriginal people cared for and lived on the land for thousands of years. Rumour has it that, in 1892, after having been gifted a gold nugget by a Watjarri man known as Governor, Michael Fitzgerald and Edward Heffernan in turn told Tom Cue about its discovery. Tom Cue – after whom the town is named – then travelled to Nannine to register their claim. Within weeks, over four hundred prospectors had clambered to the area. In doing so, a second gold-mining town, Day Dawn, which is eight kilometres south of Cue, was also established.

In 1894, Premier John Forrest visited Cue and promised to build a telegraph line, a railway and permanent government buildings. The telegraph line was completed that same year. By 1895, a number of ten-head stamp mills were in operation. The town's first water supply was a well in the centre of the main street. However, after an outbreak of typhoid fever, a rotunda was erected over the well and fresh water was carted from a well near Lake Nallan, twenty kilometres away. The first train arrived in 1897 and Cue remained the terminus for the Northern Railway until the line was extended to Meekatharra. Cue was also the junction for the branch line to Big Bell, until that line closed.

By 1900 a hospital had been built, a cemetery was operating and three newspapers were being published in the dual townships of Cue and Day Dawn. By then the population had reached ten thousand. Then came the decline: due to the number of men enlisting for World War One, the township of Day Dawn was soon abandoned. In 1918, the Great Fingall Mine closed. In 1933, due to the Depression years bringing a fall in the gold price, less than five hundred people remained. By 2006, with the main street having changed little, Cue was classified by the National Trust as being a town of significant historical value. Today Cue is a virtual ghost town with a population of around a hundred.

The only operating pub is the Murchison Club Hotel. Built in 1895, in the Victorian Georgian style, an additional storey was added in 1935.

Please note: the owners of the Murchison Club Hotel are currently in the 'slow process' of restoring the hotel back to its glory. So please inquire about opening hours as they may vary.

Finke (Aputula) – NT

Adapted from Dean Jamieson's book *They Called Me Lightning.*

Aputula, or Finke as it was known in my day, is a small remote town in the Northern Territory, down near the South Australian border. To its west, along a hundred miles of rough road, is Kulgera. Alice Springs is a couple of hundred miles to its north and Oodnadatta's an eight-hour drive to its south. The Simpson Desert almost begins at the back door of the pub and stretches out to the east. People within one hundred and fifty miles are considered locals.

Back in the mid-1950s, I went up there to work on the 1700-square-mile New Crown cattle station. Being a naive seventeen-year-old, I had the romantic notion of becoming a 'cowboy'. I eventually did make it as a cowboy – a ringer as they're called – but I must've somehow missed out on the romantic bit. Oh, that's apart from losing my virginity. But I'll get to that.

Not long after my arrival, I remember going out on New Crown with a feller called Malcolm O'Donnell to drill a borehole. Malcolm was a man of few words and, with being a new chum, I was to be his 'offsider'. During the entire week we were out there, he hardly spoke to me. Then the morning after we'd struck water, he shut down the drilling rig, changed the oil, greased the joints and packed up camp. He then rolled up his swag, threw it on the truck, jumped in and stared at me from the cab. When I shrugged as to what he wanted me to do, he motioned for me to roll up my swag. So I did and I threw it on the truck, jumped in with him, and we took off. Like I said, a man of few words.

Even then I had no idea where we were going or why – not a clue. We just bashed a track through the soft, sandy red dirt, mowing down dead mulga trees with the bull bar, until we intercepted a rough, corrugated track. I then noticed that we were running parallel to a single train line and, in the distance, perched high on a tower, stood a huge water tank the size of a small house. As we drove on, a few corrugated iron roofs started to appear, then we passed a railway platform, which had a sign reading – FINKE.

The lofty water tank and tower – a leftover relic of long-gone steam trains – dominated the town. Finke consisted of a row of fettlers' huts, a small stationmaster's house, a PMG telephone relay-post office with house attached, a police station with an attached residence and a two-cell gaol, a ramshackle general store, a single-roomed school and a teacher's house. A large galvanised shed that I later discovered was the community hall had two tarred tennis courts, then set apart was the livestock inspector's house. Set some distance from the centre of Finke was a shantytown. Many of its dwellings were upturned rainwater tanks, long ago discarded, with openings cut in the side, while others were pieced together from scrap iron and canvas.

The hotel was the town's focus: iron roofed, stonewalled, with a wide raised cement verandah half encircling the building. Our truck lurched to a stop, nose to its verandah. I dutifully followed Malcolm into the cool, dimly lit pub. The bar would've been around twelve or so foot long, with a small L section at one end. High stools lined the bar with a chrome kick rail running its length. A well-worn dartboard was clinging to the wall at one end with a set of quoits and a peg underneath. Malcolm lifted the blinds on several windows and leapt onto the bar, sitting with his back to the wall and his legs outstretched along the bar-top. While he waited for someone to turn up, I sat on a stool. After a while, a grey-haired, short, frumpy middle-aged woman entered from a side door.

'G'day, Malcolm. How long are yer stayin' 'n who's yer offsider?' she asked.

'Hi, Beat,' he said. 'We'll be stayin' a day or two. Can we have a feed 'n a clean-up? We'll camp next ter the truck.' Then, as an afterthought, he added, 'Oh, his name's Dean, city lad, just come up. He's goin' okay so far.' Which was high praise from a man who'd hardly spoken to me for over a week. While Malcolm was talking to Beat, a man walked into the bar. After two 'G'day, mates' he pulled a beer and placed it next to Malcolm, as if it was quite normal for someone to sit on top of a bar, stretched out.

The barman then looked at me. 'And what'll you have young feller?' Being under drinking age I said, 'I'd like a lemonade or a squash please.'

'Would yer now?' came the reply. 'There's not much'a that out 'ere. We're a pub. We sell beer.'

'But I'm only seventeen 'n so I'm not allowed to drink beer, sir.'

'Well, I won't tell no one if you don't tell no one,' he said. I found out later that his name was Alan Brumby and his wife's name was Beatrice. They were seasoned long-time outback people. Their son Johnny was Head Stockman out on New Crown. As Alan handed me a large glass of beer, Malcolm said, 'Put it on my tab.'

Being thirsty, the cold liquid went down almost without a pause. In fact, it tasted so good that the second glass also disappeared in seconds. Although, being a non-drinker before this day, after two beers I began to feel dizzy and uncoordinated. Worse still, when I tried to lift myself off the stool, my legs wouldn't work. So I slid downwards, with my back against the bar, before flopping into a lying position alongside the kick rail, on the barroom floor. My body was useless. I was drunk for the first time in my life and couldn't do anything about it. Upon watching me slide off the bar stool and flat onto the floor in such an ungracious manner, Alan made a comment that labelled me with the nickname that's stuck for over sixty years. 'Look at that,' he said. 'Just like lightning – one flash and it's all over,' and they all looked down at me and laughed.

I accepted the nickname of Lightning, which was often shortened to just Lite, in good humour. In the outback, most people have nicknames – some for obvious reasons, some obscure – there's Yarpie, Bulla, Wham, Dipstick, Slim, Lofty, Bluey, just to name a few. I wore mine with pride. Whenever I was questioned as to how I'd been labelled Lightning, I had several flattering versions. Though being a first-time drunk was rarely one of them.

Malcolm and I stayed in Finke for two more days, swagging it on the ground alongside our truck, and eating and washing at the hotel. And I declined any more offers of beer. During my wanderings I discovered that just a few hundred yards to the north of town was the wide Finke River. Some say it's the oldest river in the world. In my time, a low concrete and metal 'bridge-structure' sat on top of the Finke's thick, coarse sandy riverbed. Tall ghost gums spotted the bank – spectacular and healthy. The river rarely flowed, but when it did a flow of just a few inches was enough to stop the diesel electric train – The Ghan – from crossing it. When that happened The Ghan's passengers became captive, often for days, trapped in the sleepy little town.

And that was cause for celebration. Messages soon flew back and forward over the outback airwaves, causing us 'locals' to flock into Finke. Coulsen's store would almost sell out. Barbecues were organised, great slabs of beef cut up, fresh bread appeared and the stranded passengers willingly donated all proceeds to the Royal Flying Doctor Service. A huge campfire was lit and there'd be evening music with guitars, accordions and stringed tea chests. The pub stayed open all night. Jim, the local policeman, and his wife Shirley, always joined in. During these occasions, Jim always dressed in civvies so as not to put a dampener on things, and, anyway, there was rarely any trouble.

The captive train passengers loved the entertainment so much that they'd join in with the dancing in the red dust. To impress them even further, us stockmen, having suffered a drought of female companionship, would show off our moves in the hopes of snaring a young woman passenger and sneaking her off into the dark to get better acquainted. Most failed. Including me. Then, when the water level receded, the train would move on, and we'd head back out to our station properties and Finke would return to its sleepy old normal pace.

Another big event was the Finke Horse Races. People from as far away as Marree, William Creek, Oodnadatta, Kulgera and Alice Springs would turn up for the long weekend. For the women, it was a rare chance to dress up and meet people that they'd often only ever talked to over the RFDS two-way wireless network. The dance in the big community tin shed and the barbecue were highlights. Us young men would scrub ourselves as clean as a whistle and dress smartly in our R.M. Williams moleskins, big Akubra hats, colourful press-stud fronted shirts and high-heeled riding boots. And all with a twinkle in our roving eyes, looking for a damsel to 'woo'. Mind you, with the ratio of men to women being about ten to one, most, including myself, sadly ended up disappointed in our quest.

In preparation for the big event, the publican would drive his truck the six hundred miles to Port Augusta and return with a load of beer. As usual, the pub's refrigeration couldn't cope with the overload, so we'd end up drinking semi-warm beer. Still, after the first few glasses, nobody cared. The bar at the Finke Hotel was always packed. Some had been to the dance and, in their frustrated haste, had bluntly propositioned some young woman, only to be just as bluntly knocked back. Crestfallen, they'd join their mates in the pub to get 'blotto' as they all shared bullshit tales about their many conquests, or how many buck jumpers they'd ridden, or who'd win the Finke Cup.

Then at about 2 or 3 a.m. they'd stagger out of the pub to try and find their swags and pass out.

Sunup the next morning was never a pretty sight. Swags lay like lumps out in the red dust and, as the sun began to climb, it'd beat down a fiery heat. By then there'd be a gradual stirring of bodies. Many were moaning, with some holding their heads and declaring, 'That's it. Never again' or 'God I feel crook.' The few comatose bodies, who hadn't been able to make it to their swags, would be sprawled out on the concrete, in the shade of the verandah, with flies crawling over their faces and in and around open mouths as they gave forth gurgling noises.

As some of the new chums rushed for the toilets, to be as sick as dogs, their vomiting sounds would set off others. Then, with no more room in the tiny toilet block, they'd venture further out onto the red dust to join in the 'hughie' chorus. Not to be deterred, the seasoned drinkers would head for the pub to partake in 'the hair of the dog'. Even though the place stank of stale booze, cigarette smoke and body odour, at least it was cooler and dimly lit.

Another big event that happened in Finke was my first serious sexual encounter. Losing my virginity was something special. We'd come in from New Crown and were staying overnight while we waited for The Ghan to bring our station's grocery order up from Adelaide. Her name was Kay. Her father was a white railway worker, her mother part-Aboriginal. She was about my age; creamy skinned with dark hair. She was gorgeous, and I told her so, and she seemed to like me. By then I was eighteen and, after having now worked in the outback for a year, I was strong, fit and game. My swag was hidden in the darkness. We kissed and cuddled. I was clumsy, very shy and obviously inexperienced. My advances were timid and, with hers being more direct, I attempted to follow her lead. By then we were both naked and my excitement immediately reached fever pitch – so much so that the words 'premature ejaculation' would be an understatement.

Still, we stayed and cuddled in my swag. I dozed a little and, some time later, we began again. This time more leisurely and with far better results. I was now totally smitten with Kay; deeply in love, no doubt about it. Then it struck me, Have I made her pregnant? Should I ask her to marry me?

When I returned to New Crown, Kay was constantly in my thoughts. But it was nearly six weeks before I got to return to Finke; again for supplies. So there I was, dressed to the nines in my moleskin pants, polished boots, hat, fancy shirt, primed and squeaky clean. After we'd loaded up the truck at Finke Railway Station, we headed to the pub. That's when I heard there'd been an exodus of biblical proportions. The old schoolteacher had been replaced by Jeanette – young, attractive, athletic and, as rumour had it, a very good tennis player. Alan and Beat Brumby, the publicans, had handed the reigns over to Alec and Isobel Rabig. A new couple now ran the post office and telephone exchange, and Kay's parents had left Finke, taking Kay with them. And I never saw or heard of her again.

Footnote – The mostly dry Finke River was named after the German prospector, William Finke. A few kilometres from the river, and just over three hundred kilometres south of Alice Springs, is Finke, the township. Now known as Aputula, it's the farthest populated town from coastal rim of Australia and, therefore, the nearest settlement to the geographical centre of the continent.

Finke began as a small fettlers' camp around the mid-1920s, when Central Australia Railway set up a small siding. The Lower Southern Arrernte and Luritja people soon established a camp in the nearby sand hills, trading dingo scalps, wild flowers, artefacts and other items in exchange for water and food. The Indigenous people from Ernabella also began visiting Finke to pick up supplies from the train. In the late 1930s a police station was built and residents petitioned for a postal service. During the war years, Finke siding got its first repeater station operator and the north–south railway line became the main transport route for thousands of soldiers and equipment going to and from the war in the Pacific.

After World War Two, due to its better water quality and location, the government built cattle yards in Finke. The town then became a pastoral centre and its population grew. In 1947, Finke Hotel, owned by Ted Colson – the first European to cross the Simpson Desert – opened, and an airstrip provided access to the RFDS. In 1953, the school opened, and the township of Finke was proclaimed in August 1955.

Following major track damage during the floods of 1973 and 1974, the railway line was shifted westward and so, by the late 1970s, most of the Europeans had moved on. But the Indigenous population remained and, with the help of the Uniting Church mission from Ernabella, they moved off the sand dunes into houses. During this time, the town transitioned to the Aboriginal community now known as Aputula. The name is derived from the Arrernte word *putula*, which means 'a nearby soak'.

These days Finke – Aputula – has a population of less than two hundred. Most of its current inhabitants are from the Western Desert country, who acknowledge they are living on Southern Arrernte land. Due to its harsh conditions and lack of available water, the site has never been a permanent Aboriginal camping ground, even in pre-European times. In fact, Finke (Aputula) has experienced the two hottest days ever recorded in the Northern Territory – 48.3 degrees Celsius.

Finke is host to one of the Territory's biggest annual sporting events – the Finke Desert Race: an off-road, multi-terrain, two-day race for motorbikes, cars and buggies that runs from Alice Springs to Aputula. The race is held each June, on the Queen's Birthday (soon to become King's Birthday) long weekend and has the reputation of being one of the most difficult off-road courses, in one of the most remote areas in the world.

Finley – NSW

This story has been adapted from a collection of Alan 'Bronco' Brett's written memories.

Look, mate, now that I'm getting on in years, I've started writing up some of the stories about my life. The original idea was that someone might like to publish them – but that hasn't happened. No one seems interested in the past ramblings of an old codger like me. But that hasn't stopped me. You've already adapted a couple of my musings into your Great Australian Outback Stories series and, when all is said and done, perhaps my family may be interested in reading about some of the adventures that their old dad and grandfather has had during his life. So here we go: here's one in which I bare all.

Back in my day, you had to do a variety of jobs to survive. I did a fair bit of droving, another time I owned a property up in the Hunter region of New South Wales and I've been a patrol officer up in New Guinea. So I've been around a bit and done a thing or two. But during my droving years, if ever I had a home-base, it would've been in the Riverina region of south-west New South Wales. At this particular time, I was living in a shack a few miles out of a small place called Finley and, being between droving jobs, I'd earn a bob or two doing casual farm work around the area.

It was pretty basic living. So, to keep myself afloat, I'd gathered a menagerie of rangy domestic beasts around me: you know, a few chooks and ducks. I had an old house cow for milk, a couple of sheep, a couple of goats and so forth. And being in an irrigation area, I'd pump a bit of water – illegally – out of a nearby channel. So I had a pretty reasonable vegie garden.

My next-door neighbour was a feller called Lou. Lou lived in a shack a few hundred yards away from me, set back a bit further in the bush. Like me, Lou was also pretty much on the bones of his arse. To that end, he'd picked up a bit of work as the local pound keeper: meaning he was responsible for rounding up stray stock, impounding them, then attempting to extract a fine from the owners. Lou was in his forties, short and stocky and sometimes moody, and I was in my early twenties and somewhat of a dreamer. On the face of it, we were the most unlikely companions. But what drew us together was an affinity for livestock – horses and cattle in particular – and so, with Lou being that much older than me, he became a 'father-like figure'.

Anyhow, it was coming up to seven o'clock one summer's morning. I'd already milked the house cow and I was attacking a red gum log with my axe, to stoke up the fire for my traditional Sunday breakfast of bacon and eggs. A few tattered old chooks were scratching about in the dust around me and the old cockerel was managing his final hoarse cock-a-doodles for the day. It was already heading toward a scorcher and so, after I'd finished breakfast, I planned to curl up under the shade of my verandah with a good book. As I was taking an armload of wood into the house, a Muscovy drake waddled up the steps behind me. 'Piss off,' I yelled at him, to which he replied with an angry hiss and shat over my freshly swept verandah floor, as if to say, 'Get stuffed!'

'Does that mean me too?' came a voice, and Lou emerged from behind the rainwater tank.

'It's a bit bloody early for you isn't it, Lou?' I said, 'Did yer wet the bed or somethin'?'

'Gotta go ter Finley ter collect me new filly,' Lou replied. 'She's a real beaut: a two-year-old palomino. I'm not sure how she'll go bein' led behind the sulky on the way back home, so I thought yer might like ter come along with me ter keep an eye on her?'

There went any idea of my sitting in the shade with a good book. But as I said, we both shared a passion for horses so, being the good neighbour I was, it was, 'Oh yeah, all right.'

After Lou ate most of my bacon and egg breakfast, we took off back to his place to harness his old bay gelding, Jimmy, up to the sulky and we set off for Finley in the increasing heat. As Jimmy plodded down the road, the poor horse was soon covered in a lather of sweat and we weren't far behind in the sweltering stakes either. Now, about halfway to Finley, there was a huge gum tree just beside the road and just beside the gum tree was an irrigation channel – not large; perhaps only ten foot across and four foot deep.

At seeing the water, Lou wiped his brow and said, 'Geez, let's stop here a while 'n give Jimmy a break.' With a hot wind blowing up, I readily agreed. So Lou tied Jimmy to the tree and we stood under the mottled shade of the red gum, eyeing the water in the irrigation channel. It was then that we were both struck with the same idea. 'Bugger it,' we said, 'it'd be far cooler in the water than it is out here,' and so we started to strip off. First came our dusty boots, then our holey socks, our shirts, trousers, even holier underpants, the lot – except for our hats, that is – and in we went – *splash!* And I can tell you, the water was a hell of a relief from the relentless sun. So there we were, lolling about, when we heard the chugging sound of a vehicle. And before we could get out of the channel and get dressed, an old A-model Ford appeared.

'Shit,' we said as the car spattered and hissed to a stop in the shade of the gum tree, not far from old Jimmy, and not far from us.

'Hello, boys!' called out the driver, a middle-aged woman of extremely generous proportions. 'What a good idea to bring along your bathing costumes on such a hot day!'

As we sunk deeper into the water, in an attempt to hide our naked selves, all we could manage in reply was an awkward, 'G'day.'

'I hope you don't mind,' the woman said, 'but I think we might stop here a while too, just to let the radiator cool down.' 'Oh,' she went on, 'my name's Winifred.' Then, elbowing the equally buxom woman in the passenger seat, she added, 'and this is my younger sister Isabelle. We're on our way to church in Finley.'

'Oh, are you?' we squeaked, sinking further into the water.

'Do you boys go to church?' Winifred continued.

'Occasionally,' squawked Lou, which was a complete bloody lie.

Then she added, 'It's important to go to church regularly; cleanse the soul, revive the spirit and what-have-you. Good, clean living is important, don't you think, boys?'

Lou and I looked at each other and, almost simultaneously, replied, 'Yes.'

'Get the picnic things out, Isabelle,' barked Winifred, who was obviously the spokesperson and organiser.

As they got out of the A-model Ford, I noticed that both women wore long floral cotton dresses. Isabelle's was blue, and Winifred's was pink; and they both wore large straw hats, decorated with plastic fruit or flowers – pink on Isabelle's and blue on Winifred's. 'Where are you boys going?'

'We're goin' to Finley too, ter fetch a horse,' said Lou.

As Winifred made herself comfortable on a picnic blanket, she unscrewed the top off a large Thermos flask and called out, 'Boys, would you like to join us in a cup of tea and some scones?'

I loved scones and with Lou having eaten most of my breakfast, I was starving. 'That's very kind of you,' replied Lou, 'but it's not long since we had our breakfast 'n a cuppa.'

As Winifred and Isabelle settled into their picnic fare, a third figure appeared from the back of the car. It was a younger woman; tall, thin, with short straight hair, with a severe fringe having been hacked across her forehead. She also wore a cotton dress but had a tight fitting hat, which had the tiniest of brims, bound by a silk ribbon band. The thing that struck me most was that her demeanour was much less outgoing. To me, she seemed sickly and awkwardly shy – almost as if she'd like to remain invisible.

'Oh, this is Mildred,' Winifred said, offhandedly. Then she turned to Mildred and added in a scolding tone, 'I almost forgot you were there. Quiet as a mouse she is, boys. I don't know what's wrong with her but she's been like that since she was born.'

While Winifred and Isabelle got stuck into their tea and scones, Mildred sat on the far corner of the picnic blanket, sipping nervously on her tea and nibbling at her scone. Lou and I just sat, squatted, with our heads poking out above water level, hats on tight, suffering the leeches that were beginning to suck and eat at our flesh.

'Might go fer a bit of a walk, Winifred, if yer don't mind,' mumbled Mildred.

'Yes, yes, go girl, but don't get lost. We're going soon.' And Mildred got up and wandered over toward a nearby fence and was soon out of sight.

So there we were, Lou and me, squatted in the water – as naked as the day we were born – with the leeches attacking us, while Winifred and Isabelle contently had their picnic. When all was finished, Winifred called out to us, 'Well, we'd better be going boys or we'll be late for the church service. God waits for no man, nor woman. Enjoy your swim.' And while Winifred went and sat in the car, Isabelle shook the dead grass and twigs from the picnic blanket, packed up the picnic gear and put it away. When all was done, Winifred called out, 'Nice to meet you, boys. Enjoy the swim and God bless,' and off they went, the A-model Ford disappearing down the road, trailing a thick cloud of dust.

'Christ almighty,' said Lou, 'I thought they'd never bloody leave,' and we clambered out onto the bank of the channel.

Then, as we were plucking the leeches off our naked bodies, there came a soft, shy whisper from beside the gum tree. 'Excuse me, could you please take me to Finley? Me cousins have drove off 'n fergot me.'

Footnote – Finley is approximately six hundred and fifty kilometres south-west of Sydney and three hundred kilometres north of Melbourne. For thousands of years prior to European settlement, the Wiradjuri people lived on and cared for the land they named *Carawatha*, reportedly meaning 'place of pines'.

Squatters from the Port Phillip district moved into the area in the early 1840s and began cropping wheat. The first building on the future town site was a shepherd's shack known as Murray Hut. The local post office opened in 1881 and, in 1893, the name Murray Hut was changed to Finley, in recognition of F.G. Finley who had surveyed the area back in 1870.

The town grew when the railway arrived in 1898. But drought struck in 1927 and, due also to the following Great Depression, the district fell into decline. In 1935, with the construction of the Berriquin Irrigation District, the town once more began its revival. To cope with the growing wheat production, in 1941, grain silos were built beside the railway line. Although the area continued to prosper, due to government rationalisation and improved road transport and conditions, the last train to Finley ran in 1987.

There are three pubs in Finley – the Albion, the Tuppal and the Finley Country Club Hotel-Motel. All have a story: the original Albion Hotel was built in 1864. Before Allan Jeans' amazing thirty-one year career as a VFL-AFL player and coach he found himself mired in controversy when, in 1952, he accepted an offer to move from archrivals Tocumwal to Finley and work at the Albion Hotel, which was run by Finley coach Bert De Abbel. So furious about this was Tocumwal that they refused to grant Jeans a clearance, forcing him to sit out the season and miss a premiership. Three years later, with the 1954 premiership under his belt, Jeans was off to St Kilda, where he played seventy-seven games for the club, and within two decades he had transformed the course of St Kilda footy club's history.

As at August 2022, the Tuppal Hotel was up for sale. This Art Deco styled two-storey hotel with awning is featured on the Silo Art Trail. Six murals by New York-based artist Damien Mitchell picture notable local identities such as the rock band Spiderbait and former AFL player and Brownlow medallist, Shane Crawford. These two murals are located inside the Tuppal Hotel, while a large mural of a ram dominates the south side of the building.

The Finley Country Club Hotel-Motel was originally licensed in 1897 as the Terminus Hotel, under the ownership of Mrs Mary Murphy. Mrs Murphy established the hotel to capture the traffic of the new railway line. The Terminus became the Commercial, then the Finley Country Club. In its more recent years the hotel had its own barber – making a good excuse for a trip to the pub.

Forthside – Tas

In memory of John Forbes.

Forthside – or Forth as it's better known – is on the north-west coast of Tasmania, just a few kilometres from Devonport. At the time of the murder, I'd been employed at Forthside Vegetable Research Station for seven or so years. So that'd make it around 1972 or '73. Anyhow, it was either a Saturday or a Sunday evening, between half past six and seven. We were out of milk at home so I said to my wife, 'I'll go down to the shop and buy some milk.'

So I went to Forth to buy some milk. Back then Forth had three shops. We've just got the one now, plus the pub – the Bridge Hotel. Now the Bridge Hotel had, and still has, quite an intriguing past, especially concerning a ghostly female figure who started to appear in the pub around the turn of the last century. Many a hotel occupant has reported seeing the vision of a grief-stricken woman, possibly wearing a white wedding gown, gazing out across the bridge, as if waiting for her bridegroom to turn up for their wedding. Added to that, there's also been unexplained footsteps at night and the shimmering female figure who occasionally appears in the upper section of the hotel's darkened hallway – which, when all pieced together, many of us locals believe is the ghost of the intended bride.

So that's just a bit of background to the pub – the Bridge Hotel. Anyhow, back to the story. We were out of milk, so I went to the first shop and I bought the milk. When I came out, I looked across the river and saw smoke coming out of the top of the Bridge Hotel. So I rushed to the fire station. By this stage, we had a truck. And oh, when we finally got it to the scene of the fire, didn't we have some fun and games. Just to start with, we had the devil's own trouble getting our connections onto one of the hydrants. Which we eventually did. Although, unfortunately, by the time we got the fire out, all the upstairs and the roof area had been gutted.

So, after having left home at 7 o'clock at night to get some milk, I didn't get home till 2 o'clock the following morning, only to be greeted by an impatient wife, saying, 'So did you get the milk?' To which my reply was, 'Yes, dear, I did get the milk, but I don't know what I've done with it.'

So we went without milk for breakfast.

Now, getting back to the pub. That's right, the fire must've been on the Saturday night because, on the following Saturday night, when the publican – who just happened to be treasurer-secretary of the local football club – opened the safe where their footy club's accounts books were held, a fellow shot him. Yes, this's all true. He shot the publican. As it turned out, the fellow who'd started the fire the previous week and the fellow who killed the publican the following week was one and the same person.

See, what'd happened was, back when the fellow had been treasurer-secretary of the local footy club, he'd diddled the books and helped himself to five hundred dollars. And then, when the publican took over the treasurer-secretary job, the fellow decided to get rid of the evidence. Having failed to burn the pub down and destroy the accounts books, the following Saturday he went back and shot the publican dead and took off with the books. He then hid the accounts books down a rabbit hole, up on top of Braddons Lookout Road. And that's where the police found them; down a rabbit hole up on top of Braddons Lookout Road. I don't know how they worked all that out, but they did. Anyhow, the fellow was nicked before the week was out.

Now, as an aside to all this, I used to play cricket with the fellow who shot the publican. He was our wicket keeper and not a bad one at that. Anyhow, after he'd been sentenced and was sent off to the Hobart lockup, we ended up playing cricket against him. And he was still wicket keeping. Though this time for the Hobart Prison team.

But the thing I'm getting around to is that, while he was doing his time in prison, he completed his accountancy degree. Can you believe that? He became a fully qualified accountant. But as to where, when or even if he ended up practising, I wouldn't have the faintest clue. He may well have even changed his name. I don't know. Though the other sad part of the saga was that he had a wife and a young son and, of course, after he'd been sent to prison, they left him. So all in all, it was quite a dramatic turnout and follow on, especially for a small place like Forthside. I mean the dreadful things that some people do ay, and all over five hundred dollars.

Footnote – Forthside is in the north-west of Tasmania, ten or so kilometres south-west of Devonport and a couple of hundred kilometres north-west of Hobart. It has a population of less than a hundred. The Forth River runs along the western boundary and the Don River is to its eastern side.

Forthside Vegetable Research Station was set up in 1962 to provide research, help and support to the state's vegetable industries. Also, with opium poppies being best grown on the meridian of 43 degrees, Forthside Research Station was the chosen centre for poppy oil research under licence from the United Nations.

The Bridge Hotel at Forthside opened in 1872. In the September of its centenary year, fire destroyed the upper storey. The proprietor, Ernest Morrison, saved the lives of two guests and the blaze was put out by the local fire brigade. Bar trade resumed within a couple of days. A week after the fire, the Morrisons' golden Labrador – Hey You – was poisoned and Ernest Morrison was shot and killed. Papers from the hotel safe were recovered from a rabbit burrow on a nearby property, but the takings remained missing. A man was later sentenced to prison for the term of his natural life.

Georgetown – Qld

Yes, right, so it was Christmas school holidays – late '60s – and we teachers from 'down south', as Adelaide was called, only got our airfares paid every second year. With this being the end of my husband's and my first teaching year in Alice Springs, three carloads of us – three couples – decided to drive back home. Thinking that it'd be too mundane to go straight down the Stuart Highway, we decided to go the long way. We left Alice Springs and went up the Stuart Highway to Tennant Creek. Just out of Tennant Creek, we turned right at Threeway Roadhouse and headed east, across the Barkly Highway to the Northern Territory–Queensland border town of Camooweal, then across to Mount Isa and on to Cloncurry. At Cloncurry, we turned north, to take a look at Normanton and the coastal town of Karumba, then back east through little outback towns such as Croydon, Georgetown, Mount Surprise and right across, eventually to Cairns.

Now, if I may, just a quick anecdote about Cairns. By the time we arrived in Cairns, I was feeling a little off-colour and my husband had conjunctivitis. But not to worry, I sent him off to the doctor to sort out his conjunctivitis. The doctor was nice and chatty and, after he'd seen to my husband, he said, 'And how's your wife?'

My husband said, 'Oh, she's all right though she's been a bit off-colour, of late.'

When my husband returned from his appointment, he said to me, 'The doctor told me to tell you that you're pregnant!' And that was our first baby on the way.

Anyhow, after we'd spent a few lovely days in Cairns we headed south, down the east coast. By this stage, we'd parted company with the other two couples as they wanted to do different things. We'd left Alice Springs on 3 December, the day after my husband's birthday, with the aim of arriving in Adelaide in time for Christmas Day. Although, as it turned out, we ended up spending a lonely Christmas Day in Sydney, having lunch at a hotel, and we got home a few days later.

Now, before I get to the story that I'd like to tell you, just a few incidents that happened along the way. I remember arriving in Camooweal on a Saturday afternoon. There was just a little pub there and the place was jam-packed to overflowing with men out on the verandah, half of them asleep, others flaked out and some still drinking. I mean what an image: which just reminds me of some of the other different pub experiences we had along the way. This was back in the days when women weren't allowed to go into the front bar of pubs – not in Queensland anyway. At one hotel, I inadvertently fronted up at the bar with my husband and asked for a brandy and dry, or something like that. In that instant, the rowdy pub fell into deathly silence. You could've heard a pin drop. I thought, This's strange. Then my husband gave me a nudge. 'Look, everyone's staring at you. You'd better go and wait in the ladies' lounge.'

So yes, that was another pub experience, and I had to retreat to the ladies' lounge. Immediately I did, the ruckus struck up again and things returned to normal – well, as 'normal' as a packed pub was in those days. In other places, you'd see the women sitting out in the heat of the car while their men were inside drinking and every so often they'd send them out a drink. Usually a shandy. Though I never liked shandies. Another pub we went into, I asked for a brandy, lime and soda and the barman said, 'Oh, you must be from South Australia,' apparently because South Australians drink brandy, lime and soda.

Anyhow, at Camooweal, I think our men went into the pub briefly. But that was enough and we headed off soon after. Now, even though we three families were travelling together, we didn't travel in close convoy. It was more like, 'Okay, we'll see you at the next town.' And so we'd all meet up at the next town and have lunch or set up camp or whatever. We didn't stay in any of the hotels along the way. After my few experiences, I wasn't at all enthusiastic and anyway, we were well organised for camping. We never used tents. We mostly slept out in the open, on a groundsheet, tucked into our sleeping bags with a rug inside. And if it was going to be cold, we'd dig a trench and spread the coals of our campfire in it, cover it over with dirt, then we'd lay down our sleeping bags, on the groundsheet, and have a beautiful, warm, comfortable night's sleep. Far better than an electric blanket.

Although, one time, after one of our group got into their sleeping bag, I heard them say, 'Gee, I'm hot,' and they hadn't dug the trench deep enough. So you live and learn. All of us shared the chores. We'd allocated one dish of water per day to wash with. When nature called, we'd take a spade and head out bush, either behind a tree or a rock. We'd taken enough petrol for seven hundred miles and we'd had huge water tanks fitted to our Land Rover.

Another experience sticks in my mind: not long after we'd left Camooweal one of our friends got a puncture. When we'd all caught up, my husband went back to Camooweal with the other two men and one of the women to get the tyre repaired. Now, I forgot to mention that of the three women in the couples, one had a toddler, another one was very pregnant and I was yet to find out that I was pregnant. Anyhow, the one that was quite pregnant and I stayed behind in a creek bed, near the car with the puncture. We'd been sitting there for a while, when we noticed a bit of smoke down the way a bit. I said to my friend, 'Let's go for a walk along the creek.'

Which we did, and we soon came across an older couple sitting around their campfire. 'Oh,' they said, 'you must have a cuppa with us.' So we had a lovely afternoon tea with them while we were waiting for the others to get back from Camooweal with the repaired tyre. So the people you meet, ay?

Now to the incident at Georgetown. The following day we arrived in Georgetown. Back in those days, Georgetown was not much more than a pub, a couple of shops and a few scattered houses. It was mid-afternoon and, with the monsoons building, it was very hot and humid. My husband and I were travelling ahead of the others, so we were the first to arrive in town. Being wary about venturing into the pub, I spotted a little general store on the other side of the street. I said to my husband, 'Let's go and get a cold drink there.'

So we pulled up outside the store and walked to the front door, which had those flypaper strips across it. Remember the ones where the flies get stuck onto the strips? It was one of them, sticky, with dead flies – lots of them. So we pushed those aside and went in. The store itself was open, but nobody was around, and behind the old worse-for-wear counter was a long dark passageway leading to the back of the house.

I called out, 'Excuse me.' There was no answer, so I called out a bit louder, 'Oh excuse me. Is anyone there?' Still no answer. Anyhow, while we were waiting, I just happened to see something at the end of the counter that was covered with a couple of tea towels. So I took a peep under the tea towels and there were these beautiful loaves of fresh warm bread. I was just about to call out again when I heard footsteps starting to come from the back of the house. It was obviously someone in slippers because I could hear the slop, slop, slop on the lino. Then this grumpy voice calls out, 'All right. All bloody right. I'm comin'! Anybody'd think I had nothin' better ter do than ter stand there 'n serve customers all day!'

Then she appeared. She was a skinny woman, a bit older than us, with uncombed grey curly hair and a dirty apron on. Definitely not the height of fashion. We said, 'Could we please get a cold drink? What do you have?'

'Lemonade,' she grumbled.

'Okay then, we'd like two lemonades please.'

So off she goes again, sighing and mumbling about having to serve somebody. Anyhow, after a while she comes back with our drinks – lemonade and quite cold, which was a relief. Then, when we were about to pay for our drinks, I said, 'Oh, and I'd like a loaf of that beautiful fresh bread thanks.'

And back came the arrow-like reply of, 'Oh no yer won't!'

Thinking that she mightn't have heard me clearly, I said, 'Oh, but I'd really like to,' to which she folded her arms tight and gave a defiant grunt. Then to put forward my case more clearly I added, 'It's just that we've been on the road for days and it'd be a real treat to have some really fresh bread.'

And she looked me right in the eye – deadly – 'Well, you can't have it!' she snapped. 'That's tomorra's bread!'

Footnote – Georgetown is just under two thousand kilometres north-west of Brisbane and near on four hundred kilometres south-west of Cairns. It's on the Etheridge River, surrounded by beef cattle country, and is one of the best gemstone areas in Queensland.

Prior to Europeans, the Agwamin Aboriginal people lived on and cared for the land for thousands of years. Originally known as Etheridge, the town sprang up when alluvial gold was found in 1869. Within months, three thousand prospectors arrived and, by 1870, a telegraph repeater station was up and running. In 1871, Etheridge was renamed Georgetown after Assistant Gold Commissioner, Howard St George. A post office and courthouse opened in 1872 and the town's first school was built in 1874. By 1876, there were twenty-eight hotels in town and, with the continuation of gold mining, by the late 1880s, the population had peaked. The now heritage-listed Ant Bed house – an adobe, built out of crushed termite mounds – was completed in 1889. With gold mining on the wane during the 1990s, the area moved toward beef cattle. In 2004, the Agwamin people surrendered native title in exchange for access to traditional lands and housing in Georgetown.

The Wenaru Hotel is 'a neat and tidy country pub with a lounge bar, shaded beer garden and a dining room'. One visitor was surprised that, upon leaving the pub, he almost bumped into a couple of horses tied up outside, patiently waiting for their owners.

The pub apparently got its name after the original establishment was either burnt down or blown up. During the time of its temporary operation, the publican was asked repeatedly, 'When are you gonna rebuild?' so that, when he did eventually rebuild, he named it the Wenaru Hotel.

Humpty Doo – NT

Mate, I've just been getting a real chuckle out of some of the stories in your bush funerals book. One in particular got me going. If you remember, it was set in Humpty Doo, in the Northern Territory, back when there weren't many people living out there. As the story went, this Scottish feller from Darwin had been asked to play his bagpipes at a pauper's funeral, which was to be held at the gravesite. By this stage, Humpty Doo was just starting to get going and so there was a lot of infrastructure work going on; you know, stuff like curbing and guttering and sewerage and storm water systems. All that crap. Even the cemetery was being expanded and they were getting a new office and a small chapel for funeral services, along with toilets and so forth for the convenience of mourners.

Anyhow, on the morning of this pauper's funeral, the Scottish feller's car wouldn't start and he's stuck in Darwin till the NT automobile mob could come and sort him out. So by the time he got to Humpty Doo, the graveside service was over – done and dusted. No one was there apart from some gravedigger-looking-fellers filling in a hole, right over the far side of the cemetery. Now, this was smack-bang in the middle of wet season, so it'd been raining cats and dogs. So he sloshed his way over through all the mud and crap and started playing his bagpipes at the graveside. From memory it might've been 'Amazing Grace'. But whatever, when he started playing, the gravedigger-looking-fellers stopped filling in the hole and stood in respectful silence.

Now, the more the feller got into the playing of 'Amazing Grace', the more he got emotionally involved in it all. Next thing he's sobbing away, which, of course, gets these gravedigger-looking-fellers sobbing along with him. When he'd finished playing, he apologised to the fellers for being such a sop. 'Terribly sorry,' he said, 'this's the first time I've ever played at a pauper's funeral, and I'm a bit emotional.'

Then, as the gravedigger-looking-fellers were sniffling back their tears, one of them blubbered, 'Well, mate, it's also the first time we've ever had a piper play at one of our septic tank installations!'

God I laughed! I could so much identify with the situation. In fact, it brought back a few memories of my own. See, I was never actually a gravedigger as such. It's just that my farm shared a boundary fence with the local cemetery. So if ever old Tom, the gravedigger, wanted a hand, he'd give me a hoy and I'd pop over and help him out. The poor old bugger's dead now. But it was all done by hand back then, you know, pick, shovel, crowbar and whatever. And this wasn't that long ago either; probably only fifty or so years ago.

Anyway, I was saying to old Tom one day, 'Mate, how do yer know when yer've dug the grave deep enough?'

'Well,' he said, 'see the church over there through the trees?' I said, 'Yes.'

He said, 'Well, if I've been given short notice 'n I'm digging a grave 'n I see the hearse leave the church, that's when I know it's deep enough.'

So that's how deep he dug some of the graves. I mean, the council told him where to dig and all that. They had a map of the cemetery with all the plot numbers telling them where people had bought a space, or people had already been buried in a space. It was pretty accurate too, and it had to be because things were getting pretty tight. I mean, some of those plots were less than two foot apart: which leads me to the story that the Humpty Doo yarn triggered in my brain. Anyhow, like the feller in Humpty Doo, the old chap we were burying didn't have too many people turn up at his funeral service. Maybe it was because he didn't have many friends or maybe it was a bugger of a day, just like in Humpty Doo. So it's pissing down and we're digging away. We get down so far and that's when we see the hearse leaving the church.

'We're done here,' old Tom said.

Then, just as we were getting out of the hole, the whole bloody bank on the other side started to cave in. Next thing, part of the next door neighbour's coffin makes an appearance through into the hole we'd just dug. So I scooted down the track and asked the funeral feller if he wouldn't mind holding back on the hearse for a bit.

'Why's that?' he asked.

'Oh,' I said, 'we've just got some sort'a slight, minor, miniscule, technical complication back up top.'

And that was okay with him. 'Yeah, sure,' he said. 'This's the only funeral I've got on today, so I've got plenty'a time.'

Good, so I ran back up to the grave and old Tom and me, we levered the next door neighbour back into place. Then we shored up the caving-in bank with some steel posts – star-droppers – and that. So we survived that one.

Another time it was so wet that the grave we were digging was filling up with water faster than we could dig it out. The thing was, they didn't have a pump to pump the water out from the hole. Now, other than being a farmer, plus a few other odds and sods, like being an occasional grave-digging helper, I also belonged to the local bush fire brigade. In fact, I was the captain. So I shot home and I got the fire-fighting pump.

By the time I got back, the whole side of the grave had started to cave in. By then, it's near on 9 o'clock in the morning and the funeral's at eleven. Anyhow, we got the pump going flat out and we're still in there digging flat out. But, oh, they were terrible conditions; just terrible. In the end, we did the best we could under the circumstances before we saw the hearse leaving the church. And so, whoever was in the coffin came to rest in a huge puddle, down the bottom of the grave. And I can tell you, we filled the hole in pretty bloody quick, before the whole shebang started floating back to the top. So we survived that one as well.

But you know, a lot of people have funny ideas about cemeteries. Just the other day a young feller said to me, 'There's no way yer'd get me goin' int'a a cemetery, 'specially of a night-time.'

I said, 'Why?'

He said, ''Cause'a the ghosts.'

Now, I know a lot of people get uppity about ghosts and that, so I said to him, 'Mate, yer don't have ter worry about ghosts.' I said, 'What's the worst that can happen?' When he gave a bit of a shrug like he didn't know what the worst that could happen might be, I said, 'Look, a ghost's a ghost. If yer see one, just walk straight through it. They won't harm yer.'

But by the look on him, I don't think he was too convinced. And now here's something else I've just remembered: my grandfather always used to say how, during the Depression times, if you had any money or valuables, the best place to get a good night's sleep was in a cemetery. That's because, just like the young feller I was telling you about, not too many people were that keen on going into a cemetery in the dead of the night. So you'd be safe.

Though just on that, I'll tell you something else about ghosts. Back when I was helping old Tom dig the graves, we not only used the usual pick and shovel, but we also had a special crowbar. To give you some idea, this special crowbar wasn't your common old crowbar, no way; the one we used for digging graves was a real long bugger that could reach right down to the bottom of the hole. So it would've been at least six foot long and as heavy as a pregnant elephant.

Anyhow, old Tom was telling me about the time he was digging a grave. He hadn't quite finished it by knock-off time so he left all his gear there, ready for a quick start when he came back the next morning. And, when he came back the next morning, all his gear was still there – every bit of it – except for the bloody crowbar. The crowbar was gone. It'd vanished. Tom reckoned that one of the cemetery's ghosts must've nicked it because it was no good for nothing else. Like, you couldn't have even used it for post-hole digging. So I don't know what happened there, but it's never been found.

Footnote – Humpty Doo is on the traditional lands of the Woolna Aboriginal people. No one is certain how Humpty Doo got its name. It could well have been from a local station property 'Umpity Doo', or from 'Humpty Dumpty', an expression meaning 'upside down'. Another suggestion is that it was once located between two humpies i.e. 'humpy two', or that it's from the colloquial 'everything done wrong or upside down' or that it's from a Woolna word meaning 'resting place'.

The first European to explore the area was Boyle Finniss, in 1864. During the late 1860s and into the 1870s, the area was divided into large parcels of land, with the aim of growing tropical crops. By the 1880s, Chinese farmers were growing rice for the Pine Creek goldfields, to its south. By 1910, the fledgling town was known as Umpity Doo. Plans for vast irrigated areas to produce a commercial rice crop fell in a heap and, by the late 1950s, the paddy fields had been abandoned.

In 1967, a general store was opened and in 1971 the Humpty Doo Hotel-Motel opened. Above the bar's wall sits the world's biggest set of water buffalo horns. For the faint-hearted, there's also the Brahman Bulls Beer Drinking competition. As for meals, if you're game, Bill 'Swampy' Marsh recommends having a crack at the 'trio-burger': a Buffalo-Barra-Crocodile Burger combo, served with chips and salad.

Humpty Doo appears in Ted Egan's song 'Humpty Doo Boy' and Slim Dusty's 'Humpty Doo Waltz'. Its most identifiable icon is the thirteen-metre-tall, red boxing-gloved, fibreglass Big Boxing Croc. Another town feature is the Living Water Uniting Church; an open-air church built 'without walls' to help combat extreme temperature and humidity. These days Humpty Doo is a virtual satellite suburb of Darwin.

Isisford – Qld

It was during one of my early story-collecting trips back in the mid-1990s, and I'd been out on the road for two months. I'd already taken in three states. From Adelaide, I'd gone up to the west of New South Wales, to Broken Hill, on to Cobar, north to Bourke, then into Queensland via Hungerford and on to Cunnamulla, then Charleville.

When I do these big trips, I sometimes try to cadge an overnight with whomever I'm interviewing. These people are very hospitable, all with a story to tell. And as the night wears on, and the beer or the rum and coke mellows them, it's then that the real stories are revealed – the heart and soul ones that are only told when people are relaxed within your company. If by chance I don't get a bunk at someone's place, I might end up at a cheap pub or, if all else fails, I'll just park off the road, toss my swag down, and sleep under the blanket of stars. Publishers don't dish out lots of money for these trips – not for me, anyway; just a bit to help cover the petrol – so it's rare that I spend a night in a motel, with breakfast supplied.

By this stage, I was coming into Isisford, in the central west of Queensland. The previous night at Charleville had been a long one. A shearer had invited his mates around for the traditional barbecue and the yarns continued as the night drifted into morning. So I was already pretty knackered and, with the thought of the following night being another long one at a mate's place in Longreach, I decided to hang the expense and get a motel room: somewhere where I could get a good night's sleep, a decent breakfast and head off refreshed the following morning.

The only trouble was that my arrival coincided with Isisford's annual show and the place was booked out. That's until I was lucky enough to come across a cancellation.

So I settled in and had a nice long shower, and, as I felt like a change from barbecued meat, I asked the motel owner where I could get a decent feed of seafood. 'Just down the road at the pub,' he said. 'Best barramundi in Queensland.'

'Thanks,' I replied, and went back to my room to make a call home. Even before I'd left Adelaide, things hadn't been going too well on the home-front. And as my time away lengthened, our telephone conversations had become increasingly awkward. In fact, this call proved to be far more difficult than the rest and I was told that, upon my return, we needed to have a good heart-to-heart as to where our relationship was going.

After the call, I felt deflated. But knowing that it was such a busy time in Isisford, I decided to go and have dinner before the pub became too busy, and not miss out on my early night. And lucky I did, because when I arrived at Clancy's Overflow Hotel, the place was already crowded. Still, I managed to find a small table tucked away in the far corner. I then bought myself a beer and put my order in for the highly recommended barramundi. While I was waiting for my meal, mulling over the fate of my return home, a flamboyant-looking couple in their mid-fifties came over. The man was a rather large bloke, wearing a loud brown and tan suit, covered in big checks. The woman was a bird-like figure, wearing a flowery-patterned, ankle-length dress with long sleeves, frilled around the wrists.

'Excuse me, mate,' the bloke said, 'would you mind if we shared your table? All the others seem to be taken.'

'That's fine,' I replied.

They introduced themselves as Bob and Rosemary. 'G'day,' I said. 'I'm Bill. Pleased to meet you.'

I took an instant liking to Bob. He was an affable sort of bloke, full of life and fun. His bright chatter soon lightened my mood. Then, while Rosemary went off to place their meal order and get a beer for Bob and a shandy for herself, Bob asked what I did for a living.

'I'm a writer,' I said, completely letting my guard down; as soon as someone knows you're a writer they, invariably, want to tell you their entire life story, from beginning to end. Which is exactly what happened in this case. Bob started telling me how he and Rosemary were originally from Melbourne. They'd been childhood sweethearts – 'Met when we were in Fitzroy Primary School'. After they'd married, while Bob worked in finance, Rosemary stayed at home and raised the kids. But when they'd hit fifty, they decided to chuck it all in and come up north to spend the rest of their days in retirement, enjoying the beautiful Queensland weather.

By this stage, Rosemary had returned from ordering their meal. 'Rose, dear,' Bob said, 'Bill's a writer.'

'What do you write?' she asked, in a soft, wispy voice. So I gave them a brief rundown of my current project and why I was travelling through this part of Queensland. 'Oh,' was all Rosemary said, when I'd finished.

'Yes,' said Bob, jumping in to fill in the vacant space that Rosemary had left, 'Rosemary's got a story or two, haven't you, dear?'

'Maybe,' she said, and left it at that.

And that's about all I heard from Rosemary. She retreated into her shell. Bob took over again and, pitching himself against the growing pub noise, continued on from when he and Rosemary had arrived in Rockhampton. They'd bought a small block of land, with an old weatherboard house on it, which they soon discovered was infested with white ants. So they'd spent the majority of their savings on fixing it up. Then, with Bob's superannuation running out, they'd purchased a fairy floss and toffee apple van and, these days, spent their time travelling the small show cum rodeo circuit throughout Queensland.

By then my meal had arrived. But that didn't stop Bob, and I didn't actually mind because it was a fascinating story, and really well told. Bob was one of those people who'd be a dream to interview; the ones that just open up and out it all comes, warts and all, story after story, yarn after yarn. They were mostly about his and Rosemary's many adventures, travelling with the colourful characters on the circuit – the spruikers, the boxers, the store holders, the Ferris wheel operators; such a diverse community of humanity, trouping from one town to the next. And while I was listening to Bob's constant chatter about every little thing he and Rosemary did – and didn't do – and what their future plans were, I couldn't help but feel a deep sadness at my own faltering relationship.

With me being away so often, my wife and I virtually lived singular lives. Over the past couple of years, in particular, the divide between us had grown. At one stage, I suggested we should try to patch things up by going on one of my trips together so that, for once, we'd have a shared experience, just like Bob and Rosemary. The reply was always, 'But I have a business to run, right here in Adelaide.' And she was right, as usual.

'Where are you staying?' Bob asked, snapping me out of my reverie.

When I told him the name of the motel, he replied, 'That's where we're staying, isn't it, dear? Gee, you were lucky to get a room there,' he said. 'We always have to book well in advance.'

When I explained how I'd only got the room due to a cancellation, Bob said, 'That must've been Arthur and Joan's booking.' Then he told me how Arthur and his wife, Joan, were also on the rodeo-show circuit. They had one of those soft toy displays where you put a couple of dollars in the slot and a crane thing comes down and grabs at a stack of soft toys. If you were lucky, the claws on the crane might grab a soft toy and, if you hit the jackpot, it'd grab the toy that had a Rolex watch attached to it.

Apparently, Arthur had recently suffered a mild heart attack and they'd had to cancel their trip to Isisford.

'What room number?' asked Rosemary.

'Twenty-seven,' I replied.

'Yes,' said Bob, 'Arthur and Joan book that room every year, don't they, dear?'

By now, I'd finished my meal and, actually, the barramundi hadn't been too bad. It certainly made a welcome change from barbecued sausages, chops, rissoles and steak. But by now I was keen to get back to the motel to have the early night I'd promised myself. Although, when I went to excuse myself, Bob interrupted, 'Another beer, mate?'

I didn't really want one, and Bob must've seen my reluctance because he added, 'Go on. My shout. One more won't hurt you.'

'Okay,' I said. 'But make it a light beer, please.'

Bob then got up and went over to the bar to get the drinks. With Rosemary being such a shy person, an awkwardness fell between us. To fill in time until Bob returned, I tried to get some small chat happening by asking her if they had any children. Yes, they had. Two. A son and a daughter. Both were married with young children. They lived in Melbourne but, due to their own family commitments, they rarely made it up to Rockhampton, and Bob wasn't too keen on going down south because of his arthritis.

'Oh,' I said, 'that's a shame. But still and all,' I added, 'it sounds like you and Bob have a fascinating life together.'

'Yes,' she said. Then we fell into another awkward silence.

The effort of forcing conversation from someone as shy and softly spoken as Rosemary, especially within the rowdy atmosphere of the pub, was proving very difficult. So I glanced in the direction of the bar in the hopes that Bob might be on his way back. And that's when I heard a voice. 'He beats me up, you know.' Instinctively, I refocused on Rosemary, unsure if I'd heard right. But she leaned over and fixed me with a fear-filled gaze and said, 'You know, he knocks me around. I have bruises,' and she discreetly pointed to various parts of her body, hidden beneath her long flowery dress.

Being one of those who finds dealing with any form of conflict difficult, I was lost for words. 'An ostrich,' is how my wife describes me. 'Head in the sand.' What's more, the last thing I wanted was to get involved in someone else's personal problems. I already had enough of my own. So to avoid her steely stare I looked away, only to see Bob working his way back through the crowd with the beers. Suddenly embarrassed at my unsympathetic response, I tried to make it up to Rosemary. 'Can't you leave him?' I blurted out.

'It's not that simple,' she whispered, just as Bob took the last couple of strides to our table.

'Here's your beer, Bill,' Bob announced.

'And a shandy for you, dear,' he said to Rosemary.

When Bob sat down, I tried to act as if nothing had happened. I even attempted to laugh when he launched into yet another of their adventures – this time about the fairy floss recipe going haywire out near a place called Alpha. But because I now realised that Bob's easy affable manner hid something far more sinister, his stories had lost all their life, their joy and fun. I even tried to acknowledge the part Rosemary played in them. But I could no longer look at her. Then that old impulse of fright and flight kicked in and I downed my beer and made to leave. 'Great meeting you both,' I said. 'Must be off now. Big day tomorrow.'

As I walked out of the pub, into the warm Queensland evening, I breathed a sigh of relief at escaping such an awkward situation. Yet I couldn't reconcile just how wrong I'd been about Bob and Rosemary. The idyllic lifestyle I'd perceived of them being a happy couple, travelling and sharing experiences, was now shattered. But when I got into bed, I couldn't stop tossing around the complexities of my own situation. What would happen there? If worse came to the worst, what would it be like getting old by myself – living alone? Was it better to have a poor relationship than none at all? In the end, sleep proved impossible, so I turned on the bedside lamp and, in an attempt to silence my scrambled thoughts, I started reading something light and humorous. And that's when a gentle knock sounded at my door.

'Bill,' came a soft, wispy voice, 'it's Rosemary.'

Footnote – Isisford, population 200, is in Queensland's Outer Barcoo region, just over a thousand kilometres north-west of Brisbane. It has been the inspiration for many a poet, including Banjo Paterson who, in 1883, penned 'A Bush Christening': *On the outer Barcoo where the churches are few, and the men of religion are scanty. On a road never cross'd 'cept by folk that are lost, one Michael Magee had a shanty.*

The district has long been home to the Iningai Aboriginal people. The town had its beginnings when, in 1887, two travelling hawkers – brothers William and James Whitman – broke an axle while attempting to cross the Barcoo River. Instead of attempting to continue their journey they, instead, decided to settle on the banks of the river and a village soon developed.

Today Isisford is home to the Outer Barcoo Interpretation Centre Museum, which boasts fossils of the oldest modern crocodile, *Isisfordia Duncani*, at ninety-eight million years, and the bulldog fish, which has been dated as far back as a hundred million years.

The town has two hotels, The Golden West, formerly the Westward Hotel, is the only one remaining of four hotels from the early 1900s. It offers powered caravan sites, motel style accommodation, great pub meals and a beer garden with a fountain and mist fan.

Clancy's Overflow Hotel, was built by the Whitman brothers in 1876 and named the Teddington Arms. In 1884 it was renamed the Club Hotel. In 1898, a second storey was added and in 1907–08 it became the first pub in the far west to be connected to electricity. In 1965, the hotel's name was changed to Clancy's Overflow Hotel, in part to another of Banjo Paterson's poems, *Clancy of the Overflow*. Clancy's remains an iconic Queensland pub with meals plus renovated and budget accommodation.

The Isisford Sheep and Wool Show, held each May, displays the region's goods and produce including sheep, wool, cattle, goats and horse sales plus sheep and cattle dog trials. It also includes home garden competitions, school competitions, sculpture and craft, photography and a trailer pull. Another local attraction is the Big Yellowbelly: a twelve-metre scrap-metal sculpture erected by local Henry 'Cocky' Bignell and a few of his mates out on the Isisford–Ilfracombe Road.

Kagamuga – PNG

At one time I was in hotel management up in Papua New Guinea. It was a real eye-opener. This was back in the early '70s, around the time Australia was handing over control to the PNG Government. Anyhow, my husband and I applied for a job at a place up there called Kagamuga, with a hotel–brewing company. Kagamuga's in the Wahgi Valley, just out of the much larger centre of Mount Hagen.

It was an absolute disaster. We were to be the only white people there and, on the day we arrived at the hotel, a riot broke out in what's called the Boi Bar. I think the word 'boi' is a pidgin English derivation of 'boy' or 'man' because no women ever went in there; not even me and I wouldn't blame them. The riot was apparently over some sort of factional issue, which was something we were soon to find out happened quite regularly. To that end, everything in the Boi Bar that could be picked up and thrown had been bolted solidly to the floor; things like the cement tables and the cement stools and so forth. There was no glass or bottled beer sold in the place, just canned alcohol, and there was a tough, sealed mesh curtain bolted in around the bar, with just enough space for a can to be passed underneath. Even then, the barmen were often bitten.

Mind you, the bar staff were quite used to these sorts of skirmishes; well experienced you could say. In an attempt to contain a riot, large steel doors had been built around the outer-bar area, which, as soon as an incident broke out, would be bolted shut. Although, unfortunately, on this particular occasion, that didn't work and the rioters broke out of the bar area and went on the rampage. For accommodation, the hotel complex had small rondavel-type structures. These were in pairs of units, in separate little circular areas, with lovely white-painted rock pathways leading up to each of them. So of course, the rioters started chucking the rocks willy-nilly, didn't they. My unit ended up with a big hole through its front door. Car windows were smashed. Everything that could be trashed was trashed. Oh my God, like I said, nothing was safe, nothing was sacred.

It got so out of hand that someone eventually called the police and a paddy wagon rocked up from Mount Hagen. And it was the biggest paddy wagon I've ever seen. It was huge. So the natives – and that's what they were called up there – who were running riot outside, were soon rounded up and chucked in the paddy wagon. The police were both white and black. See, with this being on the cusp of Australia relinquishing control to Papua New Guinea, if you employed a white person, by law, you had to have two indigenous people in training for that job as well. Anyhow, after the police carted off the rabble-rousers, things settled down a bit. So yes, that was day one of our hotel-management stint at Kagamuga. A real eye-opener.

Another eye-opener was that, with a lot of these natives coming straight out of the mountains, their only clothing was grass skirts – 'ass-grass' as they called them – and some wore penis guards. For our first couple of days, the outgoing publican stayed on to show us the ropes. He was white, and he was gay. He'd been there for quite a while and his houseboy – his playmate – ran around in a see-through grass lap-lap, which was another eye-opener, though whenever I saw him I tried to shut my eyes.

Other than for special occasions, there wasn't much in the way of bright tribal finery. It was only when you went to the Hagen market that you'd see some of the natives dressed in all their finery. The guys from Bougainville, in particular, would be adorned in their various outfits of coloured paraphernalia. And oh, those Bougainvilleans were as black as the ace of spades, and with just the most magnificent bodies. And really lovely people. As for them wearing penis guards, I can't recall just now. I probably tried not to look.

But as horrible a time as it was, a lot of stories came out of that experience. There was the time my husband and I decided to go to the movies in Mount Hagen in the big enclosed panel van we'd been given. We usually had a driver and, whenever we went anywhere, he had to stand guard or else all the petrol would have been syphoned out of the tank. But this panel van was a real old bomb and, because no one ever bothered to fix anything, not even the window winders worked.

Anyhow, when word got out that we were going off to the movies, all the natives wanted to hitch a lift and come along with us. I forget where our driver was at the time but, as usual, my husband had been drinking so I got the job of driving. And because so many people had piled into the back of the panel van, whenever I hit a bump, the front wheels would lift right up off the ground. I was thinking, Oh my God, this is not good. I'll probably have an accident or even worse I'll run over one of their precious pigs and kill it, and then there'll be big trouble. They'll probably slit my throat. Anyhow, we made it.

Now, the way the Hagen cinema was set up was that the white people sat upstairs, in a balcony area, and everyone else was down below. And with most of the downstairs patrons having come straight out of the mountains, the smell was atrocious. To make matters worse, the film was a gruesome Cowboy and Indian epic and the natives were barracking for the Indians. I remember at one point the Indians captured a couple of the cowboys. Next thing, one of the cowboys gets upended and a fire's lit under his head and the other cowboy was spread-eagled and a fire was lit between his legs. And, oh my God, didn't they just go berserk. And the sex scenes. Oh my God. Mind you, the sex scenes back in those days were little more than a kiss and a cuddle. But that didn't matter. They were right into it. So, when we were coming back home with this carload of natives, who'd been pumped up with all the sex and murders of the white fellers, I was like, Oh my God, I hope they don't get any ideas.

There were no women employed in the Kagamuga pub. It was all men, and houseboys looked after the cleaning and the accommodation areas. But you'd often go into one of the rooms and find a towel with a footprint on it. I'd say to the houseboy, 'This towel isn't clean.'

'Yes, Missus. Is clean. Bin through laundry.'

'But look there,' I'd say, 'it's got a piccaninny footprint on it.'

'That's okay, Missus. 'Bin through laundry.'

What'd happen was; after they did the washing, they'd hang the laundry out on paddocks of grass to dry, and the piccaninny-kids would run around and trample all over the washing. But for the houseboy, that was okay because, in his mind, he'd done his job. He had put the washing through the laundry, and what happened after that was of no consequence. So I'd have to send it back. And they had the mindset where, if they didn't want to turn up for work, they wouldn't.

I'd ask, 'Where's so-n-so?'

'Haven't seen 'im, Missus. Must'a gone back to 'is place.'

Then a few days later the missing fellow would turn up and you'd say, 'Where have you been?'

'I haven't been here, Missus.' As simple as that. In his mind, he hadn't done anything wrong, so he'd just carry on as if nothing had happened. And that was their culture. When it was time to go somewhere, it was time to go. But oh, like I said, it was a real eye-opener. I knew a woman and her husband who ran a general store. And because the locals couldn't understand the concept of having to actually buy goods from the store, it was constantly being broken into. The line of thinking was, Well, if you've got it on show and I want it, I should be able to take it.'

Another difficult concept for us whites to understand was what they called the 'onetok' system. Your onetok is your best mate. How it worked was that, even though we'd actually pay each employee individually, they'd then give all their money to the onetok of the week. So for that week, the onetok was the big man in charge of all their money and so they'd come to him for loans and that. And it worked: well, for them it did. How, I don't know. But oh my God, the stuff that used to go on. Our driver, the one who usually drove our panel van, was a complete womaniser and, unbeknown to us, he'd also use the panel van to go visiting other men's wives. So every now and then, he'd be arrested and thrown into jail for appropriating another man's wife and we'd get a call from the police to come and bail him out.

Then there was the time a truck came to a screaming halt out in our car park and a white guy, from off one of the coffee plantations, was bustled into the pub and had to go into hiding. We found out that he'd been having it off with someone's wife and the natives were out to kill him. Next day he got smuggled out of the hotel; most probably to be taken to the airport and flown out of the country. Then there was the politician who took refuge in the hotel. I don't know what he'd done, but he was on the run and under threat of being murdered. The natives were after him. The parliament' was after him. Everyone was after him. So he hid in the pub while plans were made to smuggle him out of the country.

I mean, it was like living in the Wild West. If there wasn't a riot going on, it'd be something else. Never a dull moment, and so the police were coming and going, coming and going, all the time. And my husband wasn't any help. I mean, had I been with the right partner, it might've been different. But I wasn't. My husband was just there for a good time. That's if you could call it a good time. So in the end I said to him, 'Look, I'm out of here. This's not us. It's not me anyway.' I said, 'I'm heading back to civilisation with or without you.'

Anyhow, he decided to come with me and so we left Kagamuga. But the relationship fell apart soon after we got back to Australia.

Footnote – Kagamuga is just over five hundred kilometres north-west of Port Moresby and is at an altitude of around 1650 metres. It's in the fertile Wahgi Valley, in the Southern Highlands Province, a fifteen-minute drive from the centre of Mount Hagen, the third largest city in PNG. Back in 1933, on an aerial reconnaissance of the highlands, brothers Mick and Dan Leahy and a government officer Jim Taylor came across the Wahgi Valley. Not long after, they walked into the valley, becoming the first westerners to contact the local tribes.

In 1934, an airstrip was built on the future site of Mount Hagen. The first flight arrived in the same year and the first airmail flew out. The airstrip later became the main street of Mount Hagen and a much larger airstrip was built just out of town at what's now known as Kagamuga International Airport: although from time to time, the combination of altitude, midday temperatures and runway length restrict take-offs. A news report in June 2022 described how all operations and flights were suspended at the Kagamuga International Airport due to oil having been purposely spilt on the tarmac. Local police described this as, 'an act of political terrorism'. The Western Highlands 2022 Election Operations Commander dispatched a team to investigate and arrest those involved.

The Highlands Highway from Mount Hagen to other provincial capitals is 'theoretically' sealed. The word 'theoretically' is emphasised as frequent landslides and general deterioration often lead to sections of the road becoming unsealed. One of the largest cultural events in Papua New Guinea is held, annually, at nearby Mount Hagen. Regional, provincial and national tribal dance groups gather there to celebrate their cultural heritage in the form of a sing-sing. It's also one of the biggest tourist attractions of the country.

Karumba – Qld

In memory of Ron and Krys Pawlowski.

In June 1955, right after Krys and I had said our vows, I returned to the West Australian goldfields to sell all my prospecting stuff. I'd had enough of mining because, well, prospecting is not an occupation; prospecting is a disease. I always say, if you are a single man and you stay long enough in the bush, the booze will eventually claim you. So I got rid of everything except my beautiful 10 foot x 12 foot ex-army tent. It was just right for my new family of Krys and her three children, and I traded in my Morris Minor for a brand new FJ Holden.

By the time I returned to Perth, Krys had also sold up. Being the adventurous type she longed to travel, and I wanted to see more of the country too. So we decided to leave Western Australia and travel east. No details, nothing, just head east. We had a few pounds to our name and so, the three children, the doggie – Rusty the First – Krys and myself, we loaded all our belongings inside the boot and on top of the Holden. The whole thing was overloaded. The springs, instead of going upwards, were going downwards. So much so that we were riding on the rubber buffers. Then, with being so overloaded, we snuck out of Perth early one morning to avoid the police. It was exactly a month after we were married.

We travelled east, camping overnight in my sturdy ex-army tent. We passed Kalgoorlie, Norseman, Eucla. In its day, Eucla had been a telegraph station. Today it is all sand. But oh, it was beautiful country across that Nullarbor Plain. Yes, it was a rough road – no bitumen in those days – full of corrugations and potholes, though that did not matter to me. I remember when we got a flat tyre. After replacing it, I had a few wines in celebration. But I forgot to tighten the wheel nuts properly. So we were driving merrily along – all of us singing – and suddenly, here was a wheel overtaking us. Oh, the kids laughed and laughed.

Although Krys, at times, saw the Nullarbor as boring, I loved it. Well, I am a plainsman. From where I grew up in Poland there were no mountains so you could see from horizon to horizon, and that's the Nullarbor – no trees, just a bit of mulga here and there. Then, about an hour before sunset, we would pull off the road, put up the tent, gather enough wood for the night, light a fire, put the barbeque plate on and Krys would start cooking. It didn't matter under what conditions, Krys could always make a princely meal. Of course, the kids had a great time. For starters, they didn't have to go to school, so every day was Christmas. And they were involved. They were, 'Look at this' ... 'Look at that.' See, they had never been out of the city so it was all fascinating to them. And of course, the nights out in the bush; oh, to this day I love that, especially when you can lie down on a ground sheet, right under the starlit sky. It was just so beautiful.

So we travelled and travelled and, when we saw a track going north, it was 'Let's see where it goes?' There was no sign. There were no signs anywhere. At worst, we would have to travel back. But we didn't mind. We had plenty of time. No buses to catch, nothing, and we had enough provisions. So we turned up that north track till we eventually got to Coober Pedy. Back then, there were just a few tin shacks, a pub and one petrol bowser. Coober Pedy was famous for its opal mining, but opals did not excite me. I'd had enough of that sort of life. So we drove on and, oh, that's right, somewhere up the track it had rained and we got bogged. Then, when I tried to rock the FJ out of the bog, the reverse gear broke. I was very concerned about that but Krys said, 'Who on earth needs a reverse gear. We are not going back.' Krys was always positive.

Anyhow, a Hillman Minx appeared from the north with a couple of drunks in it and oh, they were happy. How they managed to miss the bog, I do not know. When they stopped, the passenger half fell out of the car door. Weak at the knees, and still gripping onto a bottle of brandy, he staggered over and said, 'Me'dis'n'le brandy. Gotta keep healthy. 'Ave a snort, mate.' As I was having a snort he examined our bogged-right-up-to-its-axles-car then he said, 'Yer buggered, aye? Wan' som' 'elp.'

Oh my God, what help could anyone that inebriated give us? They were both paralytic, so I said, 'No thanks,' and I helped him back into their car and they managed to drive off. But we eventually got out of the bog and made it to Alice Springs. In those days, Alice Springs was just a village. When we pulled up it was very hot – no air conditioning of course – and Krys thought some ice cream would be a good idea. When we came to a likely shop, she asked the shopkeeper, 'Could we please have some ice cream?' Well, he looked at Krys as if she'd just escaped from the loony bin. 'Ice cream?' he said. 'Ice cream? Where do yer think yer bloody well are, lady?'

So we settled for some lollies and we headed off again till we reached Katherine. Katherine was hardly a town. By the time we had set up camp we were too tired to do any cooking, so we had canned fish. But Krys must have eaten from the wrong end of the tin, because she took ill. Oh, she was so ill, the poor sweet. After we eventually found a hospital and they had sorted her out, the doctor then gave us a lecture on the healing properties of Vegemite. 'If you eat Vegemite you'll live forever,' he said.

We then continued north, past Pine Creek, on to Adelaide River with its crystal clear water – perfectly safe for the kids to swim in. We stopped there for about a week to catch up with our washing and all that. But we found it too humid, so we decided to head back down south. By now it was early September and

I remember it was just after 6 o'clock in the evening when we pulled up at the only petrol bowser in Pine Creek and the petrol station owner came rushing out. 'Sorry, mate,' he said, 'it's after six. I'm closed.'

I said, 'What do you mean, closed?'

He said, 'Government says I'm not allowed ter sell petrol after six, mate.'

Oh my God, here I was, stuck in an isolated, hot, small place in the Northern Territory, with a wife, three children and a dog and it was illegal to sell petrol after 6 o'clock in the evening. I then related to the petrol station owner how something similar had once happened to me in Canberra where everything shut on Sunday. And that started him off. 'Bloody politicians,' he said. 'They're the same bastards that run the Territory.' Then he softened and said, 'Tell you what, mate, go out on the road 'n if yer see a vehicle comin', sing out 'cause if the coppers catch me, they'll break me bloody neck.'

It was still a dirt road in those days, so I walked out to check for any oncoming clouds of dust. Then, as soon he had finished hand-pumping, we paid him and thanked him warmly. But I admired that guy. You know, a lot of people out there may be as rough as a piece of raw jarrah but they have golden hearts. We then continued south until we came to what is today called Three Ways intersection. Then, I don't know why, maybe we weren't interested in seeing the same thing twice, but that's where we turned east. So we drove across the Barkly Tableland. It was beautiful flat, open grass country till we came to Mount Isa. Being a mining town Mount Isa did not impress us, so we drove on. Then, just west of Cloncurry, there was a road going north to the Gulf of Carpentaria. So we said, 'Do we go east to the coastal towns or do we go north?'

I had been always been fascinated by the Gulf Country as they call it. I had read about it in the *Outdoors and Fishing* magazine. Anyhow, Krys pulled out a box of matches, broke one, and said, 'Pick. The short one is the east coast, the long one is north to the Gulf.' And I drew the one that represented the Gulf. So we drove north until we eventually stopped under a shady tree by Walkers Creek Crossing, just past Normanton. This was mid-September and the temperature ranged from 30 degrees Centigrade to 35 degrees Centigrade. The water was beautiful and clear but, when the kids wanted to go for a swim, I said, 'No, never trust tropical waters.' Of course, they didn't listen to me and they jumped straight in. Just as they did, a big croc that had been resting on a steep bank nearby made a big splash into the water. Well, they were out of there in a shot, and we immediately decided to move on.

From Walkers Flat we travelled till we reached Karumba. And when we drove out onto those open plains on 25 September '55, it just took my breath away. Those healthy trees, with the bark of a ghost gum, each looking more beautiful than the next with the green of the leaves. And very sandy, with just a bit of grey top soil. The grass was typical of the Gulf for that time of the year, parched dry and a light gold colour. Then the deep blue sky. Oh, that sky. To this day, I still dream of it. There were no road signs so we followed a dirt track till it ended up at an old flying boat slipway where a fisherman was laying out his nets. Krys immediately inquired of the fisherman, 'Where's the shop?'

'What bloody shop?' he said. 'No bloody shop 'ere.'

We found out later that it was Graham Barnett. We then found a campsite and, when Krys threw in a line, right away she caught a fish. So we put a few rocks around, gathered some wood and Krys made a beautiful salmon dinner. The following morning we woke to the singing of seagulls and the sounds of pelicans and egrets and herons and we looked out of the tent onto a carpet of flowers and golden sand. And that beautiful rising golden sun. Beyond that, beneath a cloudless sky, lay the deep blue of the sea.

We had never experienced anything like it in our lives. Everything was so calm that you didn't dare talk out aloud. And no engines, no hollering, nothing, just the occasional *splash* of a fish and the gentle *slap, slap* of the tiny waves, lapping on the shore. Little wonder we lost the desire to move on. Karumba was just too beautiful to leave. Then at breakfast a girl of about six and a boy of about five arrived at our camp and the girl handed Krys a container of fresh milk. 'Hi,' she said, 'Mum said to give you this. You might want it for breakfast.' Then she added, 'I'm Caroline Charles and this is my brother, Steven. We live at the Pilot Station. Mum said to visit sometime.'

'Thank you,' we said.

We already had a good supply of powdered milk, but this milk was fresh goat's milk. None of us had ever tasted goat's milk before, but it was delicious. So that day we visited Jock and Evie Charles. Jock was ex-RAN and Coxswain-in-Charge of the Karumba Pilot Station. It was his job to pilot the heavily laden coastal freighters, in from the Arafura Sea and up the Norman and Albert Rivers to Normanton and Burketown, often at night, with only a few feet of channel to either side. So it was a difficult job. But oh, didn't Jock prove to be a master of the art of living. He drank lots of beer, he fished, he loved life and he entertained any occasional visitors.

Evie, his wife, devoted herself to gardening and supervising the children's schoolwork. The Charleses had around three hundred and fifty goats, which supplied both milk and meat. Not that they needed all those goats but, in an isolated place like Karumba, it was wise to keep reserves. Evie encouraged us to help milk her forty or so milking goats, every day, in return for milk, and that suited us fine. The goats were quite tame. We just rounded them up into a fenced area, then we picked out the milkers. So we had ample milk which Krys also made cheese from, and then there was their meat.

For the first week we just lazed about, enjoying the scenery.

Having made the decision to stay, we began looking for alternative accommodation to our tent. So we approached one of the real old timers, Bronco. Bronco mostly sat on his verandah, drinking tea; that's if you'd call it tea. Bronco was very hospitable. Whenever he emptied the billy, he never emptied out the old tea leaves. He just left them in till they had almost built up to the top. Of course, by then, the tea resembled liquid tar. So we took up his offer of tea and inquired as to where we might stay. 'Well,' he said, 'yer can camp inside Harry Butt's old fishin' shack fer starters.'

Harry Butt was a Cloncurry soft drink manufacturer. He only visited once a year, to go fishing, and he'd already been out that year. So we packed up our tent and we moved into Harry's shack. It was standing on thin stumps, about yea thick and about three feet high. There were many similar shacks in and around Karumba and, even though it was leaning toward one side and it moved around in a strong wind, that was fine by us. Of course, being so isolated, there were very few people in Karumba at that time. But they were all characters. I have already spoken about Jock and Evie Charles and their two children. There was Burt and Patsy Ammond and their girl. Both the Charles' and Ammonds occupied houses on the Pilot Station Reserve. Burt was Jock's boatman. He was an ex-army warrant officer who carried an unlicensed US service .45 pistol on his belt because he somehow feared for his life.

Then there were the old timers. Oh, dear me, John O'Grady, the author of *They're a Weird Mob* could have written a hilarious book about each of them. One was Jim Bartell. Jim was a black powder rifleman. Later on in his life, when he had an x-ray, he couldn't account for the German World War One bullet they found in his chest. There was Chook Usher. Chook had forgotten his real name: probably because he'd changed it on so many occasions to elude the authorities. On his death, he was buried as Charles McSweenie; so one must assume that McSweenie was his original name. There was old Bronco, the man who rarely emptied his teapot. John Lindley was his real name. Old Bronco drove a 1934 Chevrolet convertible and each time he drank too much alcohol, which was quite often, he had trouble stopping his car when he drove into his garage. At times, he would hit the far end of the garage wall so hard he would push his wooden house right off its stumps. 'Premature bloody ignition,' he described it as being. So we would all arm ourselves with crowbars and whatever and help push his house back onto its stumps.

There was Lloyd Clarke and his wife. They had two daughters and a son. Lloyd owned a seventy-five-foot ex- navy vessel, which he had converted into a fishing vessel, called the *Larry Cork*. The Clarkes lived on, what is now, the town side. It was virgin country back then. They occupied what remained of the two main office buildings and the staff buildings of the old flying base. Though they didn't have to pay rent, they had to keep the buildings free of termite ants. Lloyd also employed a crew, though they lived out on the boat, fishing the rivers or out at sea. Lloyd was very successful. He could fill his twelve-thousand-pound fish freezer in three to five days. He was the man who discovered the prawn potential in the Gulf, for which he was badly treated. But that's a whole story on its own. Then there was Graham Barnett and his wife, Dot. They lived on the other side, too. Graham was a jack-of-all-trades who worked for Lloyd Clarke.

And not to forget Fred Hahn – Corned Beef Freddie. Freddie lived in a humpy that he'd built on the banks of the nearby Bynoe River. He was a very proud and independent man. He didn't like anybody and nobody liked him much, but he displayed touching compassion toward the Aboriginals. Freddie occasionally worked as a stockman, but only when his money ran out. How he survived, I'll never know. He was neither a gardener nor did he keep goats or fowls. He wasn't even much of a fisherman and, although he had an assortment of rifles, his eyesight was so poor he rarely shot anything. Freddie's sole means of transport was a small sailing boat. It had an outboard motor, which he didn't know how to use, so Freddie never hurried. If the wind died down, he simply dropped anchor and waited for another blow. Then once a year he killed, butchered and salted someone else's cow, which was why he was known as Corned Beef Freddie.

But for us there was so much abundance on our doorstep. The fish were plentiful. They'd swim right up to the edge so, when Krys wanted a fish, she'd give Steven a .22 rifle and say, 'Get me a king salmon about this big.' And Steven would put his little hands out to measure the exact size of Krys' request. Then he'd go out and twenty minutes later he would come back with a fish, the exact right size. We shot barramundi too. We'd see them swimming about. 'No, not that one, it's too big. Not that one, it's too small. This one will do.' Bang! Gotcha! And as the day heated up, the stingrays would enter the shallow waters by their hundreds to warm themselves. But we had to warn the kids that they had poison in their tails. And yes, there were lots of crocodiles; not so much along the beach, but rather more along the river.

There was also wild duck, pigeon, geese, mud crab and piglets. Because the pigs fed on yams, they tasted sweet and beautiful and were without worms because there was no rubbish to eat. Of course, we needed green vegetables as fast as possible. So right away, we planted tomato seeds and Krys raised a beautiful crop of nice juicy cucumbers. Then there was pumpkins, which the kids didn't like, and the radishes were the fastest growing vegetable of all. The kids didn't like them either so, when they sprouted, Krys would cut their leaves off and make what she called spinach. It was okay. It was edible; a little bitter maybe but it was a vegetable. She also made spinach out of pumpkin leaves, and all over the sandy ridges grew wild passionfruit from which Krys made beautiful jam, and oh the fruitcakes. And she baked the most beautiful bread. You couldn't buy any better. Krys used to get her dry yeast and flour from Normanton.

Normanton was about fifty miles away. That's where we bought our fuel and groceries. It was a rugged road, and slow going. There and back took an entire day. Most of our extra needs could be bought in Normanton. Though, in the wet season, from mid-December till the end of April, the road was impassable. So all our supplies for that period had to be purchased by early December. Burns Philp and Co was there. They were big-time traders all over the Pacific Islands. But oh, they were thieves. In season, oranges are very cheap. But the scoundrels sold oranges, all year round, at the flat rate of one shilling. And if ever we had an abundance of tomatoes we would take a few boxes into Burns Philp, which we'd be paid peanuts for, yet they would sell them at a huge profit. But oh, the manager was a real fruitcake. One time we gave him a case of tomatoes to sell and he sent us a bill for the case of tomatoes. Oh, he was a real nut case. And so we settled into Karumba very nicely. There was lots to do. The kids were happy. Krys and I were happy and so we had not a care in the world.

Footnote – Karumba is in the south-eastern corner of the Gulf of Carpentaria, just over two thousand kilometres north-west of Brisbane. The word Karumba is thought to be a derivative name of the local Indigenous peoples, the Kareldi, who had lived on and cared for the area for thousands of years. The name – Karumba – was officially adopted for the township in 1880. In the late 1930s, Karumba was a refuelling and maintenance stop for Qantas flying boats on their Sydney–London route and the RAAF operated out of there during World War Two. Karumba Post Office opened in 1889 but closed in 1919. The local state school opened in 1968 and the public library opened in 1979.

Karumba is mentioned in the Australian band Goanna's song 'Every Passing Day', and the Red Hot Chili Peppers' 'Animal Bar' is named after the Karumba Lodge's bar of the same name. Visitors to Karumba may experience the rare Morning Glory cloud that sometimes rolls through in the early hours of a September–October morning. As well as being an industrial port on the banks of the Norman River, Karumba is a very popular fishing destination.

Due to the crocodiles, ocean swimming isn't recommended. In fact, in July 1957, two years after the Pawlowskis had arrived and had begun hunting crocodiles for their skins, Krys shot the largest croc ever recorded in Australia. A replica of the 8.6-metre croc, now known as Krys, is on display in Normanton. Male hunters who had tried to shoot the croc for decades were peeved when a woman did what no man had managed to do. To add insult to injury, rumour has it that Krys could skin a croc faster than the best of them. In 1965, tired of crocodile hunting, Ron and Krys turned toward conservationism and started Australia's first crocodile farm, but were eventually forced to close. PS: The story of the Pawlowski family is currently being written by Krys' youngest son, George.

There are two main hotels in Karumba, the Karumba Lodge Hotel and the Sunset Tavern. The Karumba Lodge is in the centre of town and overlooks the Norman River. Also part of the lodge is the infamous 'Animal Bar'.

The Sunset Tavern is right on the beachfront with amazing views overlooking the Gulf of Carpentaria. Author Bill 'Swampy' Marsh remembers sinking a few there while nibbling on the special fisherman's basket and being stunned by the sunset.

Kunama – NSW

In memory of Tony Davey.

Although Kunama had a population of less than a hundred, it was still larger than some of the schools I'd taught at. For those that may have never heard of the place, and I guess there'd be quite a few, Kunama's nestled at the foot of the Snowy Mountains, in New South Wales, five miles out of Batlow, heading south, toward Tumbarumba. My recollections of the area are of tall gum trees, snow gums, mountain ash and pine forests. The cold winters, with their bitter frosts, snow, rain, hail and persistent low cloud, were compensated for by wonderfully warm summers and perfect spring days.

Back in my day, Kunama had a railway station, a small town hall and a shop or two. The primary school had a double-sized classroom and there were about eighteen pupils. When the students reached senior age, they travelled by bus to Batlow Central School. I always tried to provide activities for the kids who got to school early. One of the things I did was to build a couple of painting trestles and, of a morning, I'd take these trestles out under the gum trees and I'd get the early-to-schoolers to take in what they saw, then paint that scene. And they did some great work. Fantastic really. In fact, when one of the school inspectors came around, he was so impressed by what they'd done that he asked if I'd also take on an in-service Cultural Subjects and Art course at Wagga Wagga Teachers College. Mind you, initially the thought frightened the heck out of me. But I did it, and I believe that my student-teachers benefited.

But as with a lot of those smaller schools, we struggled for funds. On top of our wish list was a bituminised multipurpose area where we could play tennis and other ball games and the kids could do their gymnastics and folk dancing et cetera. Of course, the question was, 'How to do we raise the funds needed for such a huge project?'

The Parents & Citizens group got together and they came up with an idea. We had an extended playground area of about four or five acres, most of which was covered in bracken fern. Beneath the bracken, the soil was very rich basalt. So, with many of the P&C members being farmers, they got to it and ploughed the land and put in a crop of potatoes.

It's said that with potatoes, as with many other crops, they go in three-year cycles. The first year you get a bumper. The second year's only fair and the third year's usually a disaster. That's because, with everyone else wanting to cash in on your success, supply outstrips demand and the bottom falls out of the market. Anyhow, we planted these potatoes in a year which usually would've been the down year. But as it happened, the vast majority of the other potato growing areas were hit by drought. So their crops failed and we had this fantastic year. We struck it lucky and, when we sold the crop to the packing house at Batlow, we made a grand profit.

The parents then got right into the project. It was all volunteer. Someone had a bulldozer, so that cost nothing. We got that in and we flattened a section of the playground on which we then built a tennis court cum multipurpose area. We had to pay for the bitumen. The piping that was used to put the wire netting fence around the multipurpose area was donated. It was a real school and community effort I can tell you. It certainly was. Though unfortunately, the end result wasn't a hundred per cent success because, when the bitter frosts hit, the edges of the bitumen eventually started to lift.

And I can tell you, they were some of the most bitter winters I've ever experienced. The frosts, in particular, were extremely savage and, at one stage, it snowed for a week. And that leads me into a little story. The school residence was only about twenty-five metres from the school – an easy walk. So during the winter months, I'd get down to the school nice and early and, in an attempt to warm the double-classroom before the kids arrived, I'd light up the potbelly stove. Anyhow, this particular morning I'd already done that. So I was sitting at my desk, out the front, preparing my day's lessons, when a little fellow come up to me. His name was Ashley; he said, 'Please, sir?'

I said, 'Yes, Ashley?'

He said, 'It's snowing inside.'

When I looked at him, there he was, covered with all this silvery stuff, just like snow. What'd happened was that, as he'd crouched down close to the pot belly stove to try and get warm, the flue had caught alight and all the solder in the flue had floated off and had fallen on his shoulders. Oh gosh, I can still remember that. In fact, just last Christmas, that same kid, Ashley, came to see my wife and me down at our small holiday retreat. How that came about was that we'd lost our eldest son, Tony, to cancer a bit over twelve months prior and the locals had put up a seat along the walking trail that went along the coast. And on that seat they'd put a small plaque which read: 'In memory of Tony Davey'. Anyhow, Ashley had seen that and so he came to see us and, during his visit, he shared many happy memories of his school days at Kunama.

But, as it happened, things didn't work out too well for Kunama. In their wisdom the Lands Department, or whoever, had divided all the land up into small lots which they then encouraged farmers to come and plant with fruit trees. And it all proved to be a disaster because, as I said, the winters were extremely harsh and, just as the fruit was setting, you'd get these bitter frosts. Then the snow and hail would come and the crops would be totally ruined. Really, to be honest, Kunama was a town in the wrong place for that type of farming. And so, when the orcharding collapsed, they then closed down the railway station, and that just about put an end to the township of Kunama and its small primary school.

Footnote – Kunama is on the south-western slopes of the Snowy Valley region of New South Wales, four hundred and fifty kilometres south-west of Sydney and at an altitude of a thousand metres. The area was sited in the 1850s and after World War One it was set up as a soldier settlement area. The Kunama branch railway – also known as the Batlow Line – was completed in 1923 as an extension of the Tumut Line. When the soldier settlers' blocks failed, the government divided the blocks up and enticed people to come and plant apples and pears. Due to the harsh extended winters, that project also failed. The town then fell into decline and the railway line closed in 1957. Kunama now has a population of less than seventy and the nearest pub is nine kilometres away, in Batlow.

Larrimah – NT

G'day, Swampy, Lindy here again: Lindy and Brian, the pre-COVID Grey Nomads. Me the ex-high school teacher-cum-history-buff and my husband Brian the local council retiree and now home brewing fanatic. Thanks for printing my last story 'Blame it on COVID' in your Ambos book. As you know, Brian had his ups-'n-downs during the pandemic. But we're okay now. We're back on track and he's out of hospital. In fact, we're planning to get back on the road again this winter and head north, which may also help distance Brian from his home-brewing overindulgences.

Now, while I was planning the trip, I came across an award-winning podcast hosted by two women, Kylie Stevenson and Caroline Graham. It was called *Lost in Larrimah*. The podcast centred on the disappearance of a man, Paddy Moriarty, and his kelpie dog, Kellie, intertwined with all the various feuds that were going on within the town. I was so engrossed by the podcast that I then read their book, *Larrimah: A missing man, an eyeless croc and an outback town of eleven people who mostly hate each other.*

The story goes that, back in late 2017, an Irishman named Paddy Moriarty had drunk a few more than his usual quota before heading home with his dog Kellie, and they've never been seen since. Now, the background to all this is intriguing because, at the time, Larrimah was said to be consumed by petty squabbles and bitter neighbourhood rivalries. So the question is: who dunnit and/or where is Paddy Moriarty and his dog Kellie?

Digging into the archives, I found out that Paddy was born in Ireland back in the late 1940s, apparently out of wedlock, and was a foster child. He was eighteen when he immigrated to Australia, where he worked as a station hand, a ringer and a grader driver. After he'd moved to Larrimah, he purchased an unused service station. Then in December 2017, Paddy left the Pink Panther pub, just after 6 p.m. to ride his quadbike the eight hundred metres home. When Paddy didn't turn up at the pub the following day, the publican, Barry 'Sharpie' Sharpe, went to check on him. But there was no sign of Paddy nor Kellie and yet Paddy's bank card, wallet, glasses and keys were still on the table and a barbecued chook was in the microwave oven, ready to be heated for dinner.

Now here's a thing: it took a couple of days before anyone notified the nearest police station – seventy kilometres away at Mataranka – as to the disappearance. So then, a big land and air search began. But not hide nor hair could be found of Paddy or Kellie. Even when a reward of $250,000 was posted, no one came forward. It was a complete mystery. Now, fast-forward to the coronial inquest of April 2022 where the coroner handed down his findings.

Chief suspect was Fran Hodgetts. Paddy and Fran had been arguing for years. Fran was in her mid-seventies and owned a tea and pie shop across the road from Paddy. Over a period of time, she'd laid nine complaints to the police over such things as Paddy stealing her favourite umbrella, Paddy poisoning her plants, Paddy deliberately scaring her customers away and that he'd even tossed a dead kangaroo into her yard. On each occasion, she lost the case. At the inquest, Fran Hodgetts admitted threatening to kill Paddy but said she'd only been joking. Furthermore, she stated that, due to her chronic arthritis, she'd be unable to kill anyone and that anyhow she was a lover not a fighter. When the police searched her house, her incinerator and septic tank, no sign of Paddy or Kellie was found.

So now to Bill Hodgetts, Fran Hodgetts' ex-partner. Bill had been drinking with Paddy the night before his disappearance and said he'd told Paddy that he could borrow his lawn mower the next day. But Paddy never turned up.

At the time of Paddy's disappearance, Bill Hodgetts described the atmosphere in the town as being on a 'knife's edge'.

Then there was the pub's former bartender, Richard Simpson. Richard Simpson also denied any involvement. He said that, even though he and Paddy had had their disputes, they were mates and that, on the night of the disappearance, Paddy seemed fine, even though he had a slight 'wobbly boot' i.e. he'd drunk just a little more than he normally did.

Another suspect was Fran Hodgetts' newly appointed, former tent-boxing live-in gardener, Owen Laurie. A few days before Paddy had gone missing, Owen Laurie admitted they'd had an argument. He went on to tell the inquest that he was only joking when he'd threatened to kill anyone who came near his garden i.e. Paddy. That all flies in the face of secret police recordings played at the inquest where Owen Laurie was caught singing how he had – and I quote – 'Killer-ated old Paddy,' and he'd, 'Struck-ed him on the head and killer-ated him and bash-erated him,' and he'd, 'Smacked him on the fuckin' nostrils wiff me claw hammer.' After the recording was played to Owen Laurie, he denied it was his voice then refused to answer any further questions, in case he should incriminate himself.

Another player in all this was Barry 'Sharpie' Sharpe, the owner of the Pink Panther pub. Sharpie, whose pub included a zoo of a few hundred birds, an assortment of native animals and three crocodiles, said that yes, Paddy had his enemies and he could get prickly every now and then, especially after he'd had a few. But he insisted that he and Paddy were good mates and, if ever he wanted a hand with anything, Paddy was always there to help him out. Then there was the long-time Larrimah couple, Karl Roth – a Vietnam veteran – and his wife Debbie, who'd overheard a woman tourist saying how she'd come across a kelpie that resembled Kellie but when she'd stopped and called it, the dog wouldn't come to her.

The youngest Larrimah residents were Mark and Karen Rayner. Mark was in his sixties and Karen in her late forties. Both were regulars at the pub, as it seems everyone else in town was. Karen had been the manager of the Pink Panther until a few months prior to Paddy and his dog's disappearance and she'd continued doing the books for Sharpie, just as a favour. The Rayners said that Paddy was a very popular bloke around town who'd spin yarns for any of the tourists who dropped in for a drink. Apparently, Paddy even used to go over to the Rayners' house where they'd watch cooking shows together. During the inquest, one thing that the Rayners said they were surprised about was that Paddy had been missing for a couple of days before anyone had told the police.

Other theories abound. Karl Roth thinks Paddy and Kellie may have been abducted by aliens. Another witness told the inquest that a serial-killer mate of his – the feller who was the real, fair-dinkum killer of British backpacker Peter Falconio – had done away with Paddy and his dog. Mind you, this was despite Bradley John Murdoch already having been convicted and jailed for the murder. Another witness, who described himself as a 'psychic', said that two men, Richard and Roo Dog, had told him that they'd shot and buried Moriarty near Mataranka. Other theories suggest that Paddy and Kellie were fed to one of the pub's three crocodiles. Or they'd been minced up in Fran Hodgetts' homemade pies and sold to the tourists. Or they'd been thrown down a sinkhole. Or they'd died from snakebite and/or Paddy died from a heart attack – though that'd still leave the mystery of the missing Kellie. But whatever the case, it became obvious during the inquest that Paddy was a complex and divisive character, as was everyone else in town.

So that's basically the background to the story, which I'm keen to delve further into. Although, since the disappearance, Richard Simpson and Owen Laurie have left Larrimah. Sharpie's since sold the pub, along with its menagerie, and has passed away from prostate cancer. Fran Hodgetts was last heard of in Melbourne where she was apparently recovering from cancer.

These days, Fran Hodgetts' grandson, Brent Cilia, has taken over Fran's tea and pie house. If anyone asks about his grandmother, he tells them, with his tongue firmly planted in his cheek, that she's been on the run ever since the coroner's inquest and adds that he's willing to sign copies of a book about Paddy's disappearance. In one interview Brent wanted it made clear how Paddy and Kellie's disappearance hasn't torn the town apart – not one iota. Instead, it's reunited Larrimah, to such an extent, he said, that last year everyone gathered at the Pink Panther pub to celebrate Christmas together.

And so, Swampy, who wouldn't be drawn in by a story like that. So it got me thinking that one stopover Brian and I definitely must make is Larrimah. Of course, when I told Brian why I was so interested in stopping there, being the old stick-in-the-mud he is, he didn't want to go anywhere near the place. 'No way,' he said. 'I don't want to get involved in digging up other people's dirt!' So that was that. But when I told him that, also during my research, I discovered that the Larrimah pub was voted one of Australia's top ten outback hotels and it was themed along the lines of the Pink Panther film series, with a young bare-bummed female tennis player advertising 'the best beer in the Territory' – well that did it, didn't it? Brian's now madly packing the caravan, raring to go!

Footnote – Larrimah – population eleven – is just off the Stuart Highway, a touch over four hundred kilometres south of Darwin. The Yangman Aboriginal people lived on and cared for its land for thousands of years before Europeans arrived. John McDouall Stuart explored the region in the 1860s. During World War Two, Larrimah was not only the railhead on the North–South Railway Line – an army transit point for personnel and supplies – but also Gorrie Airfield, ten kilometres from town, became the base of both the Royal Australian Air Force and the United States Air force. During 1943, Larrimah was home to 6500 military recruits, making it one of the largest military bases in the Pacific Region. During that time, it employed near on five hundred Aboriginal men, who carried out semi-skilled work, and thirty Aboriginal women, who worked as menial labourers in hospitals et cetera.

By 2005, the invasive cane toad had reached Larrimah, threatening native wildlife. In 2020, an Australasian giant centipede was seen attacking a cane toad under a water tank in Larrimah. The sighting sparked the theory that the venom of the centipede may kill cane toads, yet the centipede is unaffected by the toad venom.

Larrimah's Pink Panther Hotel was originally built in 1930, eight kilometres south at Birdum. Rumour has it that in 1942, General Douglas MacArthur gave the order for the Battle of the Coral Sea from the pub's porch. In 1957, the hotel was relocated to Larrimah and renamed Larrimah Wayside Inn – better known as the Pink Panther pub. Adorned by a sixteen-foot-tall Darwin beer stubby, it's one of ten designated 'unique Australian outback pubs' and is reputed to have the highest bar in the Northern Territory.

During its ownership by Barry 'Sharpie' Sharpe, the hotel accommodated a menagerie of snakes, sugar gliders, birds, emus and various other native animals, including three crocodiles; plus loads of kitsch Australiana, including old beer posters, t-shirts and Akubra hats, rustic bits of farming machinery, paintings of rodeos and farm life. One of the hotel's resident saltwater crocodiles, Sneaky Sam, was purchased from a pet shop as a youngster and eventually grew to 3.5 metres in length. Apparently it leapt, with amazing agility, from its unkempt pond, to snatch chickens off a stick. Another crocodile, a freshie, was a gift from a woman who'd worked at a crocodile farm. She'd been travelling with it kept in a broccoli box until she arrived at the pub. When it was realised that the croc was blind, it was named Ray-Ray after Ray Charles. The third croc is another salty called Aggro.

'Bullshit corner' welcomes visitors to the pub and local bumper stickers read, 'If we are what we eat, I'm fast, cheap and easy.' Also out front is a sculpture of a giant pink panther, lazing in a chair, enjoying a beer. Another pink panther flies overhead in a gyrocopter and, inside the pink-panther-painted pub, three stuffed pink panthers ride a tandem bicycle.

The hotel is also a Greyhound bus stop and post office for those living on surrounding station properties. Visitors can either stay in one of the motel rooms or camp overnight. The Pink Panther pub serves an array of basic meals, featuring a variety of pies and a 'vegie burger' for those gastronomically inclined. Gravy can be added to all meals, for a minimal extra cost.

PS: At the time of writing this story, no charges have been laid concerning the disappearance of Paddy Moriarty and his dog Kellie. Though many of the residents have levelled accusations at each other, they also deny personal involvement and so the police investigation is continuing. As Detective Sergeant Matthew Allen remarked, 'Someone out there knows what happened. It's hard to keep a secret.'

That secret is yet to be told.

Latham – WA

Latham's a wheat and sheep town, on the inland railway line, about halfway between Perth and Geraldton. Oh, perhaps a bit closer to Geraldton than to Perth. Back in the 1940s, when I was a young girl, there would've only been forty or so people living in the town. Thinking about it as I am now, I can't even remember if there was a hotel. But there was definitely the one shop, a wheat bin, a few houses – mainly railway houses – and we had a little school which had just the one teacher and ten or so of us kids. Our education went up to Grade 7 then; if we wanted to further ourselves, we had to go away to boarding school, which was mainly to Geraldton.

My father, Ted Waugh, was the ganger on the railways in Latham and we stayed there until the gang closed in about 1964. Being the ganger, Dad was like the foreman-in-charge of about eight fettlers, as the workers were called, and they did repairs along that particular stretch of the railway line. As for my mother, I'd say that some of those times in Latham were more unhappy than happy. That's because she came off a farm at Greenough, a pretty town on the coast, just south of Geraldton, where she had plenty of water and plenty of food. Well, plenty of everything more or less, while at Latham, there was virtually nothing. Still, I guess the other adults there had to go through the same thing. Although, of course, as kids we never fully realised how hard it was. Kids are adaptable aren't they and so they just get on with it.

Then after the war, in about '48 or '49, a lot of what we called 'New Australians' came out from Europe to work on the railways. They were described as 'displaced people' and, to repay their fare out to Australia, they had to give the government two years' service before they could go and work at their chosen profession. I actually found them to be lovely people and they gave us a lot of new recipes, which improved our culinary skills. But I still remember when one of the New Australian couples had a little baby who died. That was very sad. I think it was due to the extreme heat. See, Latham got very hot in summer and being corrugated iron houses they got extremely hot. So I guess, coming from a country where it was a lot colder, it was too much for the little baby boy and he died.

And also, with it being so dry, the railways had to bring in our water. When that happened, everyone had to cart the water in buckets from the railway station over to their houses and pour it into the copper or the wash trough. Or, if we were having a bath, we'd put it in the bath tub. But oh, my mother was a great gardener. She'd save all the rinse water from the washing and the bath and she'd bail it out onto her geraniums and into her few pot plants, just to keep them going. Most people used to do that, and it was amazing what could be kept alive with just a little trickle of water. Mum also had a lemon tree. Oh, and that's right, Mrs Syson had both a lemon tree and a fig tree. And I remember Mrs Syson kept a cow tethered in the bush and she had a bough shed where she did her milking, and she'd give everybody her spare milk. And she was also very good with sick people. Very good, and lucky for that too, because we were a long, long way from a doctor.

But with the New Australians; I remember when my sister, Rosalie, was only three or four and she taught all the foreign children how to make mud pies. And, oh, their mothers got so upset at the terrible mess their children had got themselves into. Rosalie also used to pick up the languages of the foreign children real quick and when she'd come home Mum wouldn't have a clue what she was rabbiting on about. Of course, Rosalie used to teach the foreign children bits and pieces of English, too. It's amazing how quickly little children can learn each other's language, especially the swear words.

But dear me, it must've been so hard for some of those displaced people because most of them weren't used to labouring work. Many were well educated, like in being schoolteachers and accountants and so forth. And having come from big cities in Europe, only to arrive in Latham in summer, well, oh dear, what with the heat and the dust and the flies, the poor things must've wondered where on earth they'd come to. Of course, there was no refrigeration or anything. When they first arrived, they weren't even given a water bag. I can still see Mum sewing water bags up for them. See, even though most of us didn't have much apart from a few basic amenities, back then everybody helped each other out more than they do these days.

After the New Australians had done their two years, most of them went back down to Perth to take up their professions or whatever. After that, in about 1950 or '51, most of the men that came out to work on the railways were heavy drinkers. So there were lots of fights and their children were neglected, which was unpleasant. In fact, my mother grew quite bitter toward the types we had living around us. She reckoned it was because the government started giving the railway jobs to men who'd just come out of jail. That's what my mother said, anyway.

But one funny thing I remember; there were two old Irishmen, Paddy and Tom. Fettlers they were. I don't think they were out of a jail but they'd go on the square for a few weeks – as in no grog – then they'd go on a bender, as they called it. And with my father being English, and with the English and the Irish not being that friendly toward each other, when old Tom got drunk he used to march up and down the front of our house calling out to Dad, 'Ted Waugh you're a black 'n tan, pommy so-and-so.'

Then the other Irish fettler, old Paddy; he'd get so drunk that he couldn't even walk home. So there must've been a hotel somewhere in town. When that happened, Tom used to load old Paddy into a wheelbarrow. Oh, it was so funny. I can still see it. As a kid, I used to stand out in our front yard and watch Tom trying to wheel old Paddy home in this wheelbarrow. And Paddy was like a dead weight. He'd have his legs dangling out the front and his arms dangling out the side and his head flopping over the back. Gone for all money. And Tom would be really drunk as well and so the wheelbarrow would be zigzagging all over the street, swaying this way and that. Then they'd topple over and Tom would stumble about trying to lift Paddy back into the wheelbarrow. Then they'd head off again, zigzagging this way and that, toppling over all along the way. Sometimes it used to take them hours to get home, and they only lived just down the street.

Footnote – Latham is in the mid-west of Western Australia, approximately two hundred and fifty kilometres north-ish of Perth. Latham was named after an early pastoralist who established a watering place near a large granite rock – Latham Rock – for droving stock as they passed through the area. When the railway from Wongan Hills to Mullewa was drafted in 1913, the Public Works Department decided Latham would be a suitable site for a railway station and town. The railway opened in 1915 and the town was gazetted two years later. As the surrounding area proved suitable for wheat and other cereal crops, a bulk wheat bin was opened in 1936.

Champion wrestler George Dinnie – 1875–1939 – was a resident of Latham back in the 1920s. Latham currently has a population of just over fifty and research can't find a hotel within cooee.

Launceston – Tas

This was back in the early '60s, right. It's my first time out shearing. Well, to be more exact, at that particular time I wasn't shearing, I was roustabouting. But the point is that it was my first time away with a shearing team. I was in Tassie. I was new to the game, so I didn't know how things worked. Any rate, me and a couple of my shearing mates go into Launceston. It's a Saturday and it's the first time I'd been in there on a weekend. By the letter of the law, the pubs closed up pretty early and so, by that evening, everything was sort of dead. Any rate, we're wandering down near the Commercial Hotel. The Commercial was a huge, rambling hotel and we can hear this racket coming from inside the pub. All the blinds are drawn, but on closer investigation we find out that all this bloody noise is coming from in the bar area – dead set.

'Let's have a look,' says one of me mates.

'Okay.' The front door's locked, so we found the fire escape and we climbed up that. At the top of the fire escape, we discovered an open window. So we went through that, straight through someone's room. 'G'day, mate, sorry for the intrusion,' and down the long, winding old staircase we go, into the bar. And there's blokes everywhere, all shearers like, all drinking and carrying on, having a great time.

'This'll do us,' we said.

So we have a few beers and by about 2 o'clock in the morning the barman's falling off his perch. He's the owner like – the publican. So we give him a bit of a nudge. 'How's about another beer?' we ask.

'Go fer yer life,' he said. 'I've had it.' Then he locked the till up, stuck the day's takings in the safe and announced to all and sundry, 'Go fer it, fellers. It's now an honour system,' and off he goes to bed. From then on, someone took over the serving and we all laid our money down on the bar, and that was it. I think someone even went so far as to package up the takings to hand over to the publican the next morning.

Any rate, the thing about the Commercial was that it was totally a union pub. Like, if you were an AWU member, you were in. So after we sunk a few more beers we decided to go for a bit of a poke around the place. So we wandered up to one of the rooms and lo-n-behold it's packed with about twenty blokes, all playing poker dice – which was highly illegal mind you. Any rate, we stuck around there for a while. By this stage, it's about 4 o'clock in the morning, right. I was buggered so I just sort of found myself a spare bed and hit the sack in that. Thinking as I am now, there was a hell of a lot more shearers than there were beds so everyone must've slept in shifts or something. I don't know. I was sound asleep so it didn't worry me. Then in the morning, them who could manage it fronted up to the huge kitchen hall for breakfast. And mate, you got a real top feed. Too right you did. There was bacon, eggs, sausages, chops, the lot. Whatever you wanted, you just got stuck into it.

Now, while we were there that first weekend, on the Sunday, the pub served a beautiful lunch. Just beautiful it was. It started at about midday, and this Sunday lunch was known far and wide. Which meant you had to get there real early because just about every shearer in Tassie, who possibly could, would turn up for this Sunday lunch. Any rate, we got down to the dining room on the dot of 10 o'clock and the place was already packed.

Now, there was a bloke there they called The Birdman, and by gee he was an odd character. No exaggeration, this feller had to be at least twenty-four stone and as ugly as. A shearer he was, and a pretty good one too, or so I was told.

Any rate, The Birdman always wore this big, red, woollen jumper. It was one of them real fluffy ones, what looked like downy feathers. Other than that, the main reason why they nicknamed him The Birdman was that when he got pissed, he got it into his head that he could fly. Fair dinkum, he was absolutely convinced he could fly.

Any rate, just inside the entrance of the Commercial Hotel was this nice, big, ornate staircase, which wound up, two tiers, to the residential part of the pub, high above. Now, as I said, even by the time we got there for this Sunday lunch, the place was packed. So me and the rest of our shearing mob had to set up a table right near the entrance to the pub, which also just happened to be directly under the landing of this staircase. There was about a dozen of us at this big table, so we ordered a few jugs of beer and we're sitting there knocking them back. Now, I don't know how long The Birdman had been drinking. Maybe he'd stayed up all night. I don't know, but he was pretty much well gone by this stage. Well, he was more than that really. To be more exact, he was as pissed as a newt. Any rate, all of a sudden he calls out above the din, 'I reckon I might go fer a fly.'

So he gets off his bar stool and he wobbles over to the staircase – real unsteady like – then he proceeds to stagger up the two flights of stairs. With each step of his climb, the place goes quieter and quieter. Any rate, The Birdman somehow makes it to the top of the landing. Then, when our gun shearer sees The Birdman attempting to clamber up onto the balustrade, high up, directly above our table, he goes, 'Shit. We'd better save the grog.' So he grabs the remaining couple of jugs of beer from off our table and he calls out to us, 'Stand back fellers!' Which we did.

By now The Birdman's balancing precariously, away up on this balustrade, two floors up. 'I'm gonna fly,' he calls out.

By this stage, there's dead silence. You could've heard a feather drop. All eyes were on The Birdman. Then he fluffs up his big red jumper, gives a bit of a birdcall, then he leaps out into the air with his arms spread-eagled and flapping like they're supposed to be wings in flight. But they don't work and down he comes from this great height – *Splat!* – right, straight, smack-bang through the middle of the table we'd been sitting at. Splintered it. Belly first. *Crack!* He didn't move a muscle.

'Christ almighty, he's dead,' someone called out.

But no. Moments later The Birdman came back to life with a fluff of his woollen jumper. He opened his eyes, one by one, and gave his head a bit of a shake. He staggered groggily to his feet. Then, with glassy eyes, he looked vacantly at our gun shearer, who was standing there next to him, still clinging onto those two jugs of beer. 'What do yer reckon about that, then?' The Birdman slurred to the gun.

'Well, mate,' the gun replied, 'I must say I was very impressed with yer take off. But,' he added, 'if I were you, I'd brush up a bit on yer landings.'

Footnote – Launceston, originally named Patersonia, is in northern Tasmania, at the junction of the North and South Esk Rivers where they become the Tamar River. It's the state's second largest city and won the Australian Town of the Year awards in 2022. The original inhabitants were the largely nomadic Letteremairrener people, whose occupation and usage of the Tamar basin has been recognised for at least seven thousand years and more than likely back as far as thirty-five thousand years.

The first white explorers were George Bass and Matthew Flinders, who arrived at the mouth of the Tamar River in 1798 while exploring the possibility of a strait between Australia and Van Diemen's Land – now known as Tasmania. By 1806, Europeans began settling in the area. This caused a series of skirmishes to flare up between the settlers and the Letteremairrener people, which later led to the genocidal expeditions of between 1827 and 1831.

By 1827, Launceston had become an export centre, mainly for the pastoral industry. Small hotels and breweries began to emerge in the 1820s. By the time more 'substantial' hotels were built in the 1830s, they'd become the hub of the town's social, political, religious and sporting, churches and school group activities. Until theatres were established, even plays, musical soirees and readings were performed in the various hotels.

Tin was discovered in north-western Tasmania in the early 1870s and gold mining commenced at nearby Beaconsfield a few years later. During the following two decades, Launceston grew into an urban centre and by the late 1880s it was one of Australia's oldest cities. It chalked up a number of firsts: it boasted the first use of an anaesthetic in the Southern Hemisphere, it was the first Australian city to have underground sewers and it was the first Australian city lit by hydroelectricity.

With the number of pubs in Launceston, you'll never go short of a drink and a feed and entertainment. As for the Commercial, it was established in 1853 and is touted as being a great place to unwind and enjoy some of Tassie's best beers and wines while having a meal. The 'Mersh' as it's known these days has a menu as long as a giraffe's neck, featuring everything from Mediterranean stuffed prawns to Dagwood dogs. If you're game, have a crack at the Mersh Super Grill. As they say in their advertising, 'There's something for everyone at the Mersh!'

Learmonth – Victoria

In memory of Garry 'Gazza' Purcell.

I grew up at a place in central Victoria called Learmonth. Back then it was mostly general farming; you know, sheep, dairy cattle, oats, potatoes, et cetera. But it was a tremendous little spot, and still is. It's got a lake – Lake Learmonth – which has only been dry about three times that I can remember. All us kids learnt to swim there and, naturally enough, the local footy team's called The Lakers.

If you look at a geological map, Learmonth's right down near the bottom of the Great Dividing Range; on the southern side. It's freezing in winter. Actually, it snowed a couple of times while I was a kid – not much, but a bit. See, the way it works is that the Great Dividing Range starts right up in the northern part of Queensland. It then comes down the coast till it cuts across to Muttaburra. From Muttaburra it goes all the way down until it virtually cuts Victoria in half, before running out in the Grampians, around Halls Gap. Later on, when I visited Maryborough, which is only forty mile north of Learmonth, I couldn't for the life of me figure out why the water was running off the Great Divide the wrong way; like it was heading north, while at Learmonth it headed south. That's until I worked out that Maryborough was on the other side of the Great Divide and so the water runs south to north, on its way up to meet the Murray River.

So that's a bit about the lay of the land for you. And so, now to the story. Back when I was a kid, rumour had it that Learmonth Cemetery was haunted by some sort of a ghost. Maybe that's because our parents didn't want any of us kids to go in there. I don't know. Anyway, the thing is, we grew up believing that the Learmonth Cemetery had ghosts, so nobody ever went into the cemetery of a night for fear of what might happen to them. Now, there were two old codgers – as old as the hills. They lived next to one another in a street just the other side of the cemetery. For years and years, each night of the pub week, these two old codgers would meet up and they'd walk down the street, turn right at the southern end, then follow along another street that bordered the cemetery to go to the Stag Hotel. Yes, every night the pub was open, they done that without fail.

So this night they're in the pub. It's the middle of winter. The weather's terrible. It's cold and rainy and windy, lightning and thunder, the lot – a horrible night. Now, it might've been one of these old codger's birthdays or something because, this particular night, they really got stuck into it. Like, they'd had quite a few more than what they usually had, which would've been a lot to start with.

Anyway, just on closing time the first old codger says to the second old codger, 'I'm done,' he says. 'I'm headin' off home. See yer tomorra'.'

'Okay,' says the second old codger. 'I won't be long. I'll just have another-ie 'n head off home meself.'

'See yer,' says the first codger.

'Not if I see yer first,' says the second old codger, you know, as a sort of joke.

So the first old codger gets outside. Like I said it's a horrible, miserable winter's night; rain, hail, wind, the lot. It's as black as all hell – apart from the flashes of lightning that electrify up the sky. And so he starts to stagger off home. Down the street that borders the cemetery he goes. The wind's lashing at him, rain and hail are biting at his face. 'Bugger it,' he says. 'Not even a ghost'd come out on a night like this, so I'll take a short cut through the cemetery.'

So this old codger's staggering through the cemetery, wobbling this way and that. The thing was, a funeral was set for the following day and so they'd already dug the grave. Next thing, down the six-foot hole he goes – *plop!* – straight to the bottom. So then he starts grappling at the muddy bank of the grave, trying to get out. But the sides are so slippery, with all the mud and rain, that he can't get a grip, and before long he's all tuckered out. 'Bugger it,' he says. 'I've had enough. I may as well camp here in the back corner'a the grave fer the rest'a the night 'n someone'll get me out in the morning.' So that's what he does. He settles down for the night at the back end of the grave.

By now it's well past closing time at the Stag and so his mate heads off home. Same as before: the wind's lashing him, rain and hail are biting at his face. 'Bugger it,' he says, 'a haunted-ghost wouldn't come out on a night like this, so I'll take a short cut through the cemetery.'

So the second old codger starts staggering through the cemetery, wobbling this way and that. Next thing, down the same hole he goes – *plop!* – straight to the muddy bottom. So then he also starts scrabbling, ripping at the side of the grave, trying to get a foothold in an attempt to get out. And so there he is, trying and trying, slipping and sliding, falling down and getting back up again, when a voice echoes from the back of the grave, 'You'll never get out'a here, mate.'

Next thing – *zoom!* – straight up and out of that six-foot-deep hole he shoots, and off into the night. When he got home, he locked all his doors and windows and he scrambled under his bed, and that's where he stayed. For a whole week!

Footnote – Learmonth is in Central Victoria, around a hundred and fifty kilometres west of Melbourne. The Wadawurrung people lived on and cared for the land for thousands of years before white settlement. The township was originally named Lake Learmonth after the Learmonth brothers, Thomas and Somerville, who squatted there in 1838. Though there was a deep and bitter rivalry with the Wadawurrung people, the Learmonth brothers gained a reputation as merino and stud owners until they sold up in 1872.

The Stag Hotel opened in 1854 and, by the time the township was surveyed in 1857, there was already a Presbyterian, a Catholic and a Wesleyan church. Lake Learmonth Post Office opened in 1858, a school opened in 1859 and the town was renamed Learmonth in 1860. An Anglican church was built in 1861, a courthouse opened in 1864 and a temperance hall was built in 1867. By the mid-1860s, Learmonth had six hotels and several stores, including bakeries, saddlers and blacksmiths. Between 1888 and 1968, Learmonth was a railway branch line to Wabubra. With a falling population, the courthouse closed in 1913, the shire offices struggled on until 1964 and the school closed in 2012.

Throughout the years, Lake Learmonth has been both full and dry. Currently, as of 2022, there is water in the lake and it's open for angling and boating. The lake also boasts shoreline reserves and a caravan park. A Save Our Lake action group is actively in need of volunteers and Learmonth Bowling Club is looking for 'Local Legends' to join the club for the forthcoming season. Learmonth currently has a hotel – the Stag – two halls, three churches, a recreation reserve, tennis and bowling faculties, a general store and residential buildings that house a population of just over four hundred people.

The historic Stag Hotel has played an important part in the town's history, with such organisations as the Roads Board and the Cemetery Trust meeting there from as far back as 1858. During the gold-mining boom, a dozen coaches per day departed the Stag carrying miners to the goldfields of Ballarat. In the 1870s, the Stag was the venue for the inaugural 'champion ploughmen matches' discussions, from which people later came to exhibit their ploughing skills from as far afield as New South Wales.

The Stag closed in 2013, but has now opened with new owners. It's a 'family friendly pub' hosting, among other things, 'Save the Lake Darts Nights'. An array of beers, wines and spirits are available and the menu board is highlighted by weekly parmigiana specials. Pizzas are also available, including the popular 'Full Lake' and the perhaps less popular 'Empty Lake' as well as a 'vego' variety. Author Bill 'Swampy' Marsh was particularly drawn to the garlic prawn schnitzel with salad and chips.

Macclesfield – SA

Yes, and so how did we get to Macclesfield. Well, despite the fact that I was holding down a very highly paid, prestigious and enjoyable job in the advertising industry, a friend of my then husband, Richard, told me, 'Gaynor, if you don't support your man, you'll end up being a pencil-pusher for the rest of your life.'

So I guess with that threat, I had to stand by my man. So we sold up our lovely home in Adelaide and off I toddled to the little one-horse town of Macclesfield to become a glorified barwoman and part-owner of a pub. In the scheme of things, Macclesfield was a town time forgot. We hadn't heard much about the place other than the pub being haunted and that the locals had knocked down an old building just down the street from the pub because the walls bled. So that was pretty scary. At that time, the hotel was called the Davenport Arms – the Davvie – and in the interest of capitalising upon the rich history of the town's founding fathers, we decided to change it to the Three Brothers' Arms, in recognition of the three pioneer Davenport brothers who built the place.

So, in an attempt to return the place back to its former glory, we embarked on extensive renovations, including exposing the original local soapstone walls and roof shingles. The dining room, which had been added back the 1950s, needed work. Actually, an eighty-year-old woman who'd once been employed as a kitchen maid there told us that, back when horses and carts and bullock trains passed through on their way to and from Port Elliot, there'd been a horse trough next to the pub, which she'd had to fill daily, by means of an Anderson Lever Pump, that was attached to a well.

In fact, Richard found the well under the dining room floor. And, when he donned his SCUBA diving gear and had himself lowered into the crystal clear depths, he came across a stack of old pennies and so forth, even a half-sovereign. So we bought more pennies and halfpennies and, when we put up the new bar, we embedded them into it. As for the well itself, we decided to make a feature of it. We installed a couple of glass coffee table tops over the well, with a sign clearly stating, 'DON'T CLIMB ON THE GLASS'. Of course, when a couple of people ignored the sign and decided to dance on it – *crack!* – they went straight through, down into the well, and had to be rescued by the State Emergency Service, didn't they. It was just luck that no one was hurt.

Now, even though I'd done a short bartending and cocktail course, I'd never actually served behind a bar. It was all new to me, so I was like a fish out of water, and a very nervous one at that. On our opening day, every man, woman and their dogs turned up. You could hardly breathe. So I bravely put on my L-plates and just went for it. Anyway, I got through that – I survived – and we finally crawled into bed at some ungodly hour. At that stage, we were sleeping in the living quarters, if you could call them that. They were at the side of the hotel, on the back, and were yet to be renovated. It was pretty hideous really. You wouldn't have put your worst enemy in there. But I remember lying in the bed, completely exhausted, thinking, Oh my God, is this what the rest of my life's going to be like? And while I was mulling over that, I heard an evil, hideous, eerie-sounding noise. Having heard that the place was haunted, my immediate thought was that something demonic was about to attack me. So I'm just lying there, frozen in fear, going, Oh my God, they've come to kill me!

Anyhow, it turned out to be a colony of possums living happily in the roof space. But that just goes to show how on edge I was. Still, we carried on and after we'd made some headway, we decided to open for Sunday lunchtime. Opening on a Sunday was new to the town and, while it got up the nose of the pub across the road, it gave the locals some extra drinking time. Even so, by doing this huge overhaul and changing the pub's name, we ran into a lot of resistance and resentment. A lot of the locals viewed us as yuppies coming up from the city to disturb their idyllic lifestyle. We even had death threats at one point. Then there were the abusive phone calls. Another time a giant white penis, complete with balls and three hands, was painted outside the front of the pub. So it wasn't good.

But coming from a creative advertising background, and with Richard being a singer and entertainer, we wanted to create some sort of a music hub in the place. Anyhow, I was chatting to a guy about it and he said, 'Oh, Cyril the rabbit catcher sings real good 'n he's a local.'

I said, 'Okay, well get him to come down and we'll do an audition. If he's okay we'll start off with him.'

So Cyril comes down, fresh from rabbit trapping, adorned with a bit of spattered blood and rabbit's fur. He stood there and, I kid you not, he had a little stand, which he put his sheet music on, and he started strumming away on his guitar. When he opened his mouth, out popped a nasally voice, '*Every time I take my dog ter town, people keep kickin' my dog around.*' Then after he'd sung a few lines, he stopped, flicked the music page over, took a deep breath and picked up on the song again. I mean, it was so bad it was fantastic and he was such a lovable guy that I said, 'Cyril, I tell you what we're going to do. I'm going to market you as Cyril the Rhinestone Cowboy.' So I got a hat and I stuck rhinestones on it and the next Sunday we put him on as our feature act. And he was an absolute hit!

But oh my God, some of the patrons tested me to the limit, especially in those early days. Before the new kitchen had been built, one of the locals confronted me. 'I think yer got a nerve comin' up here 'n changin' things,' he snarled.

I said, 'Well, the place was in need of change. We've even had to close down the kitchen because the health inspectors said it's unhygienic.'

'What do yer mean unhygienic?' he said. 'Me 'n me dad have been sittin' here fer three generations, eatin' the bloody food 'n it's really good.'

I said, 'Listen, come with me, sir. I'll take you out the back and show you a few things, okay?' So I took him out to the back area and I said, 'So what's your favourite meal?'

He says, 'Snitty 'n chips.'

I said, 'Well, I'll show you how it's cooked.' So I took him into the kitchen and, I kid you not, sitting up in the congealed fat was a fried dead rat, with its mouth agape and its big eyes staring back at him. Well, he took one look at the rat, which was looking back at him, and said, 'Yeah, righto then. Got yer point.'

Another time this guy came in looking like Elvis Presley, with his four-guy entourage. They called him the Elvis of Macclesfield or something. When he fronted up to the bar with these four guys, I said, 'And what'll it be, sir?'

Well, he looked down his nose at me, lifted his eyebrow then mumbled Elvis Presley like, 'The usual.' And I'm thinking, Look, mate, I've never seen you before, let alone served you. So I said, 'And what might the usual be, sir?' So he mumbled what it was and I served him and his mates. The thing was, every time he came in, I was expected to remember what his usual was. I found out later that he lived in a house called the Ponderosa or something.

And during the weekdays, while we were still renovating, I was the only one serving. So I'd be forever scampering around, going here and there, from the front bar to the lounge bar. This time there was a woman sitting in the lounge bar. I noticed she was staring at me. Anyhow, she gave me a hoy-over, and when I did, she said in a real smug manner, 'Smile, Gaynor, the porcelain's cracking!'

And before Richard started importing English beers and genuine Guinness, we only had one beer on tap. The rest were in bottles, so I had to pour the beer into the glass by hand. I don't think we even had cans. Anyhow, there was an old guy, Albie. He'd been a regular for years. He was such a dear old soul. He lived next door to the pub. He looked about a hundred – beer worn and weathered.

He'd come in of a morning and he'd sit and drink 'ponies' all day. Oh and that's right, we had bingo tickets underneath the bar and, while he'd be sipping away on his beer, he'd buy these bingo tickets – one at a time – and very slowly. So every ten minutes I'd have to bend over and get him a bingo ticket. Then by the end of the night, this dear old man would be so stonkered that I'd have to help him out of the pub and waddle him home.

Another time a guy came up to me and said, 'Can yer ring fer a girl fer Elephant?'

I said, 'What?'

He said, 'Yeah, that guy over there, his name's Elephant. He wants a girl. Can yer ring one up for him?'

I said, 'Excuse me sir, I am not a prostitution service!'

But these were the things I was expected to do. And oh, there'd be such an uproar when Richard rang the bell for last orders. Then it'd be, 'Time please ladies and gentlemen. Thank you and good night.' And seriously, because they'd previously been allowed to stay there, drinking away till all hours, they got so upset I thought they were about to murder us.

But what put the wind up me the most were the ghosts. And oh yes, there were ghosts there, as true as I stand here. Now, imagine the male and female toilets being side by side, with a partitioning brick wall between them. So there's two doors – female and male – with bubbly glass windows in each and in between the doors is solid brick. Anyhow, this night I looked up and I saw the profiled shadow of a woman walking past the female toilet's glass window. That was okay.

But then her profile reappeared walking by the glass window in the male toilet. I kid you not: she'd walked from the female side of the toilet, through the brick wall and into the male toilet. Well, I froze. I'm thinking, holy moly. And that's as true as I stand here. You can even put me under a lie detector test. And that particular spot was always very cold, even in summer. Our two dogs, a Rottweiler and a German shepherd, wouldn't even go near those toilets.

Another night I went out the back for a bit of fresh air. There were old stables there that the horses and bullocks used in the olden days, and I spotted a shadowy figure darting around the stalls and fallen walls. And I wasn't the only one to have seen that happen. And in the backyard, there was a tyre hanging from an old tree and another time I saw this little boy standing next to the tyre. He had little jodhpurs on, with stockings, and he had curly blond ringlets. He was holding a stick and a hoop and he was forming circles with the hoop. I just froze. I couldn't believe what I was seeing. Even a young local lad said he'd seen the boy when he'd gone out to get some firewood. I remember him coming back into the bar, stammering away and literally shaking with fear! That's also as true as I stand here. You can put me under a lie detector for that one as well. And I haven't even mentioned what made our head waitress shake in her boots when she was setting up one night in the dining room.

Anyhow, we were only there for a couple of years. And there's not much good to say about the experience really, other than the people from our advertising and music background coming up and performing as a favour, God bless them. So it turned out to be a nice music–creative hub and it eventually became a sort of function centre where people could have weddings and such. And there were the Sunday nights, after closing time, when we'd sit by the open fire with friends, having a roast dinner. The chef was great. But do you know what? When we finally left that pub, I felt like I was being freed from prison – from solitary confinement. I didn't even turn around and look back.

Footnote – Macclesfield was named in honour of the Earl of Macclesfield. 'Maccy' as it's known is on the south-eastern slopes of the Mount Lofty Ranges, fifty kilometres south-east of Adelaide, with a population of around eight hundred. Prior to the arrival of European settlers in the early 1940s, the area had been occupied and cared for, for thousands of years, by the Peramangk people who named it *Kangowirranilla*, meaning 'place for water and kangaroos'.

George Davenport, a banker and director of the South Australian Company in England, together with two partners, paid for a special survey of land in South Australia. To that end, he sent out his eldest son, Francis, to select an area.

Francis arrived in Adelaide in early 1840 and selected the spot where Macclesfield now stands. In that same year, the government approved a survey. Francis Davenport returned to England in 1842, leaving Henry Giles as manager. In February 1843, Francis and his wife Sarah returned, along with Samuel Davenport and his wife and their other brother Robert – the three brothers. So began the township of Macclesfield. Interestingly, rumour has it that the willow trees that line the nearby River Angas have been grown from seeds collected from Napoleon Bonaparte's grave on the island of Elba, which were poked into the centre of raw potatoes to preserve them during the boat trip over to South Australia.

Macclesfield has two hotels. The Macclesfield Hotel is a family friendly pub, built in the 1880s to cater for, and accommodate, travellers to and from the goldfields of Victoria. The pub stocks a wide range of beers, wines and spirits and is noted for its gourmet pub grub. It has weekly specials including a curry night and the schnitzels have been rated in South Australia's top ten.

The first hotel in the area, The Goat's Head Inn, was established in 1841. Its name later changed to Macclesfield Arms, then Davenport Arms, then to Three Brothers' Arms, in reference to the three Davenport brothers. The Goat's Head Inn brewery opened by 1851, next to the hotel, and won prizes for its beers from as far away as London. In the early 1900s, the brewery was converted to a butter and cheese factory and in 1937 it was converted again. In recognition of its historic close ties, some of the ancient ironwood beams from the original brewery have been incorporated into the lounge bar of the pub.

Three Brothers' Arms is a friendly, pokie-free entertainment and arts hub that boasts an extensive beer, wine and spirit list, including its local Goat's Head Lager. Within its extensive menu, author Bill 'Swampy' Marsh recommends having a crack at the Three Brothers' Arms tasting plate.

Mount Isa – Qld

In memory of Tanya Battel.

I grew up in West Yorkshire, England, in a town called Bradford. Even though my parents were as poor as church mice, they wanted me to go to a private commercial college. It wasn't at all la-de-da because it actually should've been condemned. It was a big old Edwardian building where, for safety reasons, we weren't allowed in certain parts of the place. There were only a hundred students and, apart from four boys, we were all girls. And being a commercial college, local business people sent their kids there with the intention of them taking over the family enterprise. So we didn't do subjects like home economics or such. There was no sport. We just concentrated on commerce, languages, shorthand and typing.

So I started learning shorthand when I was ten. And I don't know, I guess I just had an aptitude for it because, by sixteen, I was up to one hundred and forty words a minute. Then, when I was eighteen and a half, I left the college and went into secretarial work. Anyhow, one day Mum saw an advertisement in the local job centre for training as a court reporter. So I went and had a chat. The deal was that they'd take me on, just as long as I got my shorthand speed up to two hundred words a minute. So I asked a couple of the teachers from my old college if they could help, and straight away they said, 'Yes.'

They were lovely people. I went twice a week after work until my shorthand got up to speed. And that's how I became a court reporter. The job basically consisted of sitting in on a trial and taking down, in shorthand, every word that's said. As you might imagine, it's quite intense and so, every fifteen minutes, we'd swap over with a fresh court reporter. We'd then go and read what we'd written down to a typist, who'd type it all up. My first year was classed as provisional training and after that, I was able to work in the high court, which, in Australia, is our Supreme Court, and the Crown Court, which is our District Court.

During my time in England, I reported on lots of bankruptcies and inquiries. You may remember the Bradford City stadium fire, back in the mid-1980s, where near on sixty people died and over two hundred and fifty were injured. I did relief reporting on that as well as working in other locations throughout the country. Anyhow, one day I just happened to mention to one of my fellow court reporters how I'd love to take a break for a while and travel.

'Well,' she said, 'you should apply to the Court Reporting Bureau in Brisbane, Australia.'

So I wrote to them and they said, 'Yes.' Next thing they sent me an aeroplane ticket. I was on a three-year contract, meaning that if I left the Bureau within that time I'd have to reimburse them. I'd just turned twenty-two when I arrived in Brisbane. It was January '86 and I remember getting off the plane and being hit by this massive blast of heat. First I thought it must've come from the plane's engine. But it hadn't. It was the normal heat of a Brisbane summer's day. And coming straight out from an English winter, it was like having my head stuck in an oven. Oh my God, I thought, What've I done? And after I'd put my makeup on for work, I'd get on the bus and, by the time I got off, it'd all be running down my face. I hadn't thought things through really and of course it was very hard for Mum and Dad. But at my age, it was like, Oh Australia sounds like a bit of fun with all its beaches and the sunshine. And that just wasn't the case.

Even though the Court Reporting Bureau usually provided accommodation for their new arrivals, I'd decided to stay with an

English female court reporter friend. We'd been great mates in England but, by the time I arrived in Brisbane, she'd hooked up with a guy. And this guy clearly didn't want me hanging around. So I found a rental – a squat – that I shared with three Aussies; a girl and two guys. In those early days, I also struggled with the Aussie lingo, and the Australians struggled to understand me. For example, during my first week in court, a police officer was asked the standard questions of name, rank and home police station.

Anyhow, he said, 'I'm John Smith. I'm a Detective Constable,' and when it got to his police station, it sounded like 'Mar-ouch-ie-doo-moo-laa-blah.' Now, as a court reporter, you have to get down every single word that's been said, and correctly. Otherwise, you have to pull up the court – meaning you stop the court's proceedings for clarification about what's been said. And you only do that under extreme circumstances. You just don't do it willy-nilly. But to me, this policeman was speaking a whole different language. Anyhow, after he'd said where he was stationed, I had to pull up the court. 'Excuse me,' I said. 'I am sorry, but what was that?' And the whole court looked at me like I was a real ninny. Then he said nice and slowly, 'Maroochydore–Mooloolaba.'

When I said, 'Could you please spell that?' everybody started laughing, even the judge. They must've thought, Who the hell is this chick? Straight off the boat from Pommy-land and doesn't have a clue. Another phrase I had difficulty with was 'fair dinkum'. Again I had to stop the court. 'Excuse me?' I asked. 'What is fairy-dinky?' Oh it was so funny, and the judge just leaned over and said, 'I think he means fair dinkum.'

I thought, Yeah okay, but what the hell does that mean?

So yes, those early days were very interesting. Then I'd only been working in Brisbane for a month when the Bureau sent me to Mount Isa. And oh, I had no idea. I hadn't even looked it up on a map. Like I said, I just thought Australia was full of beaches and sunshine. So I flew out there with another court reporter called Joy. We got off the plane at Mount Isa Airport – that's if you could call it an airport. Back then the police used to come out and pick up us court people. Then, as we were being driven back to town, I asked, 'So where's the beach?'

And oh, those coppers were real buggers for winding us up. 'Well,' they said, 'there's a real nice spot just out'a town at Lake Moondarra. You girls should hire a car 'n drive out there 'n take a look.'

Well, Joy didn't drive, and I'd failed my test in the UK just before I'd come out to Australia. I'd been rescheduled to do another one before I'd left but it'd snowed, so it got cancelled. So there we were in 'The Isa' – as they called it – and I said to these coppers, 'Well, neither of us can drive.'

'Stone the crows,' they said, 'one'a yers has gotta be able to drive?'

When I explained what had happened to me in the UK, they said, 'That's okay, Kerry'll sort yer out.'

I said, 'Who's Kerry?'

'A mate'a ours,' they said. 'He's the bloke who does the drivin' tests.'

So now I'm in a panic. 'But I don't know the area,' I said. 'And I don't know the Australian traffic rules and I don't know how to drive this type of car.'

'Oh,' they said, 'she'll be right. That'll be no problem.' And I just shrunk into the back seat of the police car, thinking, Oh Christ, what've I let myself in for?

Anyhow, as soon as we got to court, the circuit fell over. By 'fell over' I mean the accused pleaded guilty. And with no other cases scheduled that week, it was cheaper for the Bureau to fly us back to Brisbane, rather than them having to pay another week's expenses in The Isa. So I thought, Thank God for that. I won't have to do this darn driving test.

So we returned in Brisbane and we flew back out to The Isa the following Monday morning. Court was to start that afternoon at two. Well, we landed at about eleven and there's the same two coppers waiting for us. As soon as they'd dropped off Joy, they said, 'Come on, Tanya. We're takin' yer to yer drivin' test.'

I'm thinking, Oh shit, honestly. Then, when we pulled up outside where I'm going to do this driving test, they said, 'You'll be okay. We've had a word to Kerry 'n he's given us the nod.' 'But, Tanya,' they said, 'just a word'a warnin'. He's a terrible womaniser.'

I'm going, Holy shit, this's going from bad to worse. And when I got in the car with this Kerry feller, to go for my test, the first thing he said was, 'Shoes on or shoes off?' And I'm thinking, Well, I'm certainly not going to take anything off while I'm in the car with you, you randy old bugger. So in no uncertain terms, I replied, 'I will keep my shoes on, thank you very much!'

'Oh,' he said, 'it's just that out 'ere some people find it easier ter drive without their shoes on.'

And oh my God, didn't I breathe a sigh of relief. Anyhow, when I got back home to Brisbane, I said to everyone, 'Guess what?'

'What?' they said.

I said, 'I've just passed my driver's test!'

Footnote – Mount Isa – The Isa – is a mining city in the Gulf Country of Queensland almost two thousand kilometres north-west of Brisbane. Its traditional owners, the Kalkadoon people, lived on and cared for the land for thousands of years prior to European settlement. The first Europeans to pass by were members of the ill-fated Burke and Wills south to north expedition in early 1861. Later that year, William Landsborough headed a relief expedition through the area in search of the lost Burke and Wills party.

By the early 1870s, pastoral stations were being established. This caused great conflict between the Kalkadoon people and the pastoralists. And it continued right through to the mid-1880s, when Aboriginal resistance was crushed at a spot now known as Battle Mountain. By the late 1880s pastoralists had begun to 'employ' Kalkadoon and other Aboriginal people on their stations. Aboriginal stockmen thus played an integral role in the north-west Queensland cattle industry, as they have in other pastoral areas throughout Australia.

In 1923, prospector John Campbell Miles stumbled upon one of the world's richest deposits of copper, silver and zinc, and a year later the company Mount Isa Mines was formed. The name of Mount Isa was taken from one of Miles' friend's stories about the Mount Ida goldmines in Western Australia. The nearby artificial Lake Moondarra provided the town's water. Mount Isa Post Office opened in 1924 with a hospital completed the following year. By 1929, a railway line connected Mount Isa with the coastal port town of Townsville. A year later, the first Protector of Aboriginals was based in Mount Isa. Between 1933 and 1967, the majority of the region's Aboriginal population was resettled on Palm Island.

With the outbreak of World War Two and American and Australian servicemen constructing the Barkly Highway, The Isa became an important centre for supply transport into the Northern Territory. The late 1940s saw a mining boom, which led to Mount Isa Mines becoming one of the largest mining companies in Australia. As a result, The Isa became the regional centre for the entire north-west of Queensland.

In 1970 Queen Elizabeth II, the Duke of Edinburgh and Princess Anne came to town. Mount Isa City Library opened in 1974. In 2008, a Queensland Health report found that more than ten per cent of The Isa's children had blood lead levels above World Health Organization recommendations. In that same year, a rumour circulated that the ratio of males to females was five to one. This caused a former mayor to tell the *Townsville Bulletin* that The Isa was an ideal place for 'not so attractive' women to come and live. Perhaps it worked because in a later census, 47.2 per cent of the population was female.

Based on its lead, silver, copper and zinc reserves, Mount Isa Mines is today one of the most productive single mines in world history, and The Isa one of the largest towns in outback Australia. Mount Isa's Symphony Orchestra is said to be the 'most remote orchestra in the world' and The Isa is home to the region's School of the Air. As for events, every August there's the Rodeo and Mardi Gras parade and in September it's the annual Multicultural Festival.

A number of watering holes dot the town. If you're fond of XXXX beer, The Isa's the place to go. A reasonable range of wines and spirits are also available. Pubs include the Barkly Hotel, Mount Isa Tavern, Red Earth Hotel, Overland Hotel and the Isa Hotel. And you'll never go short of a feed. After author Bill 'Swampy' Marsh had partaken of the Isa Hotel's Bullring Big Breakfast, he found it a struggle to walk the ten minutes to the Riversleigh Fossil Discovery Centre and to take the short walk to attend the interactive Hard Times Mine tour.

Mount Torrens – SA

I was always drawn to the country. I'd go anywhere to get out of Adelaide. So when me and my husband, Danny, got married, we decided to bring up our kids as country kids. Originally, we were looking around the mid-north of South Australia. But when my twin sister heard about that, she said her heart would break if we moved any further away than an hour from her. So we stuck a pin in a map and circled out an hour's distance from Adelaide and we found a property up in the Adelaide Hills at Mount Torrens. And so we bought it without knowing anything about either the property or the town. As it turned out Mount Torrens is one of only three State Heritage towns in South Australia. It's unique because, whereas everywhere else around the area was settled by Germans, Mount Torrens was settled by the English. So it's a little English centre in the middle of a much larger German district, which means all the early buildings are of English design.

When we first moved up here, I was still nursing and Danny was in retail, so we commuted to Adelaide. As far as owning a pub goes, it was something Danny had always wanted to do. For me, I thought I'd be a nurse forever, but that changed when politics began to set in. So we'd been up here for near on twenty years and we'd been looking at other ventures. When we saw the hotel was for sale, we put in an offer but someone else got it. But the thing is, a lot of people think that running a pub is easy, when it's not. It's a lot of hours and a lot of hard work. Anyhow, things didn't turn out for the new owner. Don't get me wrong, he was a lovely man but he just didn't have that country town attitude. With the district steeped in such deep religious roots, you just don't go putting in topless waitresses. So when things weren't working out and he offered the hotel to us, we went, 'Why not. Let's give it a crack.'

Our plan was that every part of the heritage-listed property had to make money or contribute in some way. We began by restoring the hotel to its original condition, inside, outside, upstairs, downstairs. It's been a massive task, but a labour of love, and we're still working at it. We're presently turning the paddocks into a caravan and camping site and the old stables into a function area. The bar and interior have been brought back to their original state. Upstairs is the same. There's now accommodation.

As far as us becoming publicans goes, because I'd done volunteer bar work up at the local footy oval, people were used to me serving them, and Danny's just a natural in the kitchen. He's always been a good cook. Well, he's far more than that really: he's not only a chef but he's a handyman, jack-of-all-trades and master-of-none and, like me, he's a restorer–collector. While I collect old furniture and restore it, Danny collects other stuff and restores it. See that ornate coal bucket over there? One day a customer rang me about an old couch he had. 'I'll take it,' I said. 'It matches the ones we've got out the back.' So then I had to con Danny into going and getting it for me, and he's like, 'Yeah, all right, whatever.'

So he begrudgingly went out there to negotiate a price for the couch. While he was there, he noticed that the feller had a stack of other collectables – including the ornate coal bucket. Anyway, they were chatting away and Danny saw that he was drinking West End tinnies – the red ones. He said to the feller, 'How about an exchange: a few cartons of beer for the lot?' And the feller goes, 'All right, but it's gotta be the good stuff.' Danny went, 'Oh, the good stuff, ay?' 'Yes, the real good stuff.' So Danny's thinking he wants a far more fancy brand than your plain old ordinary

West End; something more expensive like Crown or Corona or Coopers Sparkling Ale. But the feller goes, 'No, none'a that. I want the real good stuff: Tooheys extra dry.' Which in most people's minds would be the equal of the red West End tinnies. So Danny comes home, not only with the couch but a whole load of other stuff, including the ornate coal bucket!

When we first bought the pub, it wasn't family friendly. It was very blokey. So we changed that immediately. Now the kids love coming to the pub so much that, if they're going to muck up, their parents warn them, 'You won't be able to go to the pub with us if you're naughty.' Or they'll ring up, 'Oh, can our kid come in and get a bowl of chips and a soft drink?' And they'll go and sit out the back or, if it's raining, sit inside. And with all the changes we've made to the decor, it's now very female welcoming. So the women really feel at home. Like, sometimes there'll be a bunch of women sitting around a table, cackling away, and I'll think, Yes! That's what we want. No matter where you're from or who you are or what your background is, as long as you behave yourself, you're welcome.

But gee there's some characters in the town. The guy across the road's an absolute legend. He's ninety-two and he can fix anything. He's old school. His dad lived here and he's been here all his life. He wouldn't be short of coin but each morning, whether it's forty or freezing, he gets up and lights his old-fashioned wood stove to heat up his hot water system. Then at 9 o'clock, he walks out of his house and goes down the road to his workshop to do his bits and pieces. He never used to come into the pub, and he doesn't drink. But each lunchtime at 12.15 on the dot he comes and gets his takeaway: two pieces of fish, salad, chips and tartare sauce. When he first started coming in, fish and chips was $15. And even though the price has gone up to $16.50, he still comes in and places a $10 note and a $5 note down on the counter. 'There yer go,' he says and he picks up his takeaway and off he trots back to work to eat it. Then by

5 o'clock he's back home. He calls me 'girlie' and Danny 'young feller'. I guess that's because he's known so many people over his lifespan that he can't recall everybody's real name. So it's just 'girlie' or 'young feller'. He's amazing. He remembers when his workshop was a blacksmith's and they'd bend the horse and cart wheels around in the fire and fit horseshoes over the anvil.

So much has changed in his ninety-two years. He remembers the school kids coming in off their properties on horse-drawn jiggers and carts. They'd unharness the horse, put it in the stables out the back of the pub, feed it and water it. Then they'd walk out the front to catch the much larger horse and cart to take them off to Birdwood High School. After school, they'd come back, re-harness their horse, get back in the jigger and go home, where they'd sort out the horse and jigger, feed the horse and do their farm chores and homework before dinner. Then it was off to bed, only to go through the same rigmarole the following day. When you hear stories like that, it just reminds you how hard things were back then.

Another memory is of when a horse-drawn cart delivered ice cream to the kids. It'd be packed in big canvas bags, with dry ice, and the kids would run along behind the cart with their pennies, wanting to buy an ice cream. Another guy was telling me how, when he was a kid, he broke his upper-leg. With no hospital in town, they needed to get him down to Adelaide ASAP. The only available transport at the time was the ice-cream cart. So they strapped the guy's broken leg with wood, then they loaded him onto the ice-cream cart and off they trotted. And with Adelaide being fifty kilometres away, it would've been an overnight trip. He reckons it was the most agonising experience he'd ever had. So much so that he passed out a few times along the way.

Back then the horse and jigger, or oxen and cart, was the main form of transport. Like, they grew a lot of vegetables around here. So they'd load up their horse and cart with the vegetables, ready to take down to Adelaide market. Then they'd leave before sunrise on the Friday morning, in time to get to the market and unload, ready to sell their produce on the Saturday. Late Saturday they'd leave Adelaide and travel most of the night to get back home in time for church on Sunday. Things like that.

Oh, and we've got ghosts. The guy who built the pub, George Dunn, he and his family were founding members of Mount Torrens. They came over from Devon, England, in 1839, and bought up a lot of land for sheep and wheat. He had a family house about a kilometre away. Anyhow, George was a very good businessman. By then someone had opened a takeaway alcohol store and wine bar up the other end of the town. But when George saw the amount of oxen-transport coming through Mount Torrens on its way to and from the river port of Mannum, he reckoned another pub would be a goer. And with all the other buildings in town erected in a very functional Devon-style, he said, 'I'm going to make a real show-piece of this.' So he built the hotel bigger and grander than anything else in Mount Torrens. It's exceptionally made. The carpenter was a shipwright and the town's blacksmith did all the smithy work. Even the wood architraves are hand carved – every single one of them.

Anyhow, George is one of the ghosts. I first saw him and felt his presence when we were living up in their original house. I just called him George and, when we came down to the pub, he came with us. At first, his energy was agitated. But as soon as he saw how well we were restoring their old place, he settled down.

Danny doesn't believe me, but he's not so open to things like that. But it's not just me. Other people have seen him too. The other day, a guy told me that, when he was a kid, he used to play with the ghost of an old man down by the creek. I said, 'Describe him to me?' And he described George to a T: the clothes and everything was exactly as I'd seen him, right down to his long coat.

Then we've got another ghost: Mary Turner. She was here with her husband in the pub for thirteen years. But back in the pre-1920s, the only way a woman could own a hotel was to inherit it. So when her husband died, she inherited it. This was when ladies weren't allowed in a pub and so she opened up the back room for them. Back then it had a fire, then a wall, and they knocked a small sliding window into the wall where the ladies would get served their half-strength shandies or whatever. I call it the Ladies' Parlour, in their memory.

Anyway, Mary Turner was the publican here from 1880 to 1920. Her ghost frequents the back room and she's forever shifting things around. She moves my keys all the time. I've got a photographic memory, so we did a test one day. I put my keys in a place where no one else knew where they were and by morning, they'd been moved. True. It's just her way of communicating. So then I go, 'Oh, Mary, you're so funny.' We're actually very much alike, Mary and me. I've got a wicked sense of humour as has she. Also much like me, she's quite driven and independent. So there's George Dunn and there's Mary Turner and I totally respect their presence. Mind you, Danny thinks I'm nuts, but they're here. I talk to them all the time and they respond. I'm never lonely, let's put it that way.

But the town's great and the people are friendly. We've got two children: a twenty-year-old and twenty-one-year-old and they both love it here. Our son was born in the city and now he's country through and through. He's a real ocker. You could throw him out into the middle of the outback and you'd think he grew up there. And our daughter fits in. I originally thought she'd end up back in the city, but no. We employ people with disabilities and she supports them in the pub. She also does our marketing and works front-of-house and, so Danny and me can get a day off every now and then, she does bit of cooking.

Although mind you, we don't get much time off, especially together – only Christmas Day and Good Friday.

As for anything else: well, we survived the Cudlee Creek fires. We'd already been through the Sampson Flat fires and Ash

Wednesday, so we knew there was going to be something big that day. It was 47 degrees with strong winds. The fire started twenty kilometres away at Cudlee Creek. Then it worked its way along the back of the hill face, a stone's throw away. But with it heading toward the freeway, we were like, 'Oh, we'll be okay.' Then, at 4.30 that afternoon, the wind changed. Next thing, what'd started as a twenty-kilometre fire front had whipped into a one-hundred-and-eighty-kilometre fire front and was coming over the hill toward us. We then had to choose between trying to protect either our house or the pub. Anyhow, we said, 'We can't let our precious heritage building be destroyed, no matter what.' So we chose the pub, fully expecting that our house wouldn't be there at the end of it.

By that stage, everyone had evacuated nearby Lobethal. They'd just grabbed what belongings they could, plus their dogs et cetera and had jumped in their cars and taken off. And a lot of them ended up here in the pub. They were in such a state and, because it was so hot and the fire was heading our way, we just couldn't leave their dogs outside, could we? So we had people everywhere and we had dogs everywhere and we were trying to explain to everyone, 'Don't stay here in Mount Torrens. It's not safe. Look, the fire's coming. Keep going. Get out of here.' But they were so scared, it was like their feet were planted to the ground and they couldn't move on. It was a crazy time.

Lobethal didn't fare well. It got the brunt of it. Charleston was badly hit and we were completely surrounded. Massive fireballs were going over the town. I'd never wish it upon anyone. But you deal with what you have to and we were blessed we had an amazing local CFS – Country Fire Service – and a group of people with farm fire-fighting equipment. The coordination was brilliant. Our CFS and farm fire-fighting units were continually in radio contact, 'You guys go here. You can cover that one. This's too big for us, you guys go there.'

Then after we'd finally managed to move everyone on from the pub, we left at about 6 o'clock and at about 7 o'clock it hit the town. We originally tried to evacuate via Birdwood. But because we kept running into walls of fire, we ended up going to Mannum. We were in separate cars. Danny and our son said, 'We'll follow you.' But they didn't. They turned around and headed back to help put out the spot fires. And because the police had blocked all the major roads, they drove through backroads and across burning paddocks, everywhere, just to get back and help fight the fire.

As it happened, that night was my daughter's eighteenth birthday party. She was already in Mount Barker getting supplies so, when the fire struck, I rang her and said, 'Don't come back.' Then, with my son being born at the end of the fire-burning season in October, we've always had a bonfire for him. And with my daughter being born in December, all she's ever wanted was to have a bonfire for her birthday. So I said, 'Guess what, kiddo, you've got the biggest fire ever for your eighteenth birthday!'

Anyhow, the next day we loaded up the little Kia and my four-wheel-drive with soft drinks and water and we snuck back to Mount Torrens via Tungkillo, bush-bashing through the burning paddocks. We really shouldn't have come back, but we wanted to open the pub. Even though there was no electricity, we were like, 'Our community has to have somewhere to gather, somewhere to talk and a place to get help.'

So we opened the pub with just iceboxes and, with what little food and drinks we had, we managed for a few days, feeding everyone the best we could. Then, if the CFS or any of the farm fire-fighting units were going to come by, they'd ring me on my mobile. 'We need some food,' and we'd run outside and chuck some food at them as they drove past, on their way to help put out the fires. We didn't charge them. It was like, Let's just get the town through this. But for everyone else who was sheltering in the pub, without electricity, we had no eftpos, so we ended up with a huge stack of IOUs. And you know what? Every single person came back and paid their tab.

Footnote – Mount Torrens is in the eastern Adelaide Hills region of South Australia, fifty kilometres from Adelaide. It has a population of around three hundred and, being an outstanding example of nineteenth-century English settlement, it's been declared a State Heritage area.

Although its Indigenous name is unknown, Mount Torrens was named after one of South Australia's founding fathers, Robert Torrens. George Dunn, a leading figure in the town's early history, arrived in 1839 with his wife Mary and five children. They established Barton Springs farm and raised sheep. In 1845, when copper was discovered nearby, the mine was worked in large by men from Cornwell and Devon. With Dunn's home being visited by bullock drivers, en route to and from the mines, he turned Barton Springs into the Cornish Arms Hotel and by 1850, with the added Murray River trade from Mannum, the more luxurious Mount Torrens Hotel was built.

Due to an increasing demand for land, Dunn employed a surveyor to subdivide part of his holdings and most of the town's English-style buildings were erected between 1850 and 1860, along with a flourmill. In addition to becoming a service town for passing traffic, Mount Torrens also became the centre for the rural district. With dairying becoming popular, in 1927 the old flourmill was converted into a dairying produce factory. The population of Mount Torrens reached its peak just before World War One and the entire area was badly damaged during the 2019 Cudlee Creek bushfire.

The heritage-listed Mount Torrens Hotel is being lovingly restored to its original state. In doing so, the hosts have created an inviting family atmosphere. There's always something going on at the pub including the annual Halloween party, where you don't know who might turn up – maybe even a ghost or two.

Nannine – WA

In memory of Ian Parkes.

Swampy, I think what you're doing is just terrific. As I said in my email, these sort of home-grown outback stories should be captured and recorded for prosperity. That's because the vast majority of Australians live in cities, so they have little to no knowledge of what's happening outside their tight twenty-five-mile radius, and only a few of them have ventured beyond that. Oh, over here in Western Australia, some of them may have gone to Albany or Geraldton, perhaps just once in their lives. But that's about it.

It's all very different from sixty or so years ago when Perth was much smaller, the bush was much more populated and city people had family connections who lived in some of the more remote places. So they'd jump on a ship and head up the coast, then go out and stay in towns or out on farms or on station properties, visiting family or friends. But that doesn't happen anymore. That's all gone. So these days there's no awareness – no connection. In fact, I'd go as far as to say, there's an utter and complete indifference to Australia's outback. And that's a damn shame because they're missing out on experiencing the outback's rich culture, its amazing environment and its wonderful characters. So that's why I'll be more than happy to help you.

As I wrote in my book – *A Youth Not Wasted* – I was so fascinated by my grandfather's stories about the bush that I left home at sixteen and went to work as a jackaroo on a merino stud in South Australia. That was in the 1950s, when Australia was riding on the sheep's back. After that, I spent some time on a remote property near Broken Hill, in New South Wales. That's where I first worked with, and met, some amazing Aboriginal stockmen, and when the big social event was a day at the races in Broken Hill, followed by a game of two-up. By then, bush life had solidly taken root in me. So when I returned to Western Australia, I took off to the mid-west of WA, out on Belele Station. Belele was a sheep property of around 250,000 acres – or just over 100,000 hectares – and, in a reasonable season, it could take near on twenty thousand head of sheep.

Now, Swampy, with you having written a few books about the Flying Doctor Service, you may have heard of Belele Station because it's where an old Irish stockman went missing. It was in the news and everything. It happened back in the early 1950s, just before I arrived. Anyhow, this old stockman had been working on Belele since the 1880s. And so, when he retired, the owners let him live in an old shack, out from the homestead. Then one day he went missing – just like that – and the search went on for a couple of weeks, which included an RFDS plane. But they never found him. Not a skerrick. He'd disappeared, completely, and nothing's been seen of him since. But that's just a bit of an aside because the story I want to tell you is about a place called Nannine. See, in a good season we used to get sheep railed up from Pindar. Pindar's about four hundred kilometres to the south-west of Belele, just out from Geraldton. When they got to Nannine, they were virtually just let roam until we arrived to muster them up and take them back to Belele.

Now, Nannine proved to be a fascinating place, with quite a history. To give you some idea, it's an old gold-mining town, not far from Meekatharra. But by the 1940s, the gold mining had faded and so had the town. So, by the time I arrived up there, there wasn't much of it left. It was virtually a ghost town. No one lived there. Not a soul. Structure-wise, all that remained was the railway siding. But you could still see where the streets had been laid out. You could still see some of the curbing and you could still see what remained of some of the old stone fireplaces. A lot of the old mineshafts were still there, along with the wooden framework that went around, over and above them. All that was all still there, although in very poor condition.

Anyway, after my stint at Belele, when I came back to Perth, I spent a lot of time in the J.S. Battye Library, which is in our state library. They've got archives there and they've got all the old newspapers on microfilm. So I started going through the microfilm, digging up little bits and pieces about Nannine and, back in its heyday, it was a very prosperous gold-mining town. Its water supply came from nearby Lake Anneen. It had a hospital, a Miner's Institute, a post office, a police station, a school, a Catholic church and a couple of newspapers. There was about five pubs and lots of stores. They even held regattas out on the lake and, mind you, it's dry up there nineteen years out of twenty. But in this particular microfilm clip the lake had water in it and there were boats on it.

But oh, in amongst my diggings and delvings, I came across some terrible atrocities that took place. Now, due to all this political correctness bullshit, I'm not sure if you'll be able to print this. But it's true. See, along with the Indigenous folk, there were also lots of Afghan camel drivers around in those early days. And in one of the newspapers I read where a prospector went to get some drinking water from a particular waterhole – a little soak – that all the prospectors used; right out in the bloody bush somewhere, miles from anywhere. Anyhow, when this prospector got there, there was this Afghan sitting on the edge of the waterhole washing his feet in it. So he shot him. And that's true. He shot him. Worse still was that, when it come to the trial, the prospector was acquitted for justifiable homicide. His defence went along the lines of: you can't go around washing your feet in water that other people are going to use for drinking. So, mate, if they did that to the Afghans, imagine what they did to the Aboriginals.

Footnote – Nannine is in the mid-west of Western Australia, seven hundred and fifty kilometres north-north-east of Perth. The nearest ocean, the Indian, is four hundred kilometres to its west. Although the meaning of Nannine is not exactly known, some say it came from the Aboriginal Dreaming where the Dingo bit off part of the Emu, leaving traces of the attack in a local cliff-face known as *nganiny*.

In 1890, Nannine was the site of the first gold discovery in the Murchison region, sparking a gold rush. Within a year, seven hundred prospectors had arrived. The town site was surveyed in 1892 and gazetted in 1893. At that stage, the Warden's Court and Registrar's office was still a tent, with a notice board at the front. By 1894, the town had its own electoral district. A telegraph line to Geraldton commenced service in late 1894 and work on the post and telegraph building began a couple of years later, as did the police station. At that time, six graves were in front of Judges Hotel, pending removal to the new cemetery. By 1903, a railway line between Nannine and Cue was completed. A school next to the local reverend's residence opened in early 1906 and took in boarders. By late 1906, water from Lake Annean was used for the town water supply.

In those early days, there were half a dozen hotels. The Pioneer was probably the first, being built in 1892. The Royal was listed in 1894. Although the Victoria Hotel was listed in 1895, it was later refused a licence on the grounds of there being insufficient population, so it became a boarding house. In 1896, Judges Hotel was the largest building in town. The owner of the Murchison Hotel, Mrs Ramsay, was the town's first woman publican.

The Murchison was only one of four hotels still trading by 1898. When the Nannine Hotel went up for sale in late 1899 it was advertised as being 'splendidly furnished throughout, of iron construction and containing a large bar, three parlours, a drawing room, dining room and twelve bedrooms plus appliances, and included stables, outhouses and a butcher's shop.' In early 1907 an explosion of the hotel's gasometer blew the roof off one of the outhouses. Mrs Eleanor Willows, the then live-in manager, was said to have survived 'unscathed'. 'Mum Willows' as she was known managed the hotel until she moved to Meekatharra in 1920.

With the downturn in gold production, by 1919, Nannine was also in rapid decline. The police station closed in 1922 and the building was removed to Yalgoo. The Road Board moved its headquarters to Meekatharra. Nannine struggled on until the late 1940s, with the Murchison Hotel being the town's last pub to close down. The stone ruins of the post office were among the last markers of the town site. Nannine is now a ghost town.

Naracoorte – SA

A version of this story first appeared in *Great Australian Bush Funeral Stories* under the title of 'Who Dunnit?'

Years ago, I worked as a contract gravedigger in the south-east of South Australia, around the Naracoorte area. Now, in a section of one particular cemetery, the soil was basically sand. But as that cemetery grew in size, and the grave sites were moved up the hill, the ground went into clay and, a little further on, it went into limestone rock. I never dug by hand. I always used a backhoe and, with some of the later graves being mostly in the limestone, I'd have to belt the rock with my backhoe until I'd broken through the crust. Once that was done, I was able to get in underneath and break the rock up. I'd then get a straight-edged bucket and dig the grave, square on the sides, down to the required depth. Then, finally, we'd rake out the bottom to get it nice and flat, ready to lay the coffin on – and she'd be ready to go.

The graves we dug were of varying depths. So, say, if a family wanted to lay their bodies three deep, we'd have to dig down seven foot six inches – about 2.3 metres. Mind you, these days they can even lay them down four coffins deep. That might be Mum, Dad and a couple of the kids all stacked in on top of each other. But whether they were three or four people deep, we still had to have a minimum of a foot of earth between each of the coffins. Then a four-inch concrete slab was laid on top, to deter the animals from getting in under and having a good dig around.

Now, just a little story: at one particular cemetery I dug at, the sandy soil was a very loose silvery-white. While that may make for easy digging and growing grapes, because of its loose composition, it didn't compact down too well. And with only about six inches width between some of the grave sites, if we were digging down three people deep, that could create real problems. Like, one time we'd dug down the required seven foot six inches into this loose sandy soil. Off to one side of the grave was a stack of three buried coffins and on the other side was a double stack. Anyway, we'd just finished digging this seven-foot-sixer in preparation for the burial when we saw the hearse heading toward the cemetery gate. And when we had a final last check, lo-n-behold, the three coffins on one side and the two on the other side had started to fall in on our freshly dug hole.

Panic! So one of our guys scooted down to the hearse and told the funeral director that there'd been some sort of inexplicable delay and would he mind staying put for a while. Then, while everyone waited at the cemetery gate, we went like the clappers. We scrounged up some posts and logs and we levered the neighbours back into their rightful positions and shored it all up to make room for the new coffin.

I mean, things like that happen all the time. Cemeteries take up a lot of space and it's all about saving room. Now, an interesting point of fact: some cemeteries actually lay their coffins vertically, not horizontally. Take Rouse Hill, for instance, out near Windsor, in Sydney. Right from the word go Rouse Hill's been your vertical-type and, with it being a lawn cemetery, after the burial, they fill in the hole. Then, as soon as the family's gone, to help settle the soil more quickly, they stick a hose into the ground and turn the tap on; and that makes it nice and smooth across the top for the grass to regrow. Anyhow, on this particular occasion, all had gone well until a young woman remembered she'd left her purse beside her dearly-departed mother's fresh grave. When she returned to get it, she found that a hose had been stuck down into Mum's grave. So she shot over and quizzed the cemetery people as to why they were now trying to drown her already dead-and-buried mother. So that was a bit of a funny one.

And so, back to Naracoorte: I don't know if you know or not but a gravedigger who's employed directly by the church is called the verger. Then someone who digs graves on a contract basis, like I was, is called a sexton. Anyhow, back before my time, there was this young feller down at Naracoorte who stuttered on the letter b. His name was Brock Leonard, which caused quite a bit of confusion when he tried to introduce himself to anyone. 'G'day,' he'd say, 'I'm B ... b ... b ... b ... Brock Leonard.'

Anyway, Brocky's father had been the sexton around Naracoorte for as long as anyone could remember. Then, when young Brocky was fourteen, he quit school and started helping his dad. They were still digging graves by hand back then. As the story goes, one day, just after young Brocky had joined his dad, Brocky and his father and another feller were digging this grave. It was a second burial. Like, the mother had already been buried and now they were preparing for Dad to go in on top of Mum. So, after they'd dug the grave to the regulated requirement above the mum's coffin, Brocky's dad said, 'Son, just jump in there 'n tidy it up a bit will yer?'

So, being an enthusiastic young fourteen-year-old, Brocky jumped down into the grave. When he landed on the soil above the mum's coffin, the lot gave way and Brocky went straight through, feet first, in on top of the dead mum. *Squelch.* Well, with one giant leap, Brocky rocketed out of that hole – *Bang!* – and he took off like the clappers. They reckon they could still hear him a mile down the road, going, 'You b ... b ... b ... bloody b ... b ... b ... bastards. I'll b ... b ... bloody well get you for this.'

Oh, some funny things have happened, I can tell you. And some odd ones, too. About twelve mile out of Naracoorte there's a place called Struan House, and just up the hill from Struan House there's a cemetery. It's just a small plot of about four square metres, with a stone wall around it. See, back in its day the south-east of South Australia was a very wealthy area, with abundant good soil and lots of water – meaning they had plenty of money. In fact, some of the property owners were so wealthy that they had up to a hundred people working for them. So these properties were virtually small communities. Many would've had a nurse and/or a governess for the children. Some even had their own doctor – which, a long time back, was what Struan House had. It had its own doctor.

Then many years later, when one of the doctors who'd worked at Struan House died, in his will he requested to be buried in Struan Cemetery. Anyhow, a mate and I got the job of digging the doctor's grave. To start with, we went out with the funeral director and some historical people to reconnoitre the place. Like, when we were looking around for a spot to dig the doctor's grave, these historical people would consult their mud-map, then they'd go, 'No, you can't dig there because that's where old so-and-so's grave is.'

'How about here then?' we'd say.

'No, that's where someone else is.'

Anyhow, we eventually came to a spot. 'How about here?' we asked.

'Yep,' they said, 'it doesn't look like anyone's buried there.'

Okay, good; so we got the backhoe and we began scooping out the soil. As we did, we started to build up a nice pile of dirt just off to the side of where this doctor was going to be buried. Now, back in time, those old plots would've only gone down the six foot. Anyhow, we only got down to about five feet when, as neat as you like, a skull turns up, staring at us from on top of our pile of dirt. 'Alas poor Yorick.' Although, unlike in Shakespeare's play, Hamlet, we didn't know him well. In fact, we didn't have a clue who it was. So we're like, 'What's this? Don't tell us we've dug in the wrong spot.'

The thing was, it didn't look like your normal sort of grave. Like, there was no coffin and a scattering of other bones were sticking out of the dirt. So we rang the funeral director; the feller who'd helped us peg out the site. 'No,' he said, 'there shouldn't be anyone there. It doesn't fit the map.' 'Look,' he said, 'I'm a bit concerned about this, so I might just pop down to the police station and have a chat to them.'

When he went down to the cop-shop and explained the situation, the police said, 'Gee, we'd better come 'n check it out.' So they came out and, as soon as they took a look, they said, 'Wow, this might be just what we've been looking for.'

We're going, 'So what's going on?'

'Oh,' they said, 'we can't say quite yet.' Then they grabbed the skull and a few of the bones and they whipped off to do some tests on them.

Now, in South Australia, back in those days, you couldn't charge a person with murder unless you could present a body. What's more, the state government had a statute of limitations, which in those times was seven years. So if you were under suspicion of murdering someone, and the authorities hadn't found the body after seven years, you got off scot-free.

Anyhow, as it happened, near on seven years previously – so just shy of this seven-year statute of limitations – a person down that way had gone missing, presumed murdered. The thing was that, while the police had a strong idea who'd committed the crime, they'd never been able to find the body. Anyway, they proved that the skull and bones we'd dug up were those of this missing person. Further tests showed how the person was actually murdered. From that evidence, they could prove just who the murderer was. So they arrested the person who'd been under supposition, charged him with the murder, and he was later proven guilty and sent to jail. But I mean, who'd ever think of looking for a missing body in a cemetery, ay?

Footnote – Naracoorte is in the Limestone Coast region of South Australia, three hundred and forty kilometres south-east of Adelaide. The original inhabitants and custodians of the area were the Meintangk people. The first white man to live in the area was George Ormerod who, in 1842, established a run and built a hut on a nearby creek. Naracoorte grew out of the merger of two towns, Kincraig – founded in 1845 by Scottish explorer William Macintosh – and Narracoorte – established as a government settlement in 1847. The name Naracoorte may have derived from the Meintangk words meaning 'place of running water' or 'large waterhole'. During the 1850s, Naracoorte grew as a service town for people going to and from the Victorian goldfields. A post office opened in 1853 and the town was known as Mosquito Plains until 1861. The district was proclaimed in 1879, with a primary school being built in the same year.

Historically, the region has relied on sheep, cattle and wheat farming. These days, tourism has become its major industry. This is due to the town's proximity to several wine regions and its natural features, such as the World-Heritage listed Naracoorte Caves National Park and the Ramsar-listed Bool and Hacks Lagoons. It's now believed that the Naracoorte Caves preserve the world's most complete known fossil records; spanning several ice ages, the arrival of humans to the area and the extinction of Australia's iconic megafauna, roughly sixty thousand years ago.

Struan House was the third and most elaborate house, built from local limestone for John Robertson and his family. In January 1876, local property people and those who'd worked for the Robertsons attended the housewarming ball. Dugald McCallum, John's friend and minister, christened the mansion 'Struan House' in memory of the distant Scottish Struan, the seat of the Robertson clan chief. Four years later John Robertson died, aged seventy-one, and was buried with others of his family and those of his household in the Struan House Cemetery, overlooking the creek with his home beyond. John's wife Susan joined her husband twenty-six years later.

There are three hotels in Naracoorte. The Bushman's Arms was built in 1861 as the Bushman's Inn. A year later, a grander establishment was erected on the site and renamed the Commercial Hotel. A second storey was added in the 1870s, and the eastern and western wings were built on in the

1920s. In 2006 the Commercial Hotel returned to its original name. The only remaining part of the early hotel is a wall with a historic mural painted on it.

The Kincraig Hotel is a family friendly, no pokies hotel, built by the wine and spirit merchant, Tolley. The licence from Kincraig's Globe Hotel was transferred to the newly completed building in 1934. It has recently undergone redevelopment and is under new management. Author Bill 'Swampy' Marsh suggests having a crack at Kinga's Catch.

The Naracoorte Hotel advertises itself as having 'something for everyone, with Billy Mac's Bistro serving the "finest meals using fresh local produce".'

Happy hour is weekdays 5 to 7 p.m. As of 10 August 2022, Rob Hannaford was replaced at the top of the footy tipping competition by 'Worm' McGuire! We eagerly await the season's final outcome.

New Norcia – WA

Good morning, Bill, it is Hans from Germany here. I see where you are always very active with your books. I think very fondly of having been part of your Flying Doctors and the Outback Towns and Pubs books. Now that you want to write another book about outback towns and pubs, I am pleased you have invited me to participate. This is a great honour for me, one for which I am very grateful.

To get to Australia from Germany, I have to travel halfway around the globe. Upon arrival, my destinations are mostly bases of the Royal Flying Doctor Service of Australia; an organisation so vital for outback survival and which I have supported from Germany for many, many years. The staff at the RFDS bases tell me that I am probably one of very few people who have visited all of their bases, throughout Australia. I gladly take this as a compliment and motivation for my further help.

On my tours from one RFDS base to the next, I am always on the road with a four-wheel-drive vehicle. There are so many remarkable outback towns in Australia. If you remember, on the subject of your first Outback Towns and Pubs book, I told you about Marble Bar. This time, it did not take me long to think of a town, as I have been lately remembering New Norcia, in Western Australia, and what it might look like and be like these days. So may I offer you a memory of that small community consisting of just a hundred souls, and the only monastic town in Australia. For this, I have taken the liberty of writing down some of my thoughts.

When I first came to Australia in 2006, New Norcia was not on my itinerary. On my tour south from Darwin, en route from Meekatharra to Perth, the few houses of New Norcia unexpectedly emerged from the dreary outback landscape. The impression overwhelmed me. To the left and right of the Great Northern Highway, my eyes fell upon buildings whose architecture fascinated me. And also, it was such a surprise to find a Benedictine monastery in the middle of the outback. Today, the monastery is one of the listed buildings belonging to the National Estate. Some one hundred and seventy years after it was founded, only a small number of Benedictine monks still live and pray there and, upon my walk, every now and then I met a monk among the historic buildings.

The monastery buildings, erected in the Spanish architectural style, were spectacular in contrast to the surrounding outback landscape. Also definitely worth seeing were the two architecturally designed schools that operated until 1991, and which can only be visited on a guided tour. Also magnificent were the orphanage buildings for Aboriginal children; for girls and boys separately.

Though they were closed in the early 1970s, these buildings now house the New Norcia Museum and Art Gallery. But time was short on this first tour and, keeping in mind what else I already had planned for that day, I made the decision to spend more time in New Norcia upon my next trip to Australia.

Three years later, in 2009, I invited my wife to travel with me. New Norcia was to be the crowning glory of our tour through the south-west of Western Australia. From my previously taken photos and films, my wife was aware of what to expect. And although we had prepared ourselves well, we had hoped to stay in the monastery guesthouse, along with the monks. This would give us the opportunity to participate in the rhythm of monastic life in complete silence and also follow the monks at prayer, in their private chapel.

Unfortunately, exactly on the days of our stay, a Benedictine monk, Father John Herbert, was to be ordained as the new abbot. Of course, this meant that the guesthouse in the monastery was already fully booked. Even so, we were still allowed to be present at the solemn and touching consecration of Father John in the Abbey Church. Many people were present, including, with the support of the monastic brothers, the oldest living Spanish Benedictine monk, Father Dom Paulino, who, unfortunately, passed away not long after our departure, at the age of ninety-nine. By then, our feelings were so much connected to the Benedictine monks that we were very sad to hear this news.

We were still able to participate in the monks' prayers in the monastery chapel. During this ritual, I was reminded how impressed many people are with the outback's indescribable peace. However, within prayer, the whole place radiated a completely different kind of calm – a silence so soothing that I only heard the sounds of nature and those of the ringing of church bells.

But for my wife and me, the question still remained: with the guesthouse of the monastery already being occupied, where should we stay? I have often slept in the open air, in the outback, and enjoyed the unique feeling of lying under the magnificent view of the endless starry sky of the Southern Hemisphere. My wife was not so comfortable with this suggestion, so there remained the option of New Norcia Hotel. Back in 1927, the hotel was built as a hostel for parents who wanted to visit their children attending the boarding schools in New Norcia.

Luckily we got a room there without any problems. Being heritage-listed, modern alterations were prohibited. The stone building, in neoclassical style, had two floors. There was a bar and a restaurant. Then a large staircase, several metres wide, led to a passageway with guestrooms on both sides – in all totalling fifteen – and there were communal toilets and showers. Due to its heritage status, this format was not allowed to be changed and so the installation of toilets and showers in individual rooms could not be made. From the room's windows and the verandah, which again was built in traditional Spanish style, we could look out over the monastery grounds and listen to the sounds of nature at dusk. Even though electricity had been wired in the hotel since 1952, this was switched off at 9 o'clock each evening and candles were provided.

Our guestroom had two beds, a fan on the ceiling, a fridge and a tea-making facility. You can't get more classic accommodation in the Australian outback than that. And we did not die of thirst. At the New Norcia Hotel, the monks were the first religious organisation in Australia to be granted a hotel licence. This meant they were allowed to serve alcohol. The ice-cold Australian beer tasted excellent and we still have fond memories of the food.

Over the many years I have been criss-crossing the world, I have rarely found such a contemplative and quiet place as New Norcia. New Norcia makes you reflect on your life. It gives you something that is hard to find in today's modern world: a sense of stillness and community. It refreshes and renews your soul and spirit. The only misery is that, as a traveller, you know that you will soon have to 'make tracks' and move on, and leave this remarkable meditative place behind.

Footnote – Being a Benedictine mission, New Norcia has never been officially gazetted. New Norcia is one hundred and thirty kilometres north of Perth and remains the only monastic town in Australia. Its name comes from the Italian town of Norcia, which is the birthplace of Saint Benedict. In March 1846, a Benedictine mission for the local Yued Aboriginal people, was started by two Spanish Benedictine monks, Rosendo Salvado and Joseph Benedict Serra, just to the north of where New Norcia stands today. After spending time with the local Aboriginal people, the monks came to the conclusion that they could be converted to Christianity, and so the mission was moved to where the town is today.

Over the years, New Norcia has served many purposes: a mission, a monastery, a provider of education and now as a place of spiritual retreat. It is also respected in culinary circles for its quality bakery – built in 1886 – and also for its olive oil production. Locally made wines, port and ales, can also be purchased at the community. There are two pipe organs located within the abbey buildings. In the Abbey Church of the Holy Trinity is a large German organ, built in 1922, with thirty-four speaking stops. The second pipe organ, built in 1983, has eleven speaking stops and is located in the Oratory Chapel.

New Norcia's last Spanish monk, Dom Paulino, died in January 2010, aged ninety-nine. He had worked in the monastery bakery and as a shoemaker and, in retirement, he worked in the production of olive oil. Currently there are just seven Benedictine monks occupying the monastery. They live according to the guidance and rhythms of the Rule of St Benedict, which has been followed by monks since the sixth century AD. All seven pray together, seven times a day, and remain involved in most of the town's enterprises. The New Norcia Hotel continued commercially until it closed in January 2020.

Back in January 1986, the Museum and Art Gallery mentioned in Hans' story was the scene of Western Australia's biggest art theft. While preparing to close the two-storey gallery and museum, the caretaker was attacked by two men, bound and shoved in a cupboard. The thieves then set about removing a rare collection of twenty-six paintings, depicting religious scenes from the seventeenth, eighteenth and nineteenth century. Midway through the heist, the thieves realised that all the paintings would not fit into their getaway vehicle, so they cut the canvases from the frames. As fate, or divine intervention, would have it, twenty-five of the twenty-six paintings were retrieved just as they were about to be flown out to the Philippines.

Eight kilometres south of New Norcia is the home of New Norcia Deep Space Tracking Station and a ground station for the European Space Agency. Since 1967 the agency has taken part in planning missions of more than fifty satellites. The thirty-five-metre diameter dish serves as a powerful transmitter as well as listening for the faint radio signals sent back, from so far, by the relatively low-powered satellite transmitters.

Normanton – Qld

Adapted from Bill 'Swampy' Marsh's *Goldie: Adventures in a Vanishing Australia.*

After I'd pulled the pin as head stockman out at Glenore Station, I went and stayed just out of Normanton, at the Casey's Shady Lagoons. Like, I'd just throw me swag down on the verandah and that. At that stage, the Caseys still weren't up to much as far as cattle duffing went; not that I was too worried about that because I was now looking forward to doing some more droving. That's what I really wanted to do, more droving, because, see, I sort of felt more confident with cattle than I was as head stockman, with all the responsibility of fellers under me.

So I'm at Shady right, and I goes into Normanton for a drink and I runs into a feller named Norman Smith – Smithy, we just used to call him. Now, this Smithy was no relation to Vincent and Benny Smith and all them other Smiths. This Smithy was a professional barramundi fisherman. Any rate, he'd been smacked around a bit. Like, he'd been roughed up, with a black eye and that. So I says to him, 'Geez, what happened to you, mate?'

He says, 'Goldie! Boy, am I glad ter see you.' I says, 'Why?'

He says, 'Well, I had a bit of a row with a feller, Ronny Paul, 'n he hit me about, so I said to him, "I'm gonna get Goldie ont'a you".'

Well, I didn't know nothing about all this till now, ay. So I says, 'Oh, that's very nice of yer, mate. Yer've just fixed me up fer a scrap with a feller I got no beef with.'

Actually, I was of the mind to tell Smithy to go and sort out his own problems. But apparently, word was already out about how me and Ronny Paul was going to have this bareknuckle fight out at the Normanton Golf Club. Like it was only a five or so hole golf course – you know, out on this salt-clay pan. As it turned out, Sam Henry, the Normanton copper, was also drinking in the pub that night and when he heard all this, he piped up and said, 'Well, I'll referee then.'

Then Smithy chips in with, 'Well, whoever wins out'a you 'n Ronny Paul, I'll give 'em five quid.'

So then I says, 'Yeah, all right. Okay then, I'll have a go at him.' 'Him' being this Ronny Paul feller.

From memory, Ronny would've been about thirty, just a bit older than me. I heard that he was a retired eight-rounder from Brisbane who was working around town. I forget what he was actually doing. But he had a bit of a rep – reputation – for fighting and I'd just begun to get a bit of a rep meself, too. Anyhow, news spread pretty quick and so the whole town turns out to see this fight. You know there would of been about twenty or thirty people. I mean, it wasn't race week or nothing, so the town was pretty sleepy. Not too many people lived in Normanton back in them days. At best maybe a hundred. Any rate, they're all there to see this fight and, when Ronny Paul turns up, he's got his hands all bandaged up like when you're a pro. And when he gets in the ring, there he is, prancing around, looking so pretty that one feller whispers in me ear, 'You wanta watch him, Goldie, it looks like he's been in the game a fair while.'

I said, 'He don't worry me, mate.' Because, see, I can tell by the way someone walks as to how they can fight. Like, if someone walks along real loose, you can tell he's going to be a hard hitter, but he'll be a bit on the slow side. And when you get a feller who walks along real tight, he might be fast, but he can't hit hard. That's just how this Ronny Paul was: he was fast but not a hard hitter.

Any rate, in the end Sam Henry stopped the fight ay. Oh, I was just chopping this Ronny Paul to pieces. Now, I'm not trying to make out I can scrap or nothing. Don't think that, but I just couldn't understand where Ronny got his rep from. I mean, he was supposed to be a pro eight-rounder from Brisbane. But I couldn't see it. So, yeah, Sam Henry, the copper, he came over to my corner and he said, 'Look, Goldie, I've gotta stop this.'

I said, 'Yes, please, Sam. The poor bloke's a mess.'

Now, in Normanton, you had three pubs: there was the top pub, the middle pub and the bottom pub and, after the fight, the publican from the middle pub asked us all to go back there for a drink. Any rate, after Ronny Paul had cleaned himself up a bit, him and me had a few beers together. Actually, I sort of liked the feller, so I ended up spending the five quid Smithy gave me on drinks for us both. But see, there was three coppers in Normanton at that time and one of them, Terry McMahon, he'd seen the fight and so he pulled me aside and he's on to me about going to Brisbane to train as a pro-boxer. 'Look, Goldie,' he says, 'yer've got a real future in the fight game. I'll even write yer an introduction letter ter Snowy Hill.' Apparently, this Terry McMahon knew Snowy very well. Snowy was a big-gun boxing trainer who'd trained a lot of title holders.

Any rate, I said, 'Look, Terry, thanks very much but I'll have ter put it on the backburner 'cause I promised I'd go out on Wernadinga Station ter do some drovin'.' I said, 'You know, perhaps I might go down ter Brisbane after that,' and Terry said, 'Fair enough, Goldie. Any time, mate. Just let me know 'n I'll write ter Snowy.'

So I goes back out to Shady Lagoons to get ready to go to Wernadinga. But, see, after Ronny Paul, me confidence was on a bit of a high and people were saying, 'Goldie, yer'll meet yer match if yer tangle with Tommy Edwards.'

I mean, that was like hanging a red rag out to a bull, ay. The thing was, Tommy Edwards was a good twelve and a half stone, so he was a lot heavier than me. But I'm thinking, I've gotta get this Tommy Edwards. Like, not to build up me own rep or nothing, but just to see how I'd go with him, fair and square. Because, like, if he was in a pub and a feller who didn't know him started to pick him, someone else would step in and say, 'Hey, mate, don't pick on him. He's Tommy Edwards; the King of the Gulf. He's a world-beater.'

Any rate, this time I went into Normanton and, when I went down to the bottom pub to have a drink, lo-n-behold, there's Tommy Edwards. Now, I don't know if he'd seen me fight Ronny Paul or not but, him and me, we're having a drink together and he says, 'Pity Dello isn't in town, ay Goldie, 'cause then you 'n me could have a bit of a spar in his boxing tent.'

So I says, 'Well, I'll be comin' back ter town in a couple'a days ter change me mail address, so how's about we have a bit of a spar then?'

'Okay,' he says. 'Good. See yer in a couple'a days.'

So everything's set. Me and Tommy Edwards, we're going to have this scrap behind the bottom pub. Now, I don't know if you know or not, but the township of Normanton was over the other side of the Norman River from where I was staying, out at Shady Lagoons. And to get to town, a feller by the name of Backhouse had a little hut over on the town side of the river from where he worked a punt twenty hours a day, getting traffic across from one side to the other. So I'm heading off for this fight and I gets to where the punt lands. There's a yard there for the horse and a trough for feed and there's also a big brass bell. Now, when you ring this bell, this Backhouse feller's supposed to come over in the punt and pick you up. Any rate, when I ring the bell, Backhouse sticks his head out from his hut and when he sees me he thinks, Oh, it's only Goldie. Then he goes back inside his hut where he sits down or whatever. So I'm ringing the bell and he's not doing nothing. He's completely ignoring me.

'Well, stuff you,' I says and so I took off me boots and me clothes and I tied them to me head, with me belt, and I starts to swim across the river. Now, the Norman River's pretty wide and it's pretty deep. Like you've only got to go out four foot and it's over your head. What's more, it's known for its crocs. And with the river being so muddy, a croc can sneak right up on you and you wouldn't even see it coming. That's true. At Shady Lagoons, goats was taken by crocs all the time – there one minute, gone in a flash.

So I'm swimming and I'm swimming and I'm thinking how this's probably the most stupid thing I've ever done in me whole life. Because I'm not only thinking about the crocs, but I'm starting to get washed down the river with the current and it still doesn't seem like I'm getting anywhere. So I'm swimming and swimming and I'm getting knocked up and I'm struggling. Then suddenly, me foot hits something solid ay, and, oh, I just about shot out of that water. I tell you, I was more frightened and terrified right then than what I was when that mad feller Chalkley was trying to shoot me. So now, I'm swimming like the clappers. Then I sees a bloke called Jack Smurdens. Jack'd come down to the punt to see Backhouse for some reason or other. Well, when Jack sees me out in the middle of the river thrashing about, he turns around and he takes off back to town, singing out, 'Goldie's swimmin' the river! Goldie's swimmin' the river!' And I still don't know what's happened to Backhouse. I never saw hide nor hair of him.

Any rate, I eventually got across the river. Don't ask me how, but I did. Then, with the scrap: by that stage in his life, Tommy Edwards had been drinking a fair bit and he'd gone all puffy. He couldn't even pull his riding boots on. Any rate, we goes around behind the bottom pub and everybody comes along to have a look. But he marked up real easy see. So I said to him, I said, 'Look, why chop each other to pieces just fer the enjoyment of the crowd?'

'Righto. Fair enough,' he says. So we just had a bit of a spar and in the end they stopped it and called it a draw, then we all went and had a beer.

But I found something out about Tommy Edwards that day. See, in the fight game, I'm what's called a head-hunter. I generally hit me opponent around the head. But you couldn't do that with Tommy Edwards. With Tommy Edwards, if you wanted to knock him down by hitting him around the head, you'd have to use a pick handle. But he did have one big weakness see: he was open to a left jab to the ribs and I reckon that, if I ever got a good one in there, he would've folded up like a camp stretcher.

But the real point of the story that I'm trying to tell you is: Womp Burns – remember that fat feller I once told you about, who'd stick his finger up his bum when he offered some of his mum's cake to the other ringers – well, Womp done some droving as well. And just three days later, he was swimming some bullocks across the Norman River, right where I'd swam across, and a big croc took one of his bullocks. See, there one minute, gone in a flash. Fair dinkum. Right where I swam.

What's more, up till that time, only two other people had swum the Norman River and got across safe. One was Norman Smith, the feller who'd fixed me up for the scrap with Ronny Paul. He once swam it for a bet. Then the other feller what swam it was a feller called Harry Readford. And if you know anything about your Australian history, you'll know that Harry Readford was also known as Captain Starlight. And so, there's a well-known feller for you. A drover and a cattle duffer, too he was, just like me. So yeah, Captain Starlight was the other feller who swam the Norman River. So I'm in pretty good company, ay? And they still talk about it in Normanton and there's even a photo in the bottom pub of me and Tommy Edwards sparring, and it was also written up in the newspapers. I'll even show you the piece out of the paper, if you like.

Footnote – Normanton is a port and cattle town, on the Norman River, south of the Gulf of Carpentaria and just over two thousand kilometres north-west of Brisbane. William Landsborough discovered and named the Norman River after W.H. Norman, captain of the *Victoria*, who had searched the coastline for the missing explorers Burke and Wills. The town, originally named Norman, was surveyed by George Phillips in December 1867 after Burketown, the then regional centre, was abandoned due to fever and flooding. Norman River Post Office opened in 1868 and the town was renamed Normanton in 1872. In October 1868, the first land sale was held at the police station. Normanton State School opened in 1882 and Burns Philp, general mercantile and agency office, opened in 1884, and remains the oldest intact Burns Philp store in Queensland.

During the gold rush of the late 1890s, Normanton's population rose to around 1250. The town's prosperity improved with the building of the Normanton–Croydon railway in 1889. But, with the gold boom being short-lived, by 1947 the population had fallen to two hundred and thirty-four. In 2006, Normanton had grown to around a thousand people, of which 60 per cent were Indigenous.

Normanton has a tropical savannah climate with two distinct seasons – the hot and humid wet season and the generally rainless dry season. During the wet, most roads are closed due to heavy rain and flooding. Today Normanton's main attraction is tourism. It's the terminus of the weekly Normanton to Croydon Gulflander motor rail, known as the *Tin Hare*. Among its other notable features is the six-metre replica The Big Barramundi and the 8.64-metre-long crocodile statue, named Krys, which was shot in the Norman River by Krystina Pawlowski in 1957, and is still the largest croc ever taken in Australia.

The town is on the traditional lands of the Gkuthaarn and Kukatj people. In the early twentieth century, some were relocated to Mornington Island and Doomadgee, while others were taken out to cattle stations to work as labourers. In November 2012, the traditional owners lodged a claim for native title of sixteen thousand square kilometres in and around Normanton. On July 2020, an Indigenous land use agreement was signed and the traditional owners were granted rights to fish, hunt and perform ceremonies on the land. Though pastoralists are still able to run their cattle, the Aboriginal people assist with land management and cultural heritage sites.

Orbost – Victoria

I was down in Victoria at one time, working in the High Country as a padre with Frontier Services. The Snowy River Patrol, as it was called, was run out of a place called Orbost, which is a tad under four hundred kilometres east of Melbourne. My patrol basically took in Bemm River, Marlo Plains, Cape Conran and up the Bonang Highway and associated areas such as Bonang, Bendoc, Tubbut and Buchan. It was a totally different ministry than any I've had before but, nonetheless, just as important.

One of the initial hurdles I had to overcome was that, previous to my arrival, a very fundamentalist and heavy-handed lay pastor had been working throughout that High Country. In actual fact, it was mainly due to his narrow bigoted manner and his inability to follow the party line that religious education had been kicked out of all the little schools up there. So, when I appeared on the scene, I was already pretty much up against it. So, as I always do, I started visiting.

In the main, I found the locals to be lovely people. But it was a real hard life they led, and it was tough, very tough. Yes, they may have had land, but it was extremely poor land and so a great many of them were down to the seat of their pants. But what else could these people do? This was their lot in life. Their families had been there for three or four generations and they'd been born into it. It was their home, and they knew no other. It was just unfortunate how, because they had such a hard time of it, many of their kids missed out on opportunities that the rest of us would take for granted – such as a decent education – and so they fell through the cracks, which was very, very sad.

Anyhow, one time I was asked to visit a certain family in a very remote spot, right up in this high country. When I got there, I drove up the rugged driveway of the property. I parked the vehicle, got out, and walked over to the house. After I'd knocked on the front door, I just happened to look away for a moment. And when I heard the door open, I turned back around and there was a shotgun pointed right in my face. The owner of the gun was an old guy. He'd seen that I was a priest and he immediately ordered me off the property. 'Git,' he snapped. 'Just git out'a here. Don't want nuffin ter do wiff youse mob.'

Knowing what the problem probably was, I said to him, I said, 'Look, I'm a totally different kettle of fish to the other guy, the lay pastor, who was up here. He was not part of my organisation and I just popped by to see if you were all right and that you're travelling okay.'

Anyhow, the old guy mellowed a little bit after that and he, sort of, implied I could come back and visit him again, some other time.

'Okay, that's fine,' I said.

From then on, it took quite a few visits, and a lot of talk. He was married. Actually, they were a lovely old couple. But the thing was, as it was in a lot of those remote areas, they still had that old-fashioned understanding of things. And of course, none of that had been helped by this other lay pastor, turning up on their doorstep, waving a bible under their noses. Worse still, it's that sort of bad experience that these type of people remember and that makes it extremely difficult for anyone who comes along afterwards. So, to put it mildly, it was a struggle, a big struggle.

Anyhow, a good while ago, previous to this, I remember someone in the church challenging me as to how many lost souls I'd converted to Jesus. To which my reply was, 'That's not what's important.'

In this particular case, what was important was that this old guy and his wife were struggling to survive on their farm. It was all cattle country and the place was in really bad shape. Quite run down. They had children – all grown by now and long gone, bar one. As it turned out, I was eventually able to help the last of their kids move out of home and get a job in town, and I found him board and all that. But as adults their kids were well aware that things were going from bad to worse. In fact, they were keen for their parents to get away from there; to get out of the property. They even suggested buying them a house in Orbost. But of course, these people, the old guy in particular, was as stubborn as an ox and as independent as. 'We don't need our kids ter buy us a house. We've already got this one and we're survivin' okay.'

But they weren't. Not by a long shot, and so I kept popping by every now and then, just to see how they were going. Anyhow, when I arrived one time, I spoke to the wife for a while, then I went out to find the old guy. He was trying to repair an old barn and, I tell you, this old barn, it was almost leaning right over and he was attempting to straighten up the posts. Even though I'm pretty useless at all that hands-on manual work, I still tried to help out the best I could by holding the posts in position for him. While all this was going on, we'd been chatting away – just about mundane stuff really. Then, right out of the blue, he said, 'What'll happen when I die?'

So for the next couple of hours we sat and had this in-depth theological discussion. No bible. No prayer. Nothing. As it turned out, he had a deep, strong faith and spiritual awareness and so he was concerned about the hereafter. 'What'll happen when I die?'

To cut a long story short, I was by his side when he died, and I ended up burying him. And that's when you know you've done a good job. It's not about accolades. It's not even about the pat on the back. That sort of stuff's not important. What's important was that, when this old guy died, he died well – very peacefully, with a smile on his face and with his wife and kids with him.

All that terrible fear of death had gone, and that's not done by waving a bible under people's noses. It's done by care, time, patience, love and understanding, and it's certainly got nothing to do with how many lost souls you've converted to Jesus.

Footnote – Orbost is an early-settlers' town set on the river flats of the Snowy River – three hundred and eighty kilometres east of Melbourne and two hundred and forty kilometres south of Canberra. It's essentially a one-street town with most of the town's businesses acting as service centres for the district's produce.

The local Kurnai people's Dreamtime story is based on an account of how 'Borun the Pelican and Tuk the Musk Duck' had inhabited the area. The first European settlers arrived in 1842 and took up grazing land along the fertile Snowy River Valley. Conflict between the two groups was rife and around 1851, a major massacre took place when a property worker killed a number of Kurnai.

The historic slab hut, built in 1872 and relocated in town in 1897, is now a visitors' centre and is a reminder of the early settlers' life. Gold was discovered in the mid-1850s and, by 1868, an estimated five hundred miners and squatters occupied the area. The post office opened in 1880. After sawmills were established in the early 1880s, the logged timber, plus local farm produce, was boated down the Snowy River to Melbourne. Though originally named Newmerella, the township was renamed Orbost in 1883.

In 1884–85, the Orbost Club Hotel opened for business. By the late 1880s a blacksmith's business was up and running. The township was proclaimed in 1890, and a bridge was constructed across the Snowy River. In the same year, a telegraph office was established and the newspaper – the *Snowy River Mail* – was first published. The Commonwealth Hotel – the 'top pub' – opened in 1901 and the railway arrived from Melbourne in 1916.

In the 1930s, with the rural economy in decline, there was a huge drop in the population, causing its passenger train service to cease. The railway closed in the mid-1980s and the track was dismantled in 1994. With the opening of the Snowy Mountain Scheme in the 1970s, the waters of the Snowy River were diverted into the Murray and Murrumbidgee Rivers for the purpose of irrigation. This caused the water levels in the Snowy River to fall and by the 1980s logging of the native forests was also an environmental issue.

Pilliga – NSW

Adapted from the story 'Lou's Brother' which appeared in Bill
'Swampy' Marsh's *Swampy: Tall Tales and True from Boyhood
and Beyond (Looking For Dad)*.

Lou's brother, at the Coonabarabran camping accessory shop,
reckoned that he couldn't tell stories half as well as his brother.
Mind you, at the time I didn't see how he possibly could,
certainly not after having spent the last half an hour listening to
the maestro, Lou, holding court.

When I arrived to get my gas cylinder refilled, Lou had just
begun telling everyone about the dangers of guns: everyone in
this case being the bloke Lou was serving, a lady with her three
little kids, Lou's brother and a stray dog who'd inadvertently
dropped in for an earbashing. Lou said that once, out near a
place called Tooraweenah, a grandmother was in the backyard,
hanging out the washing, while her three grandkids were
playing on the verandah. When the kids heard a sharp cry,
they looked up to see Grandma stagger, then crumble to the
ground in a heap. The kids immediately rushed over to her
side. Summing up the situation, the elder of the three rang the
local doctor and told him that their grandmother had just had
a heart attack under the clothesline. But by the time the doctor
arrived, Gran was dead. After doing a quick diagnosis, he was
stumped as to what was the cause of death. It definitely wasn't
a heart attack, so what else could it be? Then, as he lifted up
the old lady's head, something wet and sticky oozed out over
his hand.

'When the doc rolled Gran over,' Lou told us, 'there it was, a bullet, right through the back of her noggin. And the queerest thing was that it went through sideways, not straight on like yer'd expect.' I took a quick glance at Lou's audience. Everyone's jaw had dropped in shock, even the stray dog's. 'But that's not the end of it,' Lou announced in an intriguing whisper, which caused us all to take a step closer so we'd catch his every word. 'There was no murder weapon, no suspects, no nothin', just a dead old woman, lyin' beside a basket of washing, with a .303 bullet in the back of her scone 'n three bawlin' kids.'

Then came a dramatic pause as he took us in, one by one. ''N so, what do yer reckon happened?' he asked.

Well, none of us could work out how 'the murder' had occurred, especially with the bullet going through her head sideways. Just like the doctor, we were completely stumped. Capturing our blank looks, Lou proposed the theory that, just maybe, around the same time of the incident there were three pig shooters a few miles away on the outer boundaries of the Warrumbungle Ranges. Seeing how they weren't having much luck hunting down wild pigs, when a crow flew overhead, they decided to have a pot-shot at that. 'And,' deduced Lou, 'it was one of the bullets from one of those shooters that missed the crow, went miles up in'ta the air, then came back down ter earth, gatherin' velocity as it went, until it nailed Gran under the clothesline.'

There came an audible gasp from the audience. 'Yer just can't beat rotten luck, can yer?' Lou's brother chipped in, astounded at the odds of such an accident.

'No,' we all replied in agreement, shaking our heads in synchronisation with the stray dog.

After the bloke Lou was serving had sworn that he'd never again offer to hang out the washing, Lou guided him over to the cash register. The woman and her three children scampered out of the shop to go and check on their grandma, and the stray dog wandered back out onto the street still shaking its head in disbelief. And that's when Lou's brother stepped forward to serve me. As we were sorting out my gas cylinder, I asked which was the best way to get to Pilliga – through Narrabri or along the dirt past Baradine?

'Pilliga!' he recoiled in horror. 'Yer gotta be mad ter want'a go ter Pilliga.'

I then explained how I was visiting all the places where my dad had worked in the bank, in the hopes of gathering background information for a book I was writing. Pilliga just happened to be one of those places. Dad had done a relief there while he was working in nearby Narrabri.

'God,' he gasped, 'I could tell yer a few stories 'bout Pilliga.'

And before I could explain how I was in a hurry to get there before nightfall, Lou's brother began. Because Dad had been in the bank, Lou started with the one about the day the Pilliga bank was robbed by a gang of gypsies.

'Your dad was probably there at the time,' Lou's brother said. 'But anyway, along came this gang'a gypsies in a horse-drawn wagon. When they pulled up outside the bank, they called out if anyone wanted ter have their fortunes read.'

As the story went, it was a slow day in Pilliga, so the bank manager and his staff wandered outside to have their fortunes read. First up was the manager. Both he and the staff were aghast to hear that there was going to be a big change in the manager's life, and he'd soon be moved from Pilliga. Now, what the manager and his staff didn't realise was that, while this fortune-telling was going on, a couple of the gypsies had wandered in through the back door of the bank and were looting the safe.

'Cleaned the place right out,' Lou's brother announced, slapping his thigh at the twist of events. ''N that bloody old manager well, the gypsies were spot on. He got moved on all right. Head office gave him the bloody sack!'

The next story was about the Yowie. The Yowie was, and still is in Lou's brother's mind, a half-man, half-beast that runs wild out in the Pilliga scrub. Apparently, just about everyone who's spent any time in Pilliga has witnessed a Yowie. If they haven't, then they most certainly know all about it.

'Your dad was probably there at the time,' Lou's brother started. 'But anyway, early one morning an old duck came out ter feed her chooks 'n there was her prized white leghorn rooster, freshly killed 'n half-eaten to death. Blood 'n guts everywhere.' Lou's brother must have read my mind. 'Yer thinkin' that it were a fox, aren't yer? Well it weren't. It were a Yowie. 'N do yer know how they knew it were a Yowie? 'Cause right beside that half-eaten chook there was a set of false teeth that belonged to the Yowie. No kiddin'.'

From the look on Lou's brother's face, he was dead certain that the story was true. Very much doubting it myself, I asked how on earth the Yowie survived after that, without its false teeth.

'Ah,' Lou's brother replied, waving his finger at me, 'that's the funny thing. When the old duck came back inside ter call the coppers, she went to grab her false teeth out'a the glass beside her bed 'n – yer got it – while she'd been outside with her chooks, the Yowie had snuck in the back door of her house 'n pinched 'em!'

As if that wasn't enough to impress me about the existence of the Yowie, Lou's brother followed on with the one about a mate of his who was, and I quote, 'as honest as the day is long'. Apparently, this particular mate of Lou's brother was taking a load of sheep down to Coonamble. Just outside Pilliga, he pulled over to take a nap. About an hour later, he was woken by a strange tapping noise on the cab window. 'When he looked up, there it was: the Yowie,' Lou's brother said. 'Me mate reckons it were the ugliest bloody thing he's ever saw. Anyhow, the poor bugger was out of there so fast that by the time he reached

Coonamble, the truck needed a new set'a tyres 'n the sheep didn't know if it were breakfast, dinner or tea time. No kiddin'!'

I smiled, which was a grave mistake.

''N that's not all. Did yer dad ever tell yer 'bout the Pilliga Show? He'd probably been to a few, I reckon,' Lou's brother shouted, his eyes now bulbous with excitement. 'One time, when we was kids, me and Lou went ter the Pilliga Show.'

Lou's brother reckoned it was the best show they'd ever been to. Outside one particular tent there was a snake on display that had two heads. Then, after you paid to go inside, there were lots of other 'ab-norm-alities' to be seen. There was a sheep with six legs, a lizard with two tongues, a fat lady with a beard and hairy legs, a skinny bloke who wore a woman's brassiere to cover his breasts and a donkey that barked like a dog. There were also dwarfs, seven or eight of them, and the woman who wore a short dress and called herself 'Snow White' had bruises all over her legs. ''N there was an old black African fella who had two sets'a teeth growin' in his mouth; one set at the front 'n the other set behind: just like sharks' teeth they were. And this black bloke was chargin' a penny fer a look and thruppence fer a touch.'

I must have looked impressed because Lou's brother continued, ''N what's more, another woman had three breasts!' And, Lou's brother leaned over and whispered in my ear, 'She used to charge a bob fer a look 'n three bob fer a feel. I tell yer,' he shouted, 'they've taken all the fun out'a shows these days, ay!'

Footnote – Pilliga is a village out on the north-west plains of New South Wales, on the rim of the three thousand-square-kilometre Pilliga State Forest, one hundred kilometres west of Narrabri. It's said that the Gamilaraay and/or the Kamilaroi people lived on and cared for the region for 30,000 years before white settlement and the place's name was possibly derived from their word *billarga*, meaning 'swamp oaks'.

The township first came into being as a staging post along the route of the old Cobb & Co horse-drawn wagons. The Pilliga Post Office opened in January 1867. In 1902, the Pilliga artesian bore baths opened as a permanent town water supply. The baths have now become a popular swimming and therapeutic spot, for locals and visitors alike, with the water temperature averaging around 37 degrees Centigrade (99 degrees Fahrenheit). The village, with its population of around two hundred, has a store, a police station, a post office and a school with around fifteen students. There is a single storey brick hotel, the Pilliga Hotel.

The area is rife with many myths and legends. The Pilliga Princess being one: locals have described her as being a reclusive, old, grey-haired, crazy Aboriginal woman who frequently hitchhikes along the Newell Highway, between Narrabri and Coonabarabran, thumbing lifts from truckies. In 1993, it's said that she was hit and killed by a truck as she was wandering across the road in the dead of night. Since then her ghost is said to appear at regular intervals. The story of 'the bag lady' is also a familiar one, particularly among truckies. Years after her death, truckies have reported seeing 'the bag lady' walking along the highway, pushing a shopping trolley, again in the dead dark of night.

Another point of interest, relevant to the area, is the frequent sightings of the *Jingra* – an Aboriginal term for 'outback Yowie'. The Yowie is said to be a half-man, half-beast, six to eight foot tall, big-toothed, sharp-clawed, and covered in thick dark hair, akin to Big Foot. The horror film *There's Something in the Pilliga* (2014) is supposedly based on the real-life account of four people who came face to face with the Yowie after being stranded in Pilliga State Forest.

Poeppel Corner – SA, NT and Qld

Adapted from Dean Jamieson's book *They Called Me Lightning*.

One cool sunny morning before breakfast, my boss, Bob, told me to get the Land Rover ready. 'Fuel it up. Put in a forty-four-gallon drum'a diesel, a drum'a water, a drum'a oil, an extra spare wheel, fill up the tucker box, stow the portable two-way wireless, aerial, swags, rifles, ammo, make up a good toolbox 'n make sure the wheel-brace 'n jack are on board.'

'Where are we going?' I dared to ask.

'Just fer a good look around. If we get stuck we might have ter stay a couple'a days.'

This was all new and so what was he on about? I'd only just arrived on the property and already I'd been made well aware how too many questions weren't welcome – that's the way of the outback. A new chum like me never asks questions – they just watch and learn. So I just did as I was told. The next morning we left early and headed toward Abminga. Near Charlotte Waters, we drove past Boundary Bore, into country unknown to me. To my untrained eye, we seemed to be following faint wheel tracks. Now I'd see them, then they'd disappear, then they'd reappear again. Soon, our smooth sandy going gives way to rock-strewn hills and waterways. It's an ever-changing landscape. Big red sand hills. Miles of rough gibbers. Not a cow in sight. The going's slow; the ride's rough. In bad patches my head hits the metal roof of the Rover. *Ouch!* But I don't say anything – again, that's the way of the outback. Never complain. Just grin and bear it.

After hours of driving, I was still mystified as to where we were going, and why, and when the hell we'd get there. So I just sit and say nothing. Then Bob turns sharply up an extremely boulder-strewn steep hill. As we bounce our way to the top, my head repeatedly hits the metal interior of the Land Rover – *Bang! Bang! Bang!* It hurts, but I don't complain. No chance of sympathy out here. When we get to the top, Bob turns the engine off. We get out. I rush to have a piss, as does Bob. As always, hands are rinsed. 'Cut a couple'a slices'a bread 'n corned beef,' I'm ordered.

I'm glad of the rest. The going's been brutal. Bob's got a pair of binoculars and he's busy scanning the horizon. We eat fast, then we're off again. The violent movement of the Land Rover throws us about, like corks in a wild sea. On and on we go, slightly more in a southerly direction now. Another toilet stop and a long drink from the waterbag. I'm told to check the oil and water and syphon fuel from the drum to top up the Land Rover's fuel tank. Bob gets out his binoculars and has a brief look around. He gets back in the cab. Not wanting to be left behind, I jump in and we're off again. Eventually the ground levels out: more flat gibber and 'crab' holes, some damp, some show a flash of water. The sun's getting low. Bob slows the Rover to a stop and we step out. I look around and before me lies the vast expanse of the Simpson Desert.

Bob walks a short way to a cairn of stones. I follow. There's a post and, at its base, there's a raised bronze plaque with its latitude and longitude inscribed. The writing says that this is the point where the borders of the Northern Territory, South Australia and Queensland meet. I look around. This is the most isolated and desolate place I've ever been to. I gather up the courage and ask, 'What the hell are we doing here?'

Bob mumbles, 'It's Poeppel Corner, named after an early surveyor of this part of the outback.'

I can't resist a boyish temptation and spread myself across the cairn with my hands in the Northern Territory, one leg in South Australia and the other in Queensland.

Bob's not amused. 'Stop muckin' about. Gott'a get back over that bad patch'a sand 'n gullies before it's dark.'

We jump back in the Rover and off we go again. After we get over the 'bad patch'a sand 'n gullies' Bob pulls up in a sandy depression. Small hills protect us from the wind and there's enough dead wood for a campfire. I service the Rover – check the oil and water and syphon fuel from the drum to top up the fuel tank. After a good wash and a feed, I crawl into my swag. I'm totally exhausted. I feel like I've been inside a concrete mixer most of the day and I'm instantly asleep.

The following day, on the way back to the homestead, Bob confided that he took me as a backup, 'just in case we ran int'a any trouble'. "N don't tell no one we've been to Poeppel Corner,' he adds. 'If anyone asks, just tell 'em we did a wide sweep, checkin' stock feed 'n water levels.'

To this day, I never knew why we went out there. Such a long way and over the roughest of tracks. Perhaps Bob had never been there and was just curious. Who knows? We never spoke of it again and I never told anyone of our mystery tour to Poeppel Corner.

Footnote – Poeppel Corner is out in the Simpson Desert, just shy of two hundred kilometres west of Birdsville, and is the corner boundary of Queensland, South Australia and the Northern Territory.

Poeppel Corner was originally marked in 1880, during an official survey conducted by Augustus Poeppel, who was under instruction of the South Australian Government to find the exact central Australian colonial borders. In doing so, Poeppel's team used camels to drag a coolabah post to mark the intersection. Though its marking was a surveying feat at the time, with the original point being located in a salt lake, it was later found that the measuring chain used was a few centimetres too long. A second survey, conducted by Lawrence Wells, who had been Poeppel's assistant surveyor, later relocated the post to its current position – latitude 26 degrees south, longitude of 138 degrees east. The Poeppel Corner Survey Marker is now a Queensland heritage-listed site.

Because Poeppel Corner, Cameron Corner and Surveyor Generals Corner are all situated at the intersection of three different time zones, New Year's Eve occurs at those three locations three times each year, at thirty-minute intervals.

Quilpie – Qld

In Memory of Kevin O'Brien.

I wasn't ever a shearer. I was only a roustabout – a roustie – out past Quilpie, in western Queensland. Now, how a city kid like me ended up away out there is a story in itself. So I'll tell you about that first. See, by the time I was twelve, I'd represented Queensland in junior rugby league football and I'd also played cricket for New Farm State School. But we weren't rich or nothing. Dad was just a ganger on the council, so we were ordinary working-class people. Like, at home, we never had a hot water system or nothing, not even a chip heater. We had to boil the water up in the old copper, out in the laundry, then take it into the bathroom in a kerosene tin.

Any rate, I was nearing the end of junior school and, in them days, it cost a fair bit to go on to high school. But I wasn't happy at school, so I used to do a fair bit of wagging. Well, to be honest, I hated bloody school. It was a bastard of a place, and I did a hell of a lot of wagging. Any rate, one day, the headmaster got me and Dad up and he said, 'Look, Kevin.' Me dad's name was Kevin as well. 'Look, Kevin,' he said, 'I can't handle this young feller of yours. He just won't study.'

'He'll bloody study, all right,' Dad replied. 'I'll take him home 'n flog him till he does bloody study.' And Dad wasn't joking either because, by the living-Harry, he used to give me some floggings. My oath he did. He'd drag me into the bathroom by the scruff of the neck and he'd get stuck into me with one of them old razor straps, good and proper. Even today, when

I think about it, I can still feel it. And there'd be me mum, standing at the door, calling out, 'Kevin, be careful, you'll kill him.' And Dad'd shout back, 'I'll kill the little bastard, all right,' and he'd get stuck into me even harder.

Any rate, when the exam results were published, I looked in the paper and there was my name; K.C. O'Brien. New Farm – 50.5 per cent. How in the bloody hell I passed, I'll never know. Nobody knows. But see, it got Dad a bit excited. So he dragged me back up to the school with the idea of me going on to high school. 'Look, Kevin,' the headmaster said, 'let's be honest. You can't handle him. I can't handle him. So it's best to just let him go and do what he wants to do. He'll be okay, don't worry.'

Any rate, on our way home, Dad was quiet for a while, then he said, 'Well, son, what do yer want'a do?'

I said, 'I want'a go out bush.' So when we got home, Dad said to Mum, 'Mother,' he said, 'Kevin wants ter go out bush. That's what he wants ter do.'

'Well, if he wants ter go bush,' Mum said, 'he may as well go bush.'

So next morning we got a tram into Brisbane and we went to Goldsborough Mort, the old pastoral people. Dad fronts up to the office. 'The boy wants ter go out bush,' he said.

After sizing me up, they said, 'Okay, there's a job near Quilpie, out on Ray Station, as a cowboy-roustabout. The wages are two pound five a week, plus keep. We'll pay his fare out there 'n if he stays on for twelve months we'll pay his fare back home 'n he's entitled to two weeks leave.'

So Dad said to me, 'Well, what do yer think?' I said, 'Yes, that's what I want to do.'

Now, what you've got to realise is that, I'd never been out of bloody Brisbane in me whole life. So I didn't have a clue where this Quilpie place was, let alone Ray Station. So I end up on this old steam train. And I tell you, just as well Mum'd made me about a hundred sandwiches 'cause I spent the next two days and three nights sitting up in the bloody thing. Any rate, I eventually get off at Quilpie. It's night and there's no bastard around. Not a soul. So I'm hanging around the railway station when this Aboriginal fella comes stumbling along. He's as full as a boot. 'Yer waitin' fer someone?' he says.

I said, 'Yeah, me name's Kevin O'Brien.'

'Me name's Billy,' he said. 'You come this way.'

So we get in an old utility truck and we head out along this pot-holed, corrugated road. Like I said, this was me first time out of the city and pretty soon, what with all this driving in the dark, I didn't have the faintest clue as to where we were going. So I'm starting to get a bit bloody worried ay, and so I'm thinking it might be all a big trick. 'Where're we goin' Billy,' I say, 'back ter Brisbane?'

'No,' he said. 'We go long way out.'

Any rate, we eventually get to Ray Station. It's about midnight and the cook's still up. She's a big fat lady. 'Welcome boy, welcome,' she greets me. 'Me name's Mary. Yer must be hungry.'

Now, like I said, we didn't have much in the way of modern facilities back at home in Brisbane. But at least we had electricity and lights with switches on them. But out here, there was no lights, just an old hurricane lamp, and there's moths and flies all over the bloody place. But I'm real hungry ay, so I say, 'Yes please, I am hungry.' Then Mary gets out an old tin plate and she loads it up with a hunk of mutton stew from a big pot, from off a huge combustion stove. Then she grabs a pannikin. 'Do yer drink tea?'

'Yes please.'

'Get into it,' she says. So I did, and after I'd wolfed down me dinner and drunk me tea, Billy said, 'I'll take yer down to yer hut. Do yer ride a horse?'

Now the only horses I'd ridden was around New Farm, and they was very tame. But right from the start, I knew that if they found me out to be a liar, I'd be done for and I'd be sent back home. So I said, 'Yes, but only tame horses.'

'Well yer can have this one 'ere,' Billy said. 'She's a brumby, but she's tame.'

Then, because I had a small port, with some clothes in it, Billy loosely put the saddle and bridle on and he led the brumby along like that. So off we go, and we're walking and talking along the way. Any rate, we seemed to have been walking and talking for a hell of a long time, so I said, 'Where're we goin' Billy?'

'Oh, not far,' he said. 'Just up there-a-ways.'

Now, even though I'd come from an ordinary working-class family, Mum always made sure everything at home was nice and clean and tidy. So we eventually get to this old wood and rusted corrugated iron hut. After Billy opened the door, he showed me how to light the lamp. And there it was – just the one room, with a dirt floor, an old army stretcher with a coconut fibre and piss-stained mattress, a couple of blankets and a couple of fruit cases as wardrobes.

'There yer go,' says Billy. 'The mare's okay ter let roam. Be at the homestead at half past five in the mornin'. See yer,' he said, and he left.

And that was the first night I'd ever spent on me own. Like I said, I was only thirteen and here I am, stuck away out in this dirty old hut. To make matters worse, when the breeze got up, the corrugated iron banged and squeaked like buggery. I tell you, I had a lot of thoughts running through me head that night; a hell of a lot of bloody thoughts. So many in fact that I hardly slept a wink. Any rate, at some time of the morning I'd had enough, so I got up and I found a hand basin and a glass demijohn of water and I had a bit of a wash and I cleaned me teeth. After that, I put the bridle on the brumby. But, as soon as I threw the saddle over her, up she went in the air and she threw the saddle arse over. 'Gee this's not a good start,' I said. 'It's me first bloody morning 'n I gotta deal with this bastard of a thing.'

I mean, this brumby had a neck on her as thick as. So I threw the saddle on again, and up she goes again, rearing and pulling the bridle out of me hand. Any rate, after about five goes, I thought, Bugger this. By then it was just on daylight and I could see the homestead over in the distance, so I decided to lead her over. When I got to the homestead, I said to Billy, 'Billy,' I said, 'I can't get the saddle on this mare.'

'Oh,' he said, 'I fergot ter tell yer, she's got a saddle sore.'

Now, being just a youngster, I'm quite short, so there was no way I could see up that high. And I'd been throwing the saddle right smack-bang onto this huge bloody saddle sore. Any rate, when we quietened the brumby down, we put the cloth back on her, laid the saddle on nice and gentle, tightened the surcingle and she was as good as gold.

So we had breakfast which, being on a sheep station, was mutton chops. Then I had to give Billy a hand to get things sorted out for when they brung the sheep in for shearing. So off we go with this other Aboriginal fella, Joe. So then, Billy's up on this windmill, fixing something. Now, they're bloody high bastards, those windmills, over sixty foot. So Billy's working away. Next thing he slips and falls right off the bloody windmill. Down he comes and he hits the ground with an almighty *Crunch!* So we rush over. Now, at Ray Station, there was just the five of us; Billy, Joe, Mary, meself and an accountant-manager feller what basically ran the place. So Joe looks down at Billy, then he looks up at me and he says, 'Billy dead. Broke neck. You go up 'n see Mister.' The accountant feller was always called Mister.

Now, I wouldn't have known a dead man if I'd seen one. Still, I rode flat out up to the homestead. 'Mister,' I said, 'Billy's fell off the windmill. Joe reckons he's dead; broke his neck.'

Any rate, this feller comes hurrying down and he feels Billy's pulse. 'Yep,' he says, 'he's dead all right.' Then he says to me, 'Kevin,' he says, 'go 'n get Mary 'n bring a blanket down ter put over Billy, 'n be quick about it.'

Which I did. Then an hour or so later, a police sergeant, a priest and a doctor turned up in a four-wheel drive. By that stage, Joe and me were fixing the corral for the sheep. So the policeman comes over and he asks us all about it. 'Yeah,' said Joe. 'I see'd it all. Billy up 'n fell off the windmill 'n hit his head, dead.'

Any rate they announce Billy as being dead and the doctor asks Joe and me to dig a hole. So we get to it with a couple of shovels and we dig this bloody six-footer. It wasn't too difficult 'cause it's mostly sand with just a little bit of clay underneath. When that's done, we get an old sheet to wrap around Billy, and Mary brings some coffee out for the sergeant. Now I reckon, thinking back on it as I am now, that the police sergeant might've been doing some funny business with Mary, if you catch my drift. Any rate, the priest said a few nice words then we tied three pieces of rope 'round Billy – one here, one there and the other one there – and we lowered him down the hole, all wrapped up in the sheet. When that was done, we filled in the hole. There was no cross or nothing. Maybe they put one there later. I can't remember. After that, the police sergeant, the doctor and the priest went up to the homestead to sort out things with Mister. Then we had lunch and I drank a couple of pannikins of black tea, which I still drink today, and I ate some mutton sandwiches. Then this manager feller says, 'Look, Kevin,' he says, 'take the afternoon off. Grab the mare 'n go 'n have a good look around the place.'

Now Ray Station was enormous. I'm not sure how many acres it was, but it was one of the biggest properties around. The Tully family owned it. Well known they were. So any rate, I got on this brumby and I just cantered around, looking at the sheep and things. But how the bloody hell nine thousand or so head of sheep survived on that flat, sandy, bastard country had me beat. They must've lived on the mulga, because there wasn't nothing else; just mulga.

So that was my first twenty-four hours on Ray Station. I was still only thirteen and you could say that I was in a pretty sad state of affairs over it: what with being so far away from home for the first time and the way me living conditions was, then the trouble with the brumby, then Billy dying like he did. So by that stage I had it in me head to shoot through; like, bugger off out of there. But I couldn't go nowhere 'cause I didn't have any transport or money. What's more, I knew if I turned up back at home, Dad'd give me one hell of a flogging. So I thought it over and, in the end, I convinced meself that things couldn't get much worse.

But they did.

See, by now it's shearing season and I was set to do this roustabouting. What they did was, all the nearby station properties shared the one shearing shed. So the day before they started, I was sent off to this shed to settle meself in. The shearers lived in similar conditions to me, except they had kapok mattresses and lino on the floor of their huts. Everything was immaculately clean and they'd pooled in for their own cook. See, in the bush, the cook travels with the shearers. Like they'd go, say, from Quilpie to Charleville to Longreach and finish that run. Then they might go over to Western Australia or South Australia and end up with nine or ten months' straight work, which, mind you, a lot of them pissed up against the wall.

Any rate, the gun shearer was a feller by the name of Jack Malone. Jack was a real tough, hard bastard. If you looked in a shearing shed and you saw a big, strong, hairy bloke, that'd be Jack. He was only in his early fifties and he'd already been in the business for forty years. So he'd been around. He'd lived, like. I heard that he'd been married twice, maybe more. Any rate, the shearers were just about to show me what I had to do when Jack came into the shed. 'Hang on, boy,' he shouted. That was the relationship – always 'boy' and 'sir'. Anyhow, Jack grabbed a sheep out of the crush. '*Zzz-osh*,' he went. In those days, it was all belt-driven machinery. There was none of this crap they've got these days. Then, when Jack'd shore this sheep, he called out to the presser, 'Show the boy what to do.' And so, the presser showed me how to pick up a fleece and reverse it and throw it on the piece-table. It was then the piece-picker's job to take out all the shit and burrs before it was classed and went into the press. So that was okay. I now knew what I had to do.

On the first morning of shearing, the bell rings at 7 a.m. and we start – everything's by the bell. Of course, with all the shearers being paid by the sheep, the roustie's got to be real quick to keep up the pace. So I've got eight shearers to look after; four on one side, four on the other, with Jack up the top. So it's '*Zzz-osh. Zzz-osh*' and everything starts off good. But the thing is, apart from Jack, they're all about the same speed. So I'm doing this picking up, and all you wear is a pair of shorts, no shirt and just a pair of old bloody sandshoes. So I'd pick up a fleece, throw it all crooked over the table, then I'd go and pick up the next one and so on. But by the time I'd get around to the sixth fleece, the first shearer had done his second cut, and suddenly the others have also finished. So I'm going flat out and the fleeces are starting to pile up around the shearers' feet.

'Get this bastard bloody fleece out'a me way!' a shearer's calling and he's kicking the fleece out onto the boards to give himself room to get at another sheep. 'Okay, sir. Okay, sir,' I'm calling out but, of course, I'm starting to get rattled, aren't I? Then, while I'm still back down the bloody board aways, struggling with a fleece, Jack cuts a sheep and it's, 'Tar, boy!'

Now, the tar's made up by the cook, and it's kept lukewarm in a pot. And in the pot's a stick with a knob of cloth wrapped around it, which is bound by fishing line. So as soon as there's a cut, the roustie's supposed to go and paste it on the wound without touching the fleece. That seals the wound and so the blood doesn't damage the fleece. Any rate, Jack cuts this sheep and it's my job to put on the tar. I'd been told how to do it. 'Okay, sir,' I call out.

But then this next feller, the shearer on number two stand, he starts bellowing, 'Boy, get this fuckin' fleece out from under me feet!'

'Okay, sir,' I reply and I put down the tar pot and I run and grab the fleece.

'Where the fuckin' hell are yer, boy!' Jack yells. 'Git 'ere!' So I drop the bloody fleece and I pick up the tar pot again and I scamper over to Jack. 'Now, son,' he shouts, 'when I say fuckin' tar, I mean fuckin' tar, and right now!' Then he grabs the stick out from the tar pot and he scrubs tar all over me bare chest: all over, and I just stood there. I didn't know what else to do. I just stood there and took it. 'Now fix the fuckin' sheep!' Jack shouts.

So I fixed the sheep. But by now the other shearers are bluing at me. 'Get this fuckin' fleece out from under me fuckin' feet,' they're all calling out.

Any rate, I go like the clappers and I finally catch up just as the smoko bell rings. And because all the machinery's all fuel driven, to save money the Cocky turns everything off. So I go to smoko and there's hot scones, butterfly cakes – beautiful – straight out of the oven and there's tea and soft drink. There's about twelve of us in all and I'm the last to get fed 'cause I'm the roustie – down the bottom of the order – and by that stage I'm a pretty bloody miserable one at that. Any rate, I'm waiting in line and Jack calls out, 'Boy! There's some carbolic soap down there. Go 'n get that shit off a yer chest then come 'n sit with me.'

Now, a roustie never sits with the shearers. Never. A roustie sits with the presser and the piece-picker, well out of the way. The big table's only for the shearers. So I go outside: there's a tin trough and a water tank and I get to it with the carbolic soap. But the tar doesn't come off easy. It needs a lot of scrubbing. So now I'm red raw. Any rate, after I towel off, I go back inside and grab something to eat, and I go and sit with the presser and the piece-picker.

'Boy!' comes the shout. 'Git over 'ere!' So I went over and sat next to Jack.

Now, Jack didn't say another word to me during that smoko, not one word. What's more, not another word was ever spoke about how he'd scrubbed me up with the tar. And even though the week improved after that, and I was learning fast, I wasn't learning fast enough for some of the shearers. So I still copped a lot of crap. But see, the thing was, I was only thirteen and the shearers were all experienced, and I was too young and slow for them.

Any rate, Friday comes and we knock off at 2 o'clock to get ready to go into Quilpie. First, there's the shower. When I say shower, all it was, was a forty-four-gallon drum, turned upside down that you filled with lukewarm water from the copper outside. It had a nozzle on it, and that was your weekly shower. Usually, when you finished each day, you just used a washer. Like, you just had a bird-bath so you was clean. But you never got rid of that lanolin smell. It went through the whole of your body. So on the dot of half past two, we're all ready to go into Quilpie. A three-ton supply truck with seats across the tray and no bloody backs on it pulls up. There was no covering. Any rate, we're just about to get on when Jack calls out, 'Boy, come 'n sit with me.' Which was also something that a roustie never does. But Jack's word is God, so I do what I'm told. I go and sit next to Jack on the truck.

So we get into Quilpie and we go to Corones Hotel. The Corones just about owned everything in town: a couple of pubs, the post office, the service station. I remember the service station only had the one pump. It was one of them old ones where you hand-pumped two gallons of petrol at a time up into a cylinder on top, then you drained it into your vehicle. So we go into Corones Hotel. Of course, Jack's well known there. He always had room 26. Always. So Jack says, 'Twenty-six fer me 'n twenty-seven fer the boy.'

'Sorry, Jack,' the clerk says, 'twenty-seven's been taken.' And Jack eyeballed this feller, 'Well, get the bastard untaken, 'n be bloody quick about it.'

'Okay, Jack, okay,' says the clerk, 'cause you don't mess with Jack. Then Jack laid down his pay cheque, the whole lot, everything he'd earned and that was the last I saw of it. By the time we went back out to the shed on the Sunday evening, he'd drunk it all. Any rate, after we got settled, Jack came over to my room, twenty-seven, and he said, 'What're yer gonna do, boy?'

'Oh, sir,' I replied, 'I'll probably go over 'n have a couple'a malted milks 'n catch the picture show.'

'Do what you want, boy,' he said, 'but just be careful about it.'

Now this's the first time I'd ever stayed in a pub. So I said to Jack, 'Can I please have the key to me room, sir?'

'We don't use keys 'ere,' Jack said. 'Don't worry, boy. No bastard'll harm yer, not while I'm around, they won't.'

So I went to the pictures and I had a malted milk and I had a good look around Quilpie before I went back to my room. Then about midnight, up the stairs comes Jack – blind drunk. I hear him stumbling about, and he's calling out, 'Boy! Boy!' Then, when he gets to the landing, he bursts into my room, falls over, gets up again, and he calls out, 'Boy. Boy, are yer all right?'

'Yes, sir,' I said. 'I'm all right.'

'Good,' he said. 'Then that's good then.' Then he stumbled off to bed. So that was that. Then on the Sunday afternoon, we went back out to the shed and things was much better after that. And when the shearing was all done and they was cutting out, all the shearers came over and shook me hand. 'Well done, boy,' they said. 'Well done.' And Jack, well, he was the last one what came over. And he stood there and he looked down at me and he said, 'Well done, son. See yer the same time next year, ay?' And that was the first time he'd ever called me 'son'. Like I said, it was always 'boy' and 'sir'.

'Yes, sir,' I said right back to him. 'See yer next year.'

But see, it took me a while to work out what'd been going on, and it's that a shearer won't ever say he's sorry, especially to a roustie he won't. And because Jack would never have showed his emotions toward me, especially with the other shearers about, it was his way of saying 'sorry'. Because Jack regretted what he'd done on that first day when he'd scrubbed the tar all over me chest. And so, when he'd said, 'Come 'n sit with me,' it was his way of apologising for what he'd done to me. And he must've felt real bad about doing it too, 'cause like I said, a roustie just doesn't get asked to sit at the shearers' table. And all the shearers knew that as well. Too right they did. They all knew that Jack was sorry for doing what he'd done to me. And it was still on his mind when we went into Quilpie and he got rooms twenty-six and twenty-seven. Then to ask, 'Are yer all right, boy?' See, he was always keeping an eye out for me. Making sure that things was okay. A lot of shearers wouldn't think like that. They wouldn't have had the heart to. But Jack did. Jack looked over me. Jack looked over me real good.

Footnote – Quilpie, population of around five hundred, is in the Channel Country of western Queensland, a thousand kilometres west of Brisbane. Beyond the town lies endless sand dunes, scrubby mulga and gidgee vegetation and corrugated dirt roads, deep with potholes and bull dust. The town's name comes from a Margany Aboriginal word for the mainly nocturnal stone curlew. The region has an annual rainfall of less than three hundred and fifty millimetres – thirteen inches in the old money – and summer temperatures have been known to reach 50 degrees Centigrade or well over the old 100 degrees Fahrenheit in the waterbag.

Quilpie's economy is based on marginal grazing and mining, with one of the largest deposits of boulder opal in the world. It also mines gas and oil. The town site was gazetted in 1917. By 1918, Quilpie State School had opened, though it only began secondary education in 1966. A post office opened in 1921 and by 1923, the telephone had reached Quilpie. In 1927, a courthouse was built. A bore supplied the town with water from 1933, and, between 1952 and 1963, the bore's hot water generated the town's electricity.

In its heyday, Jim and Harry Corones were joint owners of three hotels in Quilpie. The Quilpie Hotel was burnt down in 1926 and was replaced by the Brick Hotel, which, these days, is an opal and art gallery. The Corones built the Imperial Hotel in 1925: the first two-storey building in Quilpie. Their third pub, the Club Hotel, was leased from 1934 and purchased in 1965. In 1992 the Imperial Hotel – which had the reputation of being 'the best pub in Quilpie' – was destroyed by fire. A second Imperial Hotel rose from its ashes.

Rawlinna – WA

This story has been adapted from a collection of Rick Darling's 'memorable journeys'.

As a keen camper, shooter-fisherman and a person who loves the outback, this story of a town that literally 'popped-up' out of nowhere has been one of my all-time favourite adventures. Now, high on my travel bucket list was to radiate out from the centre of Australia in virtually all directions. North-south from Adelaide was no big deal because it's straight along the Stuart Highway. North-west to Broome, north-east to Mount Isa, then south-east to Birdsville have had their challenges. This left one trip remaining: south-west on the Great Central Road, from Uluru to Laverton, over a thousand kilometres of unsealed track, then on to Kalgoorlie.

Along with my son, Sam, my cousin, Donn, and his son, Joel, we set off from Adelaide in two four-wheel-drive vehicles – mine being an old beat-up '96 Hilux. It took us roughly two days to get to Ayers Rock – Uluru – where, while preparing for the big push into Western Australia, we took in the sights. The following three days saw us rattle through places like Docker River, on the Northern Territory–Western Australian border, Giles Weather Station and Warburton. Along the way, we passed through a lot of country that'd been opened up by Len Beadell, the legendary surveyor, road builder, bushman, artist and author. For those who may not know, during the 1950s and '60s, Len built over six thousand kilometres of roads throughout Central Australia to which he'd given names such as Connie Sue, Heather,

Gunbarrel, Ann Beadell and Gary Junction. Anyhow, after three days of potholes, bulldust and corrugations, we were back on the black heading to Kalgoorlie via Laverton, Leonora and Menzies.

After a day's vehicle maintenance in Kalgoorlie, it was, 'Okay, so which way do we go now?'

'Bugger it,' was the conclusion. So we decided to follow the Indian Pacific railway track out as far as Haig Siding, where we intended turning south to Cocklebiddy, then back home to Adelaide along the Eyre Highway. Now, other than being a deserted railway siding, Haig has an interesting past. Back in the late 1990s, sightings of a UFO were reported just north of Haig. The story went that a two-kilometre UFO had crash-landed out in the desert, leaving three stranded aliens. On hearing this, a woman became convinced that these lost aliens needed help to fix their UFO. So she raised near-on $50,000 for lifting and welding gear and water to go out and find them – which she didn't. Following that incident, a Japanese team of UFO hunters claimed to have had satellite photos showing a strange array of lights out that way. On further investigation, the lights proved to be those of the Indian Pacific train as it passed in the night. So, unfortunately, no UFOs or stranded aliens have ever been found.

Anyhow, not long after we'd left Kalgoorlie, we came upon a veritable 'gold rush' of vehicles also heading in an easterly direction. Without knowing why, Donn remarked, 'There must be a keg on somewhere. Let's follow the trail.' So we did. And how true he was. Although, there was not just one keg, but literally truckloads of them, and everything came to a halt at the railway siding of Rawlinna – population negligible. Rawlinna being at the junction of the Trans Access Road and the Connie Sue Highway coming down from the north. It was then 'welcome to the two-day Rawlinna Rodeo and Gymkhana'.

'Quick!' Staking a camping spot was everyone's priority and, before long, a 'pop-up' town was born. The event – the Nullarbor Muster – was held around the temporarily converted sheep yards. The logistics of running such an event in such a remote location had obviously fallen on various committees and many, many volunteers. And what a great job they did. To cater for the creature comforts of well over a thousand people, everything had to be brought in. There were pop-up food stalls, pop-up toilets, pop-up showers, pop-up bars, pop-up outdoor kitchens, pop-up souvenir stalls, pop-up first aid stations, portable generators, water trucks, fuel trucks ... and lots and lots of grog.

In contrast to all these pop-ups stood relics from a past era, such as the old railway siding and building and the homestead with its outbuildings. There was also an airstrip, which was well used during the muster. The Rawlinna railway platform even played host to interstate and international guests from the Indian Pacific, with an outdoor meal, which provided them with a bit of respite from the rollicking of the train. Adding a bit more Australiana to their stopover was the kangaroos who, seemingly ignorant of all the flashing of cameras, hopped around of their own free will in the hopes of snaffling some left over salad. The roos also had free reign amongst the vast congregation of tents and caravans – after all, it was their patch – and, of course, the banning of dogs for the event would've provided them extra confidence.

To me, rodeos had seemed very macho-manly sorts of things, especially for the participants. However, in this case, the girls were no shrinking violets and they excelled in the gymkhana and other horse–man–woman events. Adding colour to the rodeo were the arena clowns. They were fascinating to watch. Their knowledge of the animals they had to deal with and their athleticism and courage held me spellbound. So much so that I now reckon, if it wasn't for those clowning unsung heroes, rodeos would not be possible.

What's more, very rarely have I been to a setting like this where the inevitable fight hasn't broken out. I mean, nothing brings the macho out of a bloke more than a few beers and pretty women. Though, to my surprise, hardly a punch landed its mark nor a wrestling hold was held too tight and the bouncers, who were only doing their job, were good-naturedly booed and heckled by the revellers. In fact, the whole rodeo gymkhana atmosphere got my son so interested that these days he's now riding in rodeos.

Now, while four-wheel-drive mode had been used in getting to Rawlinna that seemed no longer necessary. However, unfortunately, with another storm front approaching, the weather predictions weren't favourable. So, with inky black clouds building in the west, the four of us decided, 'Let's get the hell out of here.'

After a quick study of the map, we tried our luck on a one-hundred-and-fifty-kilometre dirt track heading south from Rawlinna to Cocklebiddy. And with only ten kilometres from Cocklebiddy, it started to rain heavily. Still, we made it. Then, after things had dried out a bit, it was back onto the bitumen Eyre Highway and, after two more days travel, we were home. But what a trip ay? Even though Rawlinna hadn't been on my bucket list and then, to have stumbled across it by accident, and on such a huge occasion, none of us could've wished for a better Aussie experience.

Footnote – Rawlinna is on the Nullarbor Plain, in Western Australia, along the Trans-Australian Railway, about nine hundred kilometres east of Perth and three hundred and fifty kilometres west of the Western Australia–South Australia border. The traditional owners of the land are the Mirning, Ngalea and Wangai peoples who named the region *Oondiri*, meaning 'waterless'. The actual word *Nullarbor* comes from the Latin *nullus* and *arbor* meaning 'no trees': thus the topography is flat, with sparse saltbush and bluebush outcrops and small belts of Myall and Myoporum trees. Edward John Eyre and his companion Wylie passed through the area on their 1841 expedition, with Eyre commenting that the landscape was 'a blot on the face of nature'. The annual rainfall is under two hundred millimetres – eight inches – and summer temperatures often rise above 38 degrees Centigrade, or above the old hundred in the waterbag.

Rawlinna has a population of less than thirty, at best. Australia's largest operating sheep station – Rawlinna Station – covers an area of over a million hectares and the record number of sheep ever shorn at the station is eighty thousand. There's also a small lime mine nearby and the lime is used in the gold production process at Kalgoorlie.

The Indian Pacific is the successor to the Trans-Australian; named so when the line was opened in 1917. Before the introduction of diesel locomotives in 1951, Rawlinna was one of four major towns across the Nullarbor that had Commonwealth Railways-run workshops plus facilities such as a food store, a bakery and a school. Notable derailments of trains near Rawlinna occurred in 1930, 1955, 1975, 2015 and 2016. All Commonwealth Railways buildings are now demolished, leaving only a handful of buildings remaining. Back in the 1960s, Rawlinna was also the destination of Len Beadell and his Gunbarrel Road Construction Party when they pushed the Connie Sue Highway south through Neal Junction to Warburton. These days Rawlinna's a railway stop for the Indian Pacific on its near-on four thousand-kilometre journey from Sydney and Perth.

Each year, visitors from far and wide gather to enjoy Rawlinna's Nullarbor Muster, which benefits a number of charities. For the casual traveller, please note, there are no services at Rawlinna – no shops, pubs or accommodation – and fuel is limited, so it's necessary to carry your own supplies, including grog and water.

Redhill – SA

I'm the son of a general store owner, and very proud of it. Because we lived in Redhill and there was no hospital in town, I was born at nearby Crystal Brook. Back then, Redhill was only a one-pub town – the Eureka – then it had two general stores, ours and another one, and a population of about four hundred. As for my family, my grandfather was a storekeeper just over the hill, on the coast, at Port Broughton. Then, when Dad returned from the war, he did a few odds and sods before making the shift from his birthplace to buying the Redhill general store.

I'd say Dad was probably encouraged into the business by his father with the idea of establishing a small chain of family stores. I've actually got a stencil which says 'Kerrs' Stores' though, in my grandfather's case, a heart attack put an end to that. As for myself, almost from the get-go, I helped out in all parts of our store. We sold just about everything, apart from fruit and veg. We had a large range of hardware. We had haberdashery, clothing, shoes and basic medicines. If we didn't have something, once a week Dad'd go to Adelaide to restock. And that sort of broad base of supplies and the skills that came with it made for an interesting environment to grow up in. See, during the Depression and war years people had to make-do and I was fortunate enough to be on the end of that. And because Dad was often in his shed making or repairing things, I learnt the basic of electrics, carpentry and welding. So I could turn my hand to most things and I wasn't afraid to give most things a go.

I went to Redhill Primary School. It averaged about sixty students. The schoolmaster's house was in a fenced off part of the property. At first, a husband taught upper-primary and his wife taught the lower school. After they moved on, a schoolmaster taught upper-primary and a single woman, usually just out of teachers college, would teach the juniors. I enjoyed those years. It was a two-roomed building with large grounds. There was a woodworking room, a garden, a large stony oval, an asphalt playing area and, like everyone did back then, there was a large incinerator where we burnt all our rubbish. As a kid, I guess I was a bit of a tear-about – a handful. So, whereas my sister and brother stayed at home and went to Snowtown Area School, my mother had higher aspirations for me and I was sort of pushed down to Adelaide for my high school education. It wasn't a private school, just public. Thinking as I am now, perhaps there were other things at play too. With my aging grandmother living alone, I stayed with her. So maybe there was an expected responsibility there.

Anyhow, with me going back and forward from Adelaide to Redhill, by the end of high school I was 50–50, city–country. And even though running a country store was of interest, there was no future in it. By then Redhill was struggling to support two stores and so the business was winding down and, of course, with cars being more reliable, people had started shopping in the bigger centres like Port Pirie. So in 1967, I went to uni. By then, Dad had closed the store and my parents had bought the local post office–telephone exchange. It might've even been one of the last manual plug-in exchanges in South Australia. So, just as they were at the store, my parents remained integral to the town's communication network. When a call came through to the exchange, a bell would ring to alert my parents. They'd then patch the call through to whoever it was and, if no one was at home, the caller would leave a message with us and we'd pass it on when the people returned home. It was a twenty-four hour a day job, and one of the local girls would work of a night as the telephonist. But the rest of the time, it was either Mum or Dad, or if any of us kids were around, we'd pitch in and help.

With Redhill being on the Broughton River, in an alluvial valley, it was mainly wheat and sheep, barley and beef cattle. Later on, crops like lupins and peas came in. I believe Broughton River's the longest river in South Australia and, for us kids, it was the centre of our social life. We had a series of swimming holes where we'd all meet up for a swim and swing out into the river from a rope tied to a tree. And, over generations, as we found newer and/or safer places to swim, our favoured locations shifted. Although the river had permanent water, by midsummer it'd start going green with algae, and we weren't supposed to swim in it. But kids being kids, we still did and, to the best of my knowledge, no one got seriously ill.

The Eureka Hotel was more the social centre for the adult males. It was a solidly built two-storey pub with a bar and accommodation rooms upstairs. Even though there was a little lounge area, as it happened back then, the women sat out in the car and were taken out a shandy or whatever and the kids raspberry and/or lemonade. The pub had some interesting licensees over the years – Barbara being one of them. Barbara was a real card. She was only about four foot six inches and, by gee, she could swear like a trooper. Though, whenever she was out in public, she'd change character and it'd be the full dress and makeup and she'd wear furs and strut around the place, putting on a posh accent.

Barbara's right-hand man was Harry and, oh my God, they fought like demons. They'd been together for years and rumour had it they were lovers. Harry was the barman and he had his own room – supposedly. I remember Barbara's huge black limousine, an old Humber or a Hudson maybe. Probably a pre-war model that'd been rebuilt. There was no other car like it in the district. It almost had a gangster feel to it, and it moved very slowly – crawled. Barbara parked it in the old stables, out the back of the pub. We used to go pigeoning in there. There was a lot of other stuff in there as well, including some old beer-pulls, the ones with the porcelain handles that they used to pull down the beer with. Later on I thought, Oh well, why not snaffle a relic of my hometown? And I've still got them.

Barbara had long-time connections in the racing industry. Whenever she and Harry went to the city, it was usually to do with horseracing. So there was gambling in the pub. Harry ran the SP bookie outfit, which was highly illegal. This was back in the six o'clock closing days, so everyone was kicked out at six. But between the old blacksmith's shop and the pub was a huge peppercorn tree, with enough weeping foliage to reach the ground. And that made it the perfect hiding place for those who wanted to kick on after-hours, drinking bottled beer which, no doubt, was sold through the back door of the pub.

We also had a series of interesting policemen. Redhill was only ever a one-copper town and he – as it always was in those days – was supplied with a family house. It was generally a married man with a long-suffering wife and a few kids in tow, which boosted school numbers. Some coppers, like Tom Howie, knew how to integrate into the community. Tom had two daughters and a son around our age. I was later the debutante partner to their eldest daughter. Another policeman was Copper Don. Copper Don was a real bastard. He didn't have a clue about country policing. He kept himself separate from the community and was determined to bring law and order to the place. He was married, but they didn't have any kids, which proffered the rumours about his manly prowess. And he had an unfortunate stutter and mouth shape which didn't endear him. Like, he didn't have any lips really, just a sort of slit, which made him speak in an odd sort of way.

Copper Don didn't have an official police car. He drove his old clapped out Falcon. Actually, I can't ever remember a police car being in town. It was always the local copper's car, so I guess there was compensation for mileage. And being the tight-knit community we were, word would get out when and where Copper Don was in hiding; ready to book anyone who was speeding. So, when anyone got to the spot, they'd slow down and give him a wave as they passed. Or they'd have a bit of fun and plant their foot and leave him behind, chasing in their dust in his clapped out old Falcon. It was the same with the 6 o'clock closing. Word would get out that he was on the prowl. So by the time he got to the peppercorn tree, no one would be there. In all, Copper Don and the community didn't prove compatible, so I believe he was eventually moved on.

But Redhill was quite a pretty town in many respects. It came into being in the late 1880s, as a railhead. Originally, it had two pubs: the Eureka and another, the second pub being the older of the two. It was your typical single-storey outback pub, with an enclosed internal courtyard and rooms down each side, with a big verandah and stables out the back. In my time, a local council worker lived there, as his residence. This council worker also had a block in town where he grew fruit trees and ran a few cows. Of a morning, we'd take the billy can and a couple of shillings down there and pick up our milk. He also grew hay and we'd help build his haystacks. Redhill was interesting like that. People would grow wheat or hay on their town blocks to feed their horses and cows, and so, visually, Redhill seamlessly merged in with the local rural landscape.

Other blocks were farmed by the community and the profits went back into the town. With Redhill having three churches – Methodist, Church of England and Catholic – I guess there was some sort of religious divide. But we all came together around sport and other community activities. If something needed to be done, everyone got together and got it done. Not only for the likes of sports club rooms or institutes or the school, but also individually. If you wanted a shed built, somebody would help with the cement, somebody would help with the formwork and so on. So it was good like that.

The town got its name from the red hill that appeared during summer, when the grassy knoll died off. It's marked by two quarries, which became a significant geological marker as the boundary of where two pieces of earth shifted. When they were building the town, they dug the first quarry to get rock for the houses and they'd crush the stone for the roads. Then, when the second quarry opened up on the other side of the hill, the first one became the town dump. As a kid, I spent a lot of time there. It was an interesting place. Like the saying goes, 'Someone's rubbish is another person's treasure.' But there was an etiquette to it all, like a silent barter system. If you were scouring the dump and someone arrived to offload their rubbish, you'd move well away to give them the courtesy of space. After they'd dumped their rubbish, you'd allow them time to leave. Then, after they'd left, you'd move in and start going through what they'd dropped off. So there was never any social contact. You discreetly slid past each other – ships in the night. But the dump was full of resources which everyone appreciated and everyone used. I pulled lots of stuff out of there, most of which I still have. I even have the front-door nameplate of the Eureka Hotel, which must've been tossed in the dump after Barbara sold the pub.

Anyhow, because I'd salvaged the old counter from our store and I had the original building plans, plus some of the ironwork from off the front, when I heard that someone had bought our old store and was intending to do it up and live in it, I thought, Well, these things belong back in the store. So I decided to drop by and give them to the new owner and tell him some of the history of the place. But when I got there, no one was home and the place had been stripped bare. He'd obviously started the project but then dropped it. There were things like a wheelbarrow, left lying outside, rusting and full of rainwater. It was just a mess really.

In fact, the whole town felt like that. In my time, a lot of people who lived in Redhill were retired farmers whose children had taken over their properties. So, even though it had an aging population, it was still active and people still took pride in the place. But these days, there's an influx of new people looking for low-cost accommodation, and they're generally less engaged with the community. So to see some of those lovely old stone buildings look uncared for and/or falling apart well, what can I say?

Nonetheless, a few years ago I went back for Redhill's 150th. It was a big turnout, held in the football clubrooms, and it proved to be a great occasion for formal storytelling. First up was an old bloke who presented the history of the football club, through all its iterations. 'Well, in 18-whatever-it-was, Redhill Football Club was formed,' which he elaborated on in full and minute detail. 'Then, when the numbers fell, we amalgamated with ... then when the numbers fell there, we amalgamated with ... then when the numbers fell there, we amalgamated with,' and so on and so on. It was so formally dull that it was humorous. Next was a woman who'd been in my class at school. Along with her sister, they related their family history from first settlers through to the present day. Then there was Keith. 'Oh, where's Keith?' ''E's out the back havin' a beer.' 'Well, Keith's gonna be our next speaker. 'E's got some stories.' Given time, Keith rocks up, beer in hand, with a big grin, and tells a few crackers: one of them about drinking under the peppercorn tree, another about leaving Copper Don trailing in his dust.

Keith's actually the grandson of Redhill's original blacksmith and, along with his father, Eric, they were a family of master blacksmiths. They could mend anything, invent anything, make anything. See that trailer out there? It was originally an old ex-World War Two American Willys jeep trailer that Eric modified from being a water-carrier to a cart-anything trailer, with a flap on it; just perfect for my dad to go back and forth to Adelaide to replenish his stores. And now I've inherited it. Anyhow, Keith still lives in the original blacksmith's house in Redhill, and he still works in the blacksmith's shed. These days he makes sculptures, some serious pieces and some as garden ornaments. But the thing is, he loves what he's doing. He's having a good life. In Redhill, he's found his place in the world at large, and he lives and works in the same place his dad and grandad lived and worked in.

Footnote – Redhill – population around a hundred – is on the Broughton River and is at the foot of the Flinders Ranges, one hundred and eighty kilometres north of Adelaide. The town was established in the late 1880s, under the name of Broughton, with a hotel, blacksmith, general store, a few other businesses and three churches. It was renamed Redhill in 1940. A primary school operated for many years but closed in 1994. In its day, Redhill was the terminus of the broad gauge branch railway line, which was intended to continue to Port Pirie to connect with the standard gauge Trans-Australia Railway. The link, completed in 1938, resulted in a rare triple gauge yard. In the 1980s the Redhill line was diverted to Crystal Brook.

These days the Princes Highway bypasses the town, which is recognised for its sculpture of a draughthorse pulling a plough with a pioneer farmer behind it. The Redhill Geological Site is listed on the South Australian Heritage Register and the original district council office is now a museum. The Eureka Hotel, built in 1878, is a solid two-storey building. The pub is now closed.

Rufus – NSW

In memory of George Craker.

Yes, and so about George: George Craker. He's no longer with us unfortunately, but both George and I attended teachers college in Sydney back in the late 1950s. George came from Broken Hill. He was the son of a miner and he was boarding in a house in Bondi. I was also at Bondi, though living with my family. Initially, I think George was quite lonely. As you may imagine, the Sydney lifestyle was a very different one from that of Broken Hill. But he was a gregarious sort of fellow and, once he got to know a few people, he started to enjoy the place. What also helped was that he was very active in sport. Anyhow, George and I became good mates. In fact, my parents came to embrace him as, virtually, another son.

George's first appointment out from teachers college was to a little place down in the south-western corner of New South Wales called Rufus, which is on the Rufus River. With the Rufus River being so short, the township was set in amongst a network of creeks and anabranches that led into Lake Victoria. In those days, the closest town to Rufus of any note would've been Wentworth, which is at the junction of both the Murray and Darling Rivers. Wentworth would've been a good two or three hours' drive away, along a rough dirt road. So, as you may imagine, Rufus was a very isolated place.

When George arrived to take up his teaching job, Rufus was little more than a rabbit-oh community. By that I mean, the few families who lived there somehow survived on the money they made from killing and selling rabbits. So it was a very poor community, and a very small one. I don't know what the exact population would've been but it couldn't have been too many. Actually, I remember George telling me about an incident, during an election. As usually happens, the school building doubled as the polling booth. At that stage, George was still only eighteen, which made him too young to be a returning officer. So he volunteered to be a polling clerk.

Anyhow, on this particular Election Day, when the polls had closed and they started counting the votes, the local returning officer recognised every single one of the ballot papers, either by the handwriting or the cross or the order in which they'd placed their votes. So he knew exactly how everyone had voted and George reckoned that, on a few occasions, when the returning officer looked at a ballot paper, he'd burst out with, 'I told that bloody so-and-so not to vote for that so-and-so party.' So that might give you some idea as to just how small the community of Rufus was, because this returning officer knew everyone, and he knew everything. Well, he thought he did.

Now, I can't remember George saying too much about the actual school itself, other than it was within walking distance from where he lived. Though, from what I could gather, it was only tiny, say with a maximum of ten students, and that it had very limited resources. And being a primary school, the pupils ranged from five to fourteen, and those few who did go on to high school had to go to Wentworth. Still, I believe George had a moderately enjoyable time with the children and he seemed to get on quite well with the parents.

However, I distinctly recall him describing his living conditions as 'absolutely appalling'. The place the education department found for him was a long-abandoned Main Roads Department old bark hut. It stood precariously on top of a dirt floor and was built of a basic wooden pole-frame structure, with galvanised iron tacked on as walls and a roof. So it was searing hot in summer and freezing cold in winter. As for furniture, he'd been provided with a well-worn wire-strung single bed, a well-worn horsehair mattress, a dilapidated table and one wonky chair.

For cooking, there was one of those old wooden stoves, which might've helped keep the bark hut warm in winter but, in summer, it made the place unbearable to live in. I forget now, but there must've been a shower or a wash-room somewhere in the place. Though I do remember him saying that the loo was one of those outdoor long-drop types which was a fair walk away, down a track. And that was all he had. That was his sole residence; just this rickety old shack with a dirt floor, a few sticks of furniture and a dunny down yonder. Still and all, as he said, 'At least I had a roof over my head, even if it did leak.'

However, what proved to make his living even more untenable was that, once the school day had finished, there were no social activities whatsoever at Rufus. So, at the end of the school day, he'd retreat back to his little shack, sit there all alone, and read and read and read. Come to think of it, I don't think there was even a wireless in the place that he could listen to and, what's more, I'm now wondering if the only lighting he had was an old kerosene lamp.

But, as George soon found out, Rufus had a history of young men arriving there, straight out of teachers college, and suffering mental breakdowns. This was due to them having to live such an isolated existence, under such terrible conditions. To that end, the Inspector of Schools would occasionally turn up just to make sure George was still alive. And so, with George being well and truly stuck at Rufus, unfortunately, it wasn't long before the loneliness started to get to him. Making his life even more unbearable was the fact that, with Rufus River being set amongst this network of creeks and anabranches, the mosquitoes were making a real meal of him. And, if the mozzies weren't enough to try and cope with, then came frog-mating season. Hundreds of frogs. Thousands of frogs. Millions of frogs. And with it being mating season, all these frogs became extremely hyperactive, particularly at night.

George reckoned that the gigantic gaggle of croaking frogs got so loud that his nights were chock-a-block-full of their sound. It was so unbearable that he could hardly hear himself think, let alone catch a wink of sleep. And this catastrophic cacophony of noise continued night after night after night ... until one night, George found himself running around outside his old bark hut, like a crazed madman, armed with a shovel, trying to kill every frog he could find; which, of course, was an impossible task because there were just too many of them. Far too many. Plus it was pitch dark. Plus, on top of all that, he was being eaten alive by the myriad of mozzies that were viciously attacking him. So there he stood, out in this remote place – Rufus – a desperately lonely figure, alone in the deep darkness. That's when the thought struck him, I'm going insane. Which he was. And so, like the many before him, he'd found himself on the verge of a complete nervous breakdown.

Still, he somehow managed to last out the school year at Rufus, which was some sort of miracle in itself. Then, in those days, the inducement from the Department of Education was that, if you'd survived a year or so in a remote area, they'd appoint you to a more favourable location. And that's what happened. The following year George was appointed to Frederickton, up on the north coast of New South Wales, near Kempsey. By that stage, he was recently married, and so George and his new wife headed north, to Frederickton. When they arrived, they were shown to their little school residence – their new home to be.

With no one having lived there for quite some time, the grass and garden needed work. But that wasn't a problem. A bit of gardening would be enjoyable. In comparison to Rufus, it looked great. That's until they opened the front door and discovered that the snakes, rats, spiders, mice, cockroaches, plus a number of bats and birds and just about every known and unknown sort of vermin had taken up residence inside the house. So George and his new wife spent their first couple of weeks at Frederickton cleaning the place up, in an attempt to try and make it habitable. Although as George said, 'At least the place had a wooden floor.'

Footnote – Rufus is in south-western New South Wales, near on nine hundred kilometres from Sydney, set on the Rufus River. The river itself is only five or so kilometres long, and runs from Lake Victoria into the Murray River, close to both the Victoria and South Australia borders.

Charles Sturt visited Rufus River in 1830 and named it after his red-haired – 'rufus' – travelling companion, George Macleay. A number of conflicts between Europeans and the local Maraura people followed, leading to the 1841 Rufus River Massacre. In retribution for attacks they'd made on white drovers and their stock, on the newly opened overland stock route, which followed an old Maraura route, it's been recorded that thirty or more Maraura were killed, ten were wounded and four were taken prisoner. Only one European was wounded. A subsequent inquiry, led by Sturt, deemed that the actions of the Europeans was justifiable. It also concluded that the original cause of much of the trouble had been the Europeans engaging in sexual relations with Maraura women without providing them the promised food and clothing.

Rufus has a population of less than thirty. Rufus River is reputedly an excellent spot for fishing, camping and birdwatching – though take plenty of insect repellent! There are no pubs in the town: the nearest being around forty kilometres away, in the South Australian towns of Renmark and Paringa.

Sloping Main – Tas

G'day, my name's John and being the true history buff I am, I'm afraid I can't tickle you with any rip-roaring pub yarns. If you want some, you'd best go to Hobart. Anything and everything goes in Hobart. But see, now here's a thing: Tasmania's always been divided in two – north and south. Same as the two main breweries. The rule is, you don't drink Boags beer south of Swansea and you don't drink Cascade north of Swansea. And for many, many years it's been that way. That's why the AFL reckon it's too difficult to get a united Tasmanian footy team up and going. Because, as soon as you say where a Tasmanian AFL team is going to be based – like north or south, Launceston or Hobart – you'll lose half of your supporters.

All that aside, I was born and bred here in Sloping Main. We're a sleepy little settlement, in south-eastern Tasmania, down on the Tasman Peninsula, with a population of just under fifty. To give you a better idea, Sloping Main's thirty kilometres north-west of the old convict colony at Port Arthur, twenty kilometres from Nubeena, and Frederick Henry Bay takes in our western to north-eastern shores. In saying all that, I've already created a couple of points of conjecture. I wasn't actually born here in Sloping Main; I was born in Hobart. That was in the late 1930s. My mother went up there a month or so before I was due because, back then, Sloping Main was still pretty much in the horse and cart era. And with it being mostly dirt and gravel roads between here and Hobart, it would've taken her a couple of days to cover the hundred or so kilometres to Hobart hospital.

But apart from the week I was in Hobart being born, it's true: I've lived here in Sloping Main all my life.

So now to the second point of conjecture: some people call it Sloping Main while others call it Slopen Main, and, at various stages, it's even been called Storring or Sterring. The area was first mapped in 1792 by the French explorer d'Entrecasteaux. Whaling stations were then set up in the 1820s, out in the bay, on what's known as Slopen Island. In the second edition of Matthew Flinders' 1800 map, it's written as Sloping Island. It's now written as Slopen Island on Australian charts and Sloping Island on the English and French charts. So there you go. What a mess. Though, as far as I've been able to find out, it all stems from a feller – Joshua Slopen – who I believe was the first farmer in the area. And so, from way back, my grandfather decided to retain the original name of Slopen. So the family farm's called Slopen Main Marsh and the Marsh bit is because there's a lot of marshland on it.

Actually, the area's got a lot of history. It was settled by Europeans, well before Port Arthur was built for the convicts. So the old weatherboard buildings that you can see around here are among the oldest on the Tasman Peninsula. How that all came about was that the first Attorney-General, of what was then known as Van Diemen's Land, was a feller called Joseph 'Tice' Gellibrand. I'm talking back in the early 1800s, here – forty or so years before the name of Van Diemen's Land was changed to Tasmania – and during his time, Tice Gellibrand became an early settler to this area. But being on the shores of a bay, the lower part of the property had about five hundred acres of marshland. And when he tried to drain it, there wasn't a steep enough fall for it to drain properly. So the outlet got blocked until a decent flood could flush it out.

But none of that stopped the early settlers from bringing stock here. In they came and took over the Indigenous people's land.

Then, just as the convict settlement of Port Arthur was opening up, coal deposits were discovered. With Port Arthur needing coal, the powers-that-be offered Tice Gellibrand some land on the Derwent River, near Hobart, as a swap for his land here. So he agreed to the deal and he got the better of it because the local coal turned out to be of such low grade that it spat in the home fires, which, of course, caused a few problems. So coal mining never really got up and running and, after the convict labour left in the mid-1800s, the coalmines were leased to private enterprise. And even they couldn't make a go of it.

My grandfather – old man Price – had an early association with the area. Not long after the convicts left, he started visiting in the summer months to go swan and duck shooting. Then, after he married a woman from nearby Nubeena, they came to live and farm here permanently, at Sloping Main. In those days, it was all mixed farming. Farmers did whatever they could to make a living. A regular trading boat came down from Hobart, visiting all the small settlements along the peninsula. So the locals milked a few cows, made and sold a bit of butter; they sold cream and swapped their produce for whatever they couldn't produce themselves.

As for myself, being a fair distance from the nearest school, I started out doing correspondence. Then in the late 1940s, they created an Area School and bussed us outlying kids in there. It was actually the first and only school I ever attended and, I can tell you, when you weren't used to schoolyard bullying and all the other things associated with kids' gatherings, it was a big shock. A hell of a shock actually. On the other hand, my sister did quite well. She went on to boarding school in Hobart, then got into nursing. Instead, I quit school when I was fifteen and I came back on the farm. My father needed a worker – and a cheap one at that – and I've been here ever since. So that's been my lot in life. If things had turned out different, I probably wouldn't have chosen to be a farmer. Though by necessity,

I became one. I was more interested in machinery. So after a very good wool season in the early '50s we bought our first tractor and, because Dad remained a horse man, I was the one who did all the tractor driving and maintenance. And I enjoyed that side of things.

In the earlier days, there wasn't a lot of fencing and it was pretty much all sheep. In our case, we had an overall area of around 3000 acres. And as I was going to tell you when you were writing the volunteer firies book – as the Aboriginals had done for thousands of years – us farmers used to do patch burning. Patch burning's basically where you burn certain patches of land. So when you burnt an adjacent patch the next season, it was less likely to escape. It was like a patchwork quilt or a checkerboard method of burning really. And, with not wanting the burn to get away – also as the Aboriginals had done – we lit what's called a cool fire. A cool fire's lit where there's not a great deal of vegetation or fuel load on the ground. So the fire just dawdles along in the lower scrub, making it easier to control. Which is what we wanted because, if there was too much of a fuel load on the ground, we'd get a fire of a greater height, which could easily get into the canopy of the trees. And once a fire gets up into the tree tops – *whoosh!* – it can get away from you.

The other advantage of patch burning is that, when it came to mustering, the sheep tended to group around the younger shoots that'd germinated on a previously burnt patch. And this is where the Aboriginals and our forebears had it right. They were always burning. Although, for the Aboriginals, I don't think they were doing it so much to prevent wildfires. They did it more so to attract wild game to come in and nibble on the freshly germinated vegetation which, in turn, made for easier hunting. I mean, who'd want to chase a kangaroo for miles and miles when you could just spear one in your own backyard so to speak.

Anyhow, that's just a bit of history about Sloping Main and how my family come to live here and how I come about and how I'm still living here. But like I said, if you want some real rip-roaring pub yarns you'd better go to Hobart. But just be mindful of what type of beer you drink!

Footnote – Sloping Main is a small settlement, set upon a sandy beach, in a wide bay bound by Black Jack Point and Lobster Point. As Van Diemen's Land's Attorney-General, Joseph Tice Gellibrand attempted to make changes that he believed were needed to the new colony's legal system. When this brought him into conflict with Lieutenant-Governor George Arthur, he was dismissed from his position. He then continued to work as a barrister and editor of the *Tasmanian*. Over this time, he purchased a number of properties, including on the Tasman Peninsula, where Sloping Main is today. In 1837, Gellibrand and a companion disappeared on a summer expedition into the bush country. The thinking is that they might've lost their horses and died in the heat. The mystery remains unsolved.

In 1833, coal was discovered near Sloping Main, and so began Tasmania's first operational mine. For fifteen years, convicts worked in trying conditions, in two eight-hour shifts, having to extract the day's quota of twenty-five tonnes per shift – or else be punished. By 1847, the main shaft was at a depth of over three hundred feet. By 1893, a hundred and fifty convicts and twenty-nine officers lived at the mine site. Carts ran along rail tracks down to the jetties for loading. Large stone barracks housed the convicts and a chapel. A bakehouse and a store were erected. Solitary cells were dug into the underground workings to punish those who'd committed crimes at the mines. On the hillside above stood the comfortable quarters of the commanding officer, a surgeon and other officials.

The coal mines were closed in 1848 – on 'moral and financial grounds'. The Coal Mines Historic Site is one of eleven sites that, together, form the Australian Convict Sites World Heritage Property.

Tarnagulla – Victoria

In memory of Wayne Kennedy.

Dad was the eldest of eleven. He was born in 1920, in the gold-mining and farming area of Newbridge, a little place twenty-five mile west of Bendigo. The story goes that, in readiness for Dad's birth, my grandfather put Grandma in their horse-drawn wagon – a dray – and headed off to Inglewood Hospital. Anyhow, they only got a couple of mile down the track before Dad decided to pop out. With no longer having a reason to go to Inglewood, Grandad then turned the dray around and they came back home. So that may give you some idea as to the life Dad was about to lead – a very independent one. Like, later on, in his early teenage years, he decided school wasn't for him. 'Bugger this,' he said, 'I'm out'a here.' So he went woodcutting and things around the place.

When Dad was old enough to get his driver's licence, he headed off to Melbourne and got work in a munitions factory in Footscray. The war had started by then and, with that sort of job being an essential service, he was encouraged to stay there and do his bit for the war effort. Dad met Mum when he was twenty-five and Mum was nineteen and, after they married, they worked around Footscray for a while before coming back to Newbridge. Dad then took on itinerant work like timber-cutting, out in the bush, or he'd go grape picking up at Mildura or, when the spuds were ready to be dug up by hand and bagged, he'd head down around the Ballarat area to do that.

I came along in '47 – the first of three boys – and, when I was ten, Dad bought an old house, five mile up the road from Newbridge, at Tarnagulla. It cost five hundred quid, which was a lot of money back then. Dad was still cutting timber: mainly ironbark and box for railway sleepers, fence posts and firewood. With no chainsaws in them days, Dad used a swing-saw blade and a pull-push crosscut saw. Dangerous bloody things they were too. So they'd fell a tree with the blade, then log it off. But Dad was forever telling us kids, 'To make a quid yer've always gotta have somethin' goin' on, on the side.' So while he was timber-cutting, he befriended the local copper and, on the side, he started running an SP – single price – bookie set-up at the pub. Being highly illegal, Dad'd grease the copper's hand with beer. The old man was pretty shrewd like that. In fact, we were the first family in Tarnagulla to have a TV. I don't know how that came about but, from then on, the house was always full of adults and kids who'd drop in for a look-see.

Then, when they were laying the rail line from Dunolly, through the Mallee, to up Quambatook way, Dad got a job in the railways. So he'd go away during the week and leave Mum at home with us three boys. Then Dad had an accident. A Casey – a single-cylinder coffeepot type trolley – jumped the tracks and it ran over him and smashed up his arm. They made him a flagman then: like he'd flag the trains in and out and, if something was happening further up the line, he'd warn the oncoming train driver by laying detonators on the track. So Dad was still with the railways when my middle brother – Preston – got killed in a truck accident in 1977. And that hit him real hard. Knocked him really. In them days, as soon as you got to sixty-five in a government job, you were out – so he soon retired. But still being fit as a mallee bull he went back woodcutting and, as a sideline, he bought a small property and ran some sheep and cattle and a few pigs.

Dad and Mum were still in the old house at Tarnagulla then and, because I was away so much, my other brother would go back up from Melbourne each weekend to make sure they were okay. Mind you, their living conditions were still pretty rugged. The kitchen had a dirt floor. There was no hot water, except for what you boiled on the stove. So they done it tough. Any rate, when they decided to renovate, Dad got help from some of his old mates, from back in the war days, when he was in the munitions factory. And mate, some of them were real buggers. They'd pinch the eye out of a needle if you gave them half a chance. One story goes that, when Dad needed some materials for the house, one of his old mates drove his truck into this big Melbourne warehouse. When no one was looking, he went into the change room, nicked a dustcoat and clipboard, then went over to the forklift driver and said – all official like – 'Load this 'n this 'n that on the truck.' And when it was all loaded up, he drove out of the warehouse and straight up to our place.

So they were pretty colourful characters. I mean, when another of Dad's old mates noticed how the newly arrived Italian immigrants didn't have Australian driving licences, he started forging them and flogging them off to them for fifty quid. True. He even made it onto the front page of the *Truth* newspaper, which was a famous paper back in them days. And when I got older and got a car, if ever I needed anything mechanical, Dad'd just spread the word and it'd somehow materialise. Oh, there was lots of other stuff too. But I'd better just leave it there. Then, when Mum got really crook and went into Maryborough Hospital, my brother and me decided they'd be better off in a retirement place. So we found a lovely little unit in Maryborough and we got it all set up and, much against Dad's grain, he went into the place. When we got Mum out of hospital, we took her to the unit to be with Dad. But she only lasted twenty-four hours and she died. So then the old man said, 'Nup, not gonna live here. I want'a go back home ter Tarnagulla.'

So we loaded him up and took him back home. But he'd done bugger all around the house. Mum'd done the cooking and everything for him. He just provided all the gear. So by the time Mum died, Dad had procured a microwave and all the bloody press-button kitchen gadgetry you'd ever need. Dad had no idea. All he could do was turn on the TV and boil the jug. So we stayed with him for a few weeks, to get him used to things. Then one day I got a call from my brother, 'You'll never believe this.'

I said, 'What?'

He said, 'The old man's so proud of himself.'

'Why?'

'He's made a jelly.'

I said, 'Anyone can make a jelly.'

He said, 'Not the old man.'

From then on, every time we visited, it'd be jelly and ice cream. And each pension day, he'd drive into Maryborough. And mate, that was scary. We were just lucky that his brother-in-law lived in Maryborough because, whenever Dad went to town, the brother-in-law would run him about everywhere. But on his way back home, Dad always dropped into the supermarket to buy a big bag of sausages, a big bag of carrots and a big bag of spuds. When he got home, he'd stick a few snags in a pot, toss in a couple of the spuds and a couple of the carrots, all as they were; no peeling, nothing. He'd boil them up, strain off the water and that was his tucker. Nothing fancy, except for his ice cream and jelly. Oh, and also his bloody McCain TV dinners for when he didn't feel like cooking. I tell you, the old man had a three-hundred-litre deep-freeze and, fair dinkum, he would've had more frozen dinners stacked in there than McCain's had in their entire bloody factory!

It was that independence thing again. Anyhow, he fended for himself until he hit his nineties, and that's when he started to get forgetful. At one point we had Home Care coming in to look after him. But he'd say, 'They do bugger all, so why the bloody hell should I have ter pay fer them?' Oh, he was tight, was the old man. As kids, he'd go crook at us for leaving the lights on, and he'd say, 'Only put enough bloody water in the jug for what yer need or yer'll be wastin' electricity.' And when he got older, during the winter months, he wouldn't get out of bed till it was daylight, because he didn't want to turn the lights or the heater on. Oh, he was a shocker like that. But when we got word that he wasn't looking after himself, we said, 'Dad, what do yer reckon about going into a retirement village?'

He said, 'Can I take me ute?

I said, 'I don't know. I suppose it depends on the place.'

So off we go. We pull up at the first place. We met some of the people and after he'd had a look around, he said, 'Nup. Can't go in here.'

I said, 'What's wrong?'

He said, 'I can't see any cars 'n they've got big fences all 'round the place.'

That was the end of that one, so we took him another place. We pull up, go in and meet some of the people. He was uneasy, so I said, 'What's wrong?'

'Have a bloody look,' he said. 'These people can't even walk. They're all in wheelchairs. So I'm not goin' in here.' Mind you, he could still run a fair distance at ninety, and at ninety-three, he could still skip. I said, 'Well, let's just go 'n have a look at one of the rooms.' And that was very nice. But when he saw the communal dining room, that was it. 'I'm not gonna eat with all these people. Look,' he said, 'most of 'em can't even feed 'emselves.' 'Anyway,' he said, 'What's it all gonna cost?'

Now this's a man who went crook at us for not turning the lights off. So I knew what was going to happen. I said, 'It's a hundred 'n seventy thousand dollars plus eighty-three per cent of your pension.'

'Like bloody hell it is!' he yelled. 'I'm not payin' that sort'a money just fer a bloody roof over me head.'

So off we go, back home. Dad was on a restricted licence by then. One time he'd driven into Bendigo to do some shopping.

He'd got himself in there okay. But on the way back out, instead of going down a road to a traffic island, then turning left to go down to some traffic lights to turn around and come back on the other side of the road to head home, he went straight down the road, straight across the traffic island, up the wrong side of the road and turned at another set of traffic lights. Even when he got outside of the city limits, he was still putting along at sixty k's and wandering all over the road. So the police pulled him over. 'Have you been drinking, sir?'

'No, I don't drink.'

'Why are you driving so slow?'

He said, 'Is that a crime?'

The copper said, 'Where do you come from?'

'Tarnagulla.'

'Have you got a licence?'

'Yes,' and he produced his licence.

When the copper saw it he said, 'Holy Jesus, it says here yer ninety somethin'.'

'Yes,' Dad said. 'And is that a crime too?'

Anyway, we got word from the local copper that, while he could still drive around Tarnagulla, under no circumstances was he allowed to leave town. By then Tarnagulla might've only had a population of seventy. The shop was long gone so there was just the pub and a post office. But that was it. You could get your milk, a newspaper and a few spuds and stuff from the post office. And I must say the post office people were great. Any bills that came in, they'd fix them up for us and we'd pay them back later. But when he really started to go downhill, we were strongly advised that he should go into care.

Much against his grain, we eventually got him into respite at a little old nursing home–hospital at Dunolly, with only a dozen or so people in it. But from the moment he moved in, he really went downhill. He kept on about how he didn't need care and that they locked him in so he couldn't get out. It was that independence thing again. He just wanted to go back home to Tarnagulla. Then one night he must've had a nightmare and, as he jumped out of bed, he fell and broke his hip. They took him to Bendigo Hospital but he died the next morning. Quick as that, no suffering, and he was gone.

Footnote – Tarnagulla is an old gold-mining town in central Victoria, one hundred and eighty kilometres north-west of Melbourne, with a population less than a hundred. European squatters arrived during the 1840s and, in 1852, one of the richest gold reefs in the world was discovered, causing a rush of five thousand prospectors, including some one thousand Chinese plus people of Greek and Italian origin. The post office opened in 1856 as Sandy Creek and was renamed Tarnagulla in 1860–61. The word Tarnagulla is said to be the phonetic spelling of the Polish word for 'black mountain' and it was also the name of a local station property.

Local government was established in 1864 and, by the following year, Tarnagulla had two banks, five bakers, three butchers, four blacksmiths, two bootmakers, one corn factory, four crushing machines, two chemists, two drapers, a fruiterer, a gold broker, an ironmonger, a miller, a painter, nine general stores, three surgeons, a share broker, a steam saw miller, a tailor, a tobacconist, two wheelwrights, a watchmaker, two breweries and four pubs. Gas street lighting was established in 1869 but electricity didn't arrive until 1950.

In 1870 the council built a swimming pool and granted licences to locals to fish in the town reservoir. A state school opened in 1874, and by 1888 the railway had arrived. In 1906 the Poseidon nugget – weighing 26.6 kilograms – was found and named after the winner of the 1906 Melbourne Cup. In 2020 two nuggets, with an estimated worth of $350,000, were found. Today the major industries include agriculture, fruit growing and flax oil production and it's near the box–ironbark forests of the Waanyarra Nature Conservation Reserve.

Tarnagulla's Golden Age Hotel was built by Joseph Foos in 1857–58, and licensed as Foos' Family Hotel. In 1861 it was renamed the Golden Age Hotel, and Foos added a hall to it.

Three Springs – WA

It's Edna here: Mad Mick's wife. Remember, we had a story in your first book of Outback Towns and Pubs – Three Springs and Arrino Siding. Now, I'm not sure what the rules are here, like whether you can also include the same town in your second book of Outback Towns and Pubs, but I've got another couple of Three Springs' stories to add.

When I first came to Three Springs, I'd say there might've been five hundred people in town. Then, by the time Mick and I left to come down to Tassie in '76, it was a lot bigger: mainly because Western Mining had moved in and they'd put in bitumen roads and they'd air-conditioned the school and there was a couple of butcher's shops, a Wesfarmers, plus another grocery store. Of course, since Western Mining's moved out, most of those places have closed. I don't think there's even a butcher now. And since the new highway's been put in along the coast way, these days, hardly anyone passes through town.

The Commercial Hotel's still up and running, and that was always a hive of activity. After they'd won the grand final, I didn't see Mick for two days. He'd gone off celebrating. That's when someone dared him to mow the top of the front bar. Always up for a challenge, he purloined a lawn mower from God-knows-where and he got to it, full throttle, running the bloody mower up and down the top of the front bar. See, back then, Mick was a bit on the wild side, so his mates would egg him on to do crazy things. But he's sort of settled down a little bit now, since we've moved down to Tassie.

But Three Springs was a great place to live and it certainly had its characters. Just the other night Mick and I were having a laugh about a mechanic feller called Jack. Jack's nickname was 'Ripper'. I mean, no one ever called him Jack. It was always Ripper, which, I presume, came from 'Jack the Ripper'. Anyhow, Ripper worked for a bloke called Don Hosken and Don had a little son, David. Of course, kids being kids, young David used to hang around the garage where Ripper fixed all the cars and that. So David knew Ripper very well and they spent a great deal of time together.

Then one Christmas, Ripper landed the job of Santa. So he got all dollied up; you know with the flowing white beard, red coat and pants, hat, boots – the whole palaver. Then as each kid's name was called out, they'd go and sit on Santa's knee and Santa would say, 'Have you been good this year?' and then ask them what they wanted for Christmas. Then it was, 'Ho, ho, ho,' and Santa would give them a small gift and the kid'd jump down off Santa's knee and run outside to open it. Anyhow, when David Hosken got called up, he goes and sits on Santa's knee. Ripper, alias Santa, says, 'Ho, ho, ho have yer been a good boy this year?'

Before he answers, young David gives Santa a good looking over, has a think, then blurts out, 'Hey, you're not Santa.'

'Ho, ho, ho, yes I am,' says Ripper. But, as quick as a flash, David says, 'Well, if you're Santa, how come yer got Ripper's watch on. What, did yer nick it off 'im or somethin'?'

So that was that one. Anyway, as you may have guessed, Mick was also a bit of a character. Back then, he drove a manual Holden sedan and I had an old bomb that I'd cart our two little boys around in. By then we were living on a farm about a mile out of Three Springs. Now, in summer, the Commercial Hotel used to have a family barbecue on Friday nights. As usual, Mick'd gone in early to warm up the bar and I came in later with the boys. Anyhow, after the barbecue, I said to Mick, 'I'm off home now to put the boys to bed.'

'Okay,' he said. 'Won't be long. After I finish up here I'll just pop int'a the bowls club 'n grab a carton of beer fer the weekend, then I'll come straight home.' See, a carton of beer was cheaper at the bowling club.

I said, 'Righto, see you soon then.'

Like I said, we were only a mile or so out of town. So after I'd put the boys to bed, I thought, I may as well stay up 'n wait for Mick. So I waited, and I waited. But no Mick. Mind you, I wasn't overly concerned because, Mick being Mick, he'd often get stuck in the pub or the club, catching up with his mates. So I wasn't bothered too much. Then it would've been after midnight – I'd just gone to bed – when I heard all this ruckus going on. I thought, Oh Lordy, here we go again, and I got up and had a look out through the front window. And down the bottom of our driveway, I could hear Mick going off something chronic. Next thing, the dogs are going off. Next thing after that I hear Mick going off at the dogs; then I hear him going off as he stamped up the steps. So I open the front door. 'Mick,' I said, 'what's happened?'

Of course, he's inebriated – as usual. 'Oh,' he slurred, 'the bloody gear box is stuffed in me car 'n I've bloody well lost all the forward gears, so I had ter reverse all the bloody way home.'

I said, 'How did you manage that?'

He said, 'Well, Pam' – Pam was Irish and, of course, Mick's Irish too – He said, 'Pam was good enough ter drive in front– behind me with her headlights shinin' so I could see where I was goin'.'

So he'd reversed all the way out of town, then home, virtually in complete darkness. The thing was, he couldn't get the car up the driveway because, when he'd got to the front gate, he'd inadvertently backed the thing into the table drain. And, with no forward gears to drive out of the drain, he'd got stuck, hadn't he. So he decided to leave it where it was and sort it out in the morning. Anyway, he wasn't much in a mood for talking, so he went to bed and, as soon as he'd hit the sack, he was snoring.

Next morning he got up with a rip-roaring hangover. 'Well,' he said, 'I'd better go 'n have a look at this bloody car. Can yer grab some rope 'n come down in your old bomb 'n help pull me out'a the ditch?'

By now the boys had woken up. So while Mick went down to inspect his car, I went and got some rope and got the boys in the car, jarmies and all, and off we went. By the time we got there, Mick's in the car, fiddling around with this, that and the other, and he'd started it. Then very sheepishly, he said, 'It's okay. Yer can go home now.'

Next thing he drives straight out of the table drain and he heads off, into town. So I'm thinking, What the hell's going on? He said that the car had lost its forward gears and now he's driven straight out of the drain and headed off to town. Anyhow, a while later, he turns up home with the Sunday paper. I said, 'Mick, what's going on? I thought the car had lost its forward gears?'

'Oh,' he said, 'so did I. But it's all right now. Must'a fixed itself overnight.'

I thought, Oh yeah. The only reason why you couldn't get the car into a forward gear was because you were too inebriated to find them, mate. And so he'd driven all the way home in reverse and had roped in poor Pam to help him out. So, that's the Irish for you. I mean, you could almost make a joke out of it, couldn't you?

Now, before Mick and I could get married, we had to do all the paperwork. And because Mick was Catholic, we had to book an appointment to see the local priest; you know, to give him our particulars and what have you. From memory, the priest's name was Father O'Brien – another Irishman. Anyway, we arrived at the seminary, or whatever it's called, at the appointed time, on the appointed night. As we're pulling up, a car drove out past us and headed down the street. I said to Mick, 'That looks like Father O'Brien's car.'

'Yes,' said Mick, 'I reckon yer might just be right.'

Anyway, we went up to the seminary door and we knocked. But no answer. Knocked again. Same thing, no answer. Anyhow, we'd just been up the coast, fishing with some friends, and so Mick said, 'He's probably ducked down the street ter grab a packet of fags or somethin'. So let's wait in the car 'n I'll show yer some'a the photos I took while we were away.'

So we went and sat in the car and looked at these photos. After about twenty minutes, I said to Mick, 'Well, I wonder where he's gone?' I said, 'How about we go down the street and see if we can see his car parked anywhere.' So off we go, down the street, and there, right outside the Commercial Hotel, was Father O'Brien's car.

I said to Mick, 'What'll we do now?'

He said, 'Let's go in 'n find out what's goin' on.'

So we went inside. Pat Kelly – yet another Irishman – was the owner of the Commercial back then, and Mick said to Pat, 'Is Father O'Brien around? His car's parked out the front 'n we've got an appointment ter see him.' And Pat said, 'Yeah, he's here all right. But yer'd better not disturb him. There's an illegal poker game going on upstairs.'

So we left him to it. Anyhow, I rang Father O'Brien the next morning and told him that, when we'd arrived for the appointment, he wasn't there. Like, I didn't let on that we knew where he was or anything. 'Oh,' he said, 'I was unexpectedly called out on some very urgent church business.' I thought, Oh yeah, you lying so-and-so. So you think an illegal game of poker is more important than our wedding arrangements do you?

Anyway, we made another appointment and this time Father O'Brien was there. After we sat down, the first thing he said – in his thick Irish brogue – was, 'Well d' Arch Bishop may well not approve of dis marriage.'

I said, 'Why not?'

He said, 'Well, lassie, I believe yer ter be of Church of England faith 'n in d' strict eyes of d' Catholic Church it's deemed ter be a mixed marriage.' And I thought, Well, bugger me, here's this feller going on about the rules and regulations of the Catholic Church and yet, at the drop of a hat, he's off playing an illegal game of cards. I mean, it didn't worry me in the least. I think it's a whole lot of hogwash anyway, and I doubt if Mick'd been anywhere near a church since he was baptised.

Anyway, I played along with the entire charade and told Father O'Brien how I was willing to convert to the Catholic faith and that I'd attend church every Sunday and follow the strict letters of Catholic law from here till eternity. So I survived that bit. But then he started rabbiting on about the do's and don'ts of the Catholic faith; you know, about contraception and abortion and about how your child has to be baptised into the Catholic faith and all that sort of crap. By then, I'd had enough. So when he'd finished, I said, 'And what about having a flutter every now and then, Father; such as in playing illegal card games like poker and so forth? Is that a sin against the Church too?'

And that stopped him dead in his tracks. He looked at me as if he was wondering if, perhaps, maybe, I just might've somehow known about his illegal poker games down at the Commercial Hotel. Then, after what seemed like an eternity of contemplative silence, he said, 'Lassie,' he said, 'I think yer should go down to Fremantle ter get married, dey may be more understandin' on matters of the faith.'

Footnote – Three Springs is in the West Australian Wheatbelt region, just over three hundred kilometres north of Perth. Prior to European arrival, the Amangu Aboriginal people had lived on and cared for the land for thousands of years. The area was explored in 1846, by the Gregory brothers – Angus, Henry and Francis – who were looking for new country to settle. By 1894, the railway had passed through. In 1905, the government opened up land known as the Kadathinni Agricultural Area. Prior to that, the only residents were a few railway employees. In 1907 the town site – named Kadathinni –

was declared next to the railway siding. It was gazetted in 1908; the same year as a school opened and Kadathinni Farmers and Progress Association was formed.

A newsagency opened in 1909, as did a general store. The town's postal service opened in 1910 – in the local store – and the Catholic Church was consecrated. 1910 also saw the upgrading of the station's railway siding, and a stationmaster installed. In 1911, a town dam was constructed, a resident police officer arrived and a local Justice of the Peace appointed. A town hall was built in 1912. In 1914, the telephone was connected to just six subscribers. The Three Springs Road Board was established in 1929, and in the 1931–32 harvest, the district produced the highest average wheat production in the state. By 1946, the town's name of Kadathinni was changed to Three Springs, after three nearby freshwater springs.

These days Three Springs is known for its talc mine and its wildflowers and, like most Wheatbelt towns, life focuses on the grain silos, the railway line, the main street and the hotel. The Commercial Hotel was built in 1910 and, after extensive alterations, secured a general publican's licence.

Please note: in December 2021, the hotel's alarm and security cameras were upgraded, so no longer will tolerance be given to those who choose to break in and steal from the hotel. If you went to the Commercial Hotel on 8 December 2021, fully expecting 'the skimpy' to turn up, she apologies for her non-show as she was sick that night and had to cancel.

Tilpa – NSW

I've been reading your first book of Flying Doctor stories and there's a story in there that's set in Tilpa, called 'Peak Hour Traffic'. If you remember, it's about an old bushy from off a station property who had a few health issues. And so the RFDS recommended that he move into Tilpa caravan park, where they could keep a closer eye on him. Which he did. Problem being, because he'd spent most of his life out on remote properties, the traffic in Tilpa got too much for him. So he packed up and left the caravan park and moved further down the Darling River. And like, you'd be lucky to get half a dozen vehicles go through Tilpa in any one day!

Though I reckon you might've changed the bushy's name because I've been living here for yonks and the name just doesn't ring a bell. That's unless it's about old Clem. And what's more, there's never really been a caravan park in Tilpa; just a couple of powered sites over next to the old Flying Doctor clinic. I mean, there's accommodation at the Tilpa Hotel and the people who own the Tilpa Trading Post – the store – have a couple of cabins with a couple of sites for caravans. But that's it.

Just on that, the funny thing is what's now the store was originally the pub and what's now the pub used to be the store. So they've sort of swapped. That happened a heck of a long time ago now, because the pub became the pub in 1894, after it'd been the store. And the last owner, before it became a pub, was David Jones & Co. Yes, the big department store mob. Mind you, I haven't been able to categorically prove it's the one-and-the-same David Jones & Co. But I've been in touch with their archivist and she told me that, back in the 1800s, DJs did have stores out in the bush, though she found no record of anything out as far as Tilpa.

But the intrigue didn't stop there because see, the old store also included a post office. This was back when the railways only got out as far as Bourke and the paddle steamers were still plying the Darling. And my thinking is that, the bloke who owned the store-cum-post office was getting his supplies from DJs. So maybe it got to the stage where the store-post office owner got so deep into debt that the only way he could dig himself out of the poo was to hand it all over to DJs. So David Jones inadvertently became the owners of the Tilpa store-post office.

I've actually seen the original letters that were written by the bloke who owned the store-post office, personally notifying the Postmaster General how the new owners were David Jones & Co. Then three months later he notified them that David Jones had sold the lot to a feller called Edmund Montgomery Perrott and he'd turned it into a hotel. Of course, then there were the protests about having a post office in a pub. Like, they were worried that some bloke, out on a sheep station, might say to his missus, 'Look, I'm just gonna pop int'a Tilpa 'n get the mail,' and he mightn't turn up back home till a week or so later, still stinking of grog. So with that kind of thinking, the post office and the store were shifted to another building.

See, I know all this stuff because Col and I have been writing books on Tilpa for yonks. We wrote one for the Post Office Centenary back in 1980. Then we did another one in '94 for the Hotel Centenary, and we did another one after the Tilpa cricket team pulled out of the Cobar cricket competition because we couldn't muster up a team anymore. Oh, I tell you, me and Col, we've done heaps. We also wrote a book on the Tilpa War Memorial, and last year we did one for the sesquicentenary of the first settlers in the Tilpa district. So there's a lot of history around the place, because it's near on two hundred years since the explorer–surveyor Thomas Mitchell came down the Darling.

So it's been fun. Like, because the Post Office Centenary was also a fundraiser for the RFDS, Clyde, their chief pilot, flew their Nomad up from Broken Hill to do a short take-off display. And because someone knew the right person in the right place, a Caribou also turned up with eight blokes to put on a parachute display. Anyhow, just before these displays got underway, there was a car accident just out of town and so the only short take-off display we saw was when Clyde took off in the Nomad to take the injured up to Bourke Hospital. So yes, we've had quite a few celebrations. Like, in 2002, The Year of the Outback, we had a show called *The Stars on the Darling*, which was a country music concert headlined by Lee Kernaghan. And for a village with a population of six, two thousand people turned up for that one. I tell you, it was a fantastic weekend. The place was bursting at the seams.

But normally she's a pretty quiet place and not much changes. Like, the six people who live here now were also around for the 1976 floods, and that's near on fifty years ago. And of those six, three are now in their nineties and the other three are well into their eighties, or darn well close to it. So a complete generation have left the area. A lot of the females have either got married or gone to uni or got jobs away from the district. Same with the blokes: a lot of them have gone and got jobs elsewhere or, in some cases, have bought properties elsewhere. So yes, it's the same old story ay; while the properties are getting bigger and bigger, our local community doesn't.

Though in saying that, I recently heard that Tilpa might be about to go through a boom. Up until the beginning of this year, there were only three residences in town: the hotel, the store and a homestead that belongs to a property. And now it looks like there might be three new places going up in town. One's for a chap from down Griffith way, in the Riverina. He's bought a block in Tilpa and he's putting up a demountable so that, when he and his family or mates come up fishing, they've got somewhere to stay. Then, with the other two, the land's been bought by people who are working on stations around the district. One belongs to a roo shooter, but I forget what the other person does.

But look, if the story 'Peak Hour Traffic' was about old Clem, I can understand it now because he was a very private sort of bloke. He was a Rat of Tobruk who hailed from out Tibooburra way. Or maybe it was Broken Hill, because I know that a couple of his sisters taught piano there. But old Clem had been a fencing contractor around here for about forty years. And oh, he was a perfectionist. The words 'Oh, she'll do' weren't in his vocabulary. If a fence post wasn't spot-on, he'd pull the bugger out and put it back, perfect, and at his own expense and in his own time. He was that sort of a bloke.

Old Clem's dead now, of course. But he was a bit of an institution, and an independent bugger too. On one occasion he got crook and needed to see a doctor in Cobar. But rather than ring up one of us locals to see if we could give him a lift, he walked over to the edge of the road and hitched a ride to Cobar. And that's where he died; in Cobar. And in his will he'd expressed the wish to be buried in Tilpa Cemetery. And what a debacle that turned out to be; because see, the cemetery in Tilpa was on private ground and the people who owned it didn't want him buried there. So in the end he had to be buried in Cobar, which we were all upset about. As it happened, my wife and I were away at the time and when we got back and heard about it, I said, 'Well this's never gonna happen again.' I said, 'I'm gonna get onto the shire and get them to put a cemetery in Tilpa so whoever wants to get buried here, can be buried here.'

Anyhow, I spent the first seven years fighting the Environmental Protection Agency, filling out heaps of bloody forms, mainly due to them being worried about bodies being washed down the river. But while yes, the old cemetery was on the banks of the river, the proposed new one was going to be way out near the airstrip. So they didn't have much to worry about there. But I stuck with it and after eight years we eventually got our own cemetery. And we're quite proud to say that, currently, it's the only official town cemetery in Australia that's got no body buried in it. So, if you ever get around to writing another book of outback towns and pubs, keep Tilpa in mind because I'd like to throw out the challenge as to how many other towns in Australia can say that they're likely to double their residences in the next few months, and there's still no body buried in their town cemetery.

Footnote – Tilpa is on the western bank of the Darling River, in the far west of New South Wales, nine hundred kilometres from Sydney. In its heyday, it was an important river port, with paddle steamers delivering supplies to nearby sheep stations and returning downstream loaded with bales of wool. In 1886, it was reported that Tilpa had 'a good store', a telegraph office and 'a commodious hotel'. Before the bridge was completed in 1963, a punt crossed the river and the punt operator charged twenty-five shillings per thousand head of sheep.

Sheep stations still surround the town, and tourists come for the scenery and wildlife. Fishing is also popular, with the Murray cod apparently being partial to the local witchetty grubs. A feature of Tilpa is a Boer War memorial that includes an acknowledgement to drover, horseman, bush poet, military officer and war criminal, Harry 'Breaker' Morant, who was controversially executed by the British Army for murdering Boer prisoners. Tilpa also claims to have the smallest heritage trail in Australia and the only cemetery in Australia which has, currently, no interments.

The corrugated-iron-and-timber Tilpa pub was built in 1894 to service the riverboat trade. The inner walls are adorned with the personal autographs, dry-witted comments and messages of the many hundreds of people who have visited over the years, including from author Bill 'Swampy' Marsh. For a small fee – which raises money for the RFDS – you can also add your name to the wall.

Torrowangee – NSW

In Memory of Ray Cook.

Look, I'm in the middle of tasting some of George's homemade wine, so I'm a bit pressed for time just at the moment. But as for our previous communications, I did find out some historical facts about Torrowangee. But, unfortunately, the chronology didn't fit and nobody wanted to own up to being involved in the particular incident. *Oh, yes, it's a true story, all right, isn't it, George?* I'll even send down a map which will show you where the limestone quarries were.

Now, keep in mind that this was back when Big Melva's Brothel was still doing a roaring trade in Broken Hill, which may give you some idea as to the date and time of the event. In actual fact, I now live in the house that was Big Melva's Brothel.

Thanks, George, don't mind if I do.

Anyhow, do you want me to read what I've scribbled down so far?

George, would you mind not being such a cheapskate and put a bit more in my glass, thanks. I've got Swampy on the line and so this may take some time.

Okay. Are you still there? Good, here goes. It'd rained and it'd rained and it'd rained, then it'd rained some more, just to get on everyone's goat. Boots were soled, and soiled, with two-inch-thick, brown-black muddy conglomerate. The thing was, due to the torrential downpour, loading operations at the Torrowangee Limestone Quarries had ground to a halt. This meant that the train hadn't gone to Broken Hill for a couple of weeks because, as the boss stated, 'If there's no limestone ter deliver then the train doesn't run. It's company policy 'n that's that.'

Mind you, the boss was a downright bastard. Nobody liked him. He ruled Torrowangee with a dictatorial iron fist and an even stronger dictatorial iron will. In today's language, he might be termed as being a psychotic-manipulative. So much so that even Albert Brady's three-legged kelpie took cover when the boss strode down the street. And so, the aged train – Bucephalus, Pegasus, the mighty iron equine and the town's only link to the outside world – remained parked in the goods shed; there to sit, a sad and sorry sight, without fire nor steam and with its trucks hollow and bare. To that end, the driver, the fireman and the guard spent their days sitting on empty fruit boxes, shuffling damp, waxy playing cards and puffing on scrag ends of roll-me-owns. Not only did the company pay its workers poorly, it paid its train crew even less.

Top-up please, George, if you don't mind.

Anyhow, such was the situation that, by Monday, food stocks and supplies were running low at Scofield's Grocery. And still it was raining. To such an extent that there were murmurs amongst the workers, 'If things keep goin' like this, the unthinkable might happen.'

As you may well know, Swampy, in times of extremes, outback towns such as Torrowangee act like magnets to every liar, shearer, thief, roustabout, murderer, cook, cheat, cattle duffer, prospector and swaggie. They drifted in to town, laden with whatever heartache they may bear, or simply to cadge a fag, pole a drink, scab some food and, in this case, also hoping to find a little shelter from the deluge by bludging a free train ride into Broken Hill. Alas, even Abdul, the Afghan, appeared from out of the downpour that Monday, leading his blind camel, and took up camp under a sad-eyed and sodden gidgee tree, on the outskirts of town.

By Tuesday, Scofield's Grocery had run out of food. Not one scrap remained on the shelf. Not even a crumb, can, canister or cockroach. Then the unthinkable. 'That's it,' called Ted, the alcoholic publican, a thin and sickly man, with a dodgy past as long as his crooked leg. 'We've run out'a grog!'

At this remark, the pub plummeted into a deep quagmire of despair and Ted was caroused by a protesting cacophony of Gaelic grumbles, Cornish curses, Welsh wails, Aussie oaths, Irish irony and plain old English whingeing. 'It can't be so,' they called.

'But it is,' replied Ted, scratching his leg.

By Wednesday, the townsfolk had mustered for the cause and had elected a committee of tongue-dried miners, bellowing bludgers and parch-throated hangers-on to confront the boss. 'Sir,' they said, 'the town's out'a supplies. The train needs to get int'a Broken Hill or we'll all be famished.'

At this, the boss stood to his tallest. He puffed out his beefy chest and looked down upon the pitiful gathering before him, as if they were wriggling maggots. 'If there's no limestone ter deliver, then the train doesn't run. It's company policy 'n that's that,' he barked.

That night, while the boss dined on roasted chicken and the finest of wines, the townsfolk partook of the last of their left-over, left-over scraps before holding another meeting. By the next day – Thursday – a different tack had been decided upon and, in the vague hopes that the boss had some sort of a heart, townsfolk began knocking on his door to regale him with some tale of woe or other.

Knock. Knock. 'Sir, me wife's in terrible pain. She's about due wiff our fifth 'n she needs to get int'a Broken Hill Hospital quick.'

Knock. Knock. 'Sir, I need ter get int'a Broken Hill 'cause I'm supposed 'ta be gettin' married there on Satur-dee.'

Knock. Knock. 'Sir, me poor mother's ailin' in the Hill 'n, oh God, I need ter be by her side as her spirit rises up int'a the heavens or she'll never speak to me again.'

And so on and so forth it continued, all to which the boss growled, 'If there's no limestone ter deliver, then the train doesn't run. It's company policy 'n that's that.'

Pour us another one will you, George. I'm just starting to warm up here.

Now, in Joseph Conrad's *Heart of Darkness* he writes of *an implacable force brooding over an inscrutable intention.* And such was the case in the small outback township of Torrowangee; in large part caused by either the grip of an icy-cold liquid-gold beer or the burning desire to bed Big Melva or the tug of the two-up game – or all of those rolled into one. As they say 'desperate times need desperate measures' and so the townsfolk met again – the *implacable force.* A midnight gathering at the railway barracks. In-depth discussions. All hush-hush. A little graft and corruption. A little bit here, a little bit there, along with much persistent pleading.

'But we'll be sacked,' said the train driver.

'So what,' said the fireman.

'Yeah,' replied the driver. 'So what.'

The guard stammered, 'If I don't get a flippin' drink, 'n get it soon, I'll die 'a bloody thirst.'

Thanks, George, just a top-up, mate.

And so, after a hearty lunch on the Friday, the boss walked out of his front door and looked down the street, to the end of town. By now, Campbell's Creek was running a real banker. Through the blinding rain, he could just make out Abdul's blind camel standing forlorn, trying to hide under an even more forlorn gidgee tree and a downright depressed Abdul. The boss, appropriately attired against the wicked conditions, grunted his contempt, stepped off the verandah and strode down the street. At seeing his approach, Albert's three-legged kelpie scampered for safety. Tom, Jack and the site foreman, Colin Cook, turned their heads to shield themselves from the boss' piercing gaze. 'G'day, sir,' they mumbled.

The boss looked through the window of the pub. A straggle of shearers, despondent workers and layabouts sat, heads hung low, watery-eyed, sniffing to the now distant memory of an icy-cold beer. At the sight of the boss' face Ted, the crooked-legged publican, instinctively grabbed a cloth and began rewiping some already well-wiped beer glasses. The boss walked over to Scofield's Grocery. Upon seeing him, young Meredith Worth grabbed a straw broom and began resweeping the bare earth floor. The boss then idled home, self-satisfied. He had them all exactly where he wanted. 'Power. Power. Power,' he whispered, under a sly smile. He then repeated those words, just a little louder, as if saying a mantra, 'Power. Power. Power.'

As it happened, it rained heavily again that particular Friday night. Even the boss was woken a couple of times by loud cracks of thunder, blinding sheets of lightning and corrugated tin roofs flapping. But this only caused him to smile the smile of an absolute downright rotten bastard. 'Good, no train for a few more days yet.' Then he rolled back to sleep, as sound as a baby.

Quick, George, another top-up, mate. I'm just about to hit the punchline. Good.

Thanks.

And so, Saturday morning, the boss was up early. He felt good. As fit as a fiddle. He cooked himself a hearty meal of bacon and eggs. After breakfast, he washed and shaved. He donned his finest suit. He preened his moustache in front of the mirror. 'I'll see how the low-life's are sufferin' ter-day,' he quipped to his own reflection.

He then slipped into his fancy galoshes and donned his immaculate mackintosh and opened his front door and stepped out onto the verandah to sniff the breeze. The rain had stopped, though momentarily. A hint of sunshine peaked through the clouds and a certain quiet had settled over Torrowangee. The streets lay empty. Bare. When he looked into the distance, he couldn't see Abdul or his blind camel – just a deserted gidgee tree. His pace quickened as he strode along the street to Albert's wagon – but no three-legged dog. With panic on the rise, he put his face to the window of the pub. No, not a sign. Not a soul. He rushed over to Scofield's Grocery. A straw broom lay abandoned on the floor. Nothing else. No Meredith. Not even a cockroach. Then, far in the distance, he heard the sound of a train whistle heading south toward Broken Hill.

George, a top-up please, mate.

Footnote – Torrowangee is in the far west of New South Wales, sixty or so kilometres north of Broken Hill and at the headwaters of Campbell's Creek. The town was established in 1889 and, a year later, the Torrowangee Flux and Tramway Company Limited began conveying limestone, via rail, to be used as flux in the Broken Hill smelters. In its heyday, Torrowangee was home to around five hundred people, a post office, two pubs, a police station, a courthouse and a school. In 1898, the limestone quarry closed and smelting operations were moved to Port Pirie in South Australia. Under pressure from local landowners and picnic-goers to Stephens Creek, the New South Wales Government took over the tramway and one train per week, plus special picnic trains, ran along the line until January 1929. The last train ran in April 1931 and the line closed in 1932. The rail tracks had been removed by 1959. The town's short ten-year quarry-life accounted for seven fatalities, five of them related to the use and/or misuse of explosives.

Today Torrowangee is a virtual ghost town, with only the foundation stones of a few buildings remaining; the rest is just piles of rubble. The town site is now part of Poolamacca Station's property. The nearest airport is in Broken Hill. Its nearest railway station is twenty kilometres away at Mt Gibbs Railway Station, the nearest school is Broken Hill's Morgan Street Public School, the nearest beach is over two hundred kilometres away at Telowie, in South Australia, and the nearest pub is in Broken Hill.

Tottenham – NSW

In memory of Victoria Grace Marsh.

As a young girl back in the 1920s, I lived in Tottenham, a small town in the central-west of New South Wales. My father worked for the railways as the ganger over three men whom he termed fettlers. Dad and his team tended the rail line about thirteen miles either side of the Tottenham Railway Station. For transport, they travelled on a rail trike: a contraption that ran on the railway tracks that had a flat base for the driver to sit on and a plank for the workers. To get it going, they had a handle to pull back and forward and two pedals to push with their feet. So it was like a push–pull sort of thing.

A mixed goods–passenger train came to Tottenham mid-afternoon, three days a week, and its arrival, as was its departure, was a big event. On train day, us kids would listen out for its first distant bleating hum. From that moment on, as the train sounds grew into a rumble, our excitement levels would rise.

Eventually there'd be a long whistle-wail and the train would come into view, puffing smoke. Just about everyone in town gathered at the railway station to greet the train. It was a real social occasion: a chance to meet up with friends and swap news, while simultaneously keeping an eagle-eye on who got off the train and what goods were being unloaded.

My family lived along the approach line to town and, when the train had finished unloading at the railway station, they'd shunt the carriages back along the western side of the line, where they'd be left empty overnight. I actually recall Mum remarking to someone how the empty carriages were sometimes patronised at night by young courting couples. Many was the rumour about some poor girl being pregnant with a 'carriage baby'.

Other than the chance of an unexpected pregnancy, the process of shunting the carriages was an extremely dangerous operation. I'd heard that, over time, more than one railway worker's life had been lost. With the buffers between the carriages and the luggage vans being linked by heavy chains, the men's timing had to be spot-on when they were connecting these links, while the train was still in motion ... or else. Anyhow, after the shunting had been completed, the loco was driven onto a turntable, where it was reversed, ready for next morning's return journey. Because the train's crew had to overnight in Tottenham, they stayed in special railway barracks. These were within easy walking distance from our place. I still picture Dad, sitting by the front gate, in his old rocking chair, waiting for a certain type of coded whistle, which meant that an illegal game of cards was on in the barracks, and Dad was included.

The following morning, when the train was ready for its departure, it'd notify the town with a blast of steam, followed by a loud whistle. It was fun to watch the passengers scurrying across to the station, to be first on the train. There were two main reasons for being early; one was to get on the train as soon as possible to avoid having to sit near the toilet. Secondly, was to grab the seats facing away from where the soot came in through the windows. Even still, there were always the stragglers. These were mainly men who'd slept in after the previous night's late-night card game or had been hanging around for the final throw of the two-up coins or enjoying a few late-late-night beers in the pub. If a male came on board who needed to recover from his previous night's shenanigans, he'd often try to take over the upper luggage rack where he could sleep it off.

But, oh it was a scream. As the train was moving away from the station, some of the wives or girlfriends would be hanging out the windows shouting for their delayed partners to get a move on. And there'd be children in tears, worried that their fathers were going to be left behind. Events such as marriages or births or families who were moving away were always acknowledged by an array of train whistles and either one, two or three detonators being placed on the rails to explode. Weddings were the highest on the whistle-detonator scale. So the train would depart Tottenham amid an array of bangs, whistles and clunks before it settled into its beautiful clickety-clack rhythm as it gained speed toward Albert, then on to Tullamore. As the train got further and further away, in my child's eye, I can still recall the huge white cloud coming out of the funnel, rising up like a giant meringue, before evaporating into the blue sky.

Our house – well, it wasn't much more than a hut, really – was built on government land, on the outskirts of town. Everybody knew it as the 'Ganger's House', and the land it was on was termed the 'railway paddock'. Because the railways employed my father, Dad had the privilege of renting this land for just one shilling per year and not having to pay council rates. Now, as to exactly how much land he had, I can't now recall, except that it was large enough for him to build a racecourse on it and a dam for his horses. As you may guess, he loved his racehorses. The house itself was constructed from boards and logs, with the logs being cut in half as they do in log homes, and there was lots of corrugated iron. We had three small bedrooms and a kitchen. One bedroom, known as 'Dad's Room', joined the kitchen, and there was a breezeway between there and the other two bedrooms. The breezeway was an open space, with a roof over it. That was more of a communal area really, because it's where we ate and washed and all those sorts of things.

As far as our family went, there was … well, my mother had nine children … wait a minute … one died and Lorna went to live elsewhere. So there would've been at least seven children in the house at any given time. And on hot summer nights we'd move our old iron framed beds outside to sleep under the stars, while Mum and Dad had one of those lovely big old-fashioned iron beds with porcelain knobs on it. But oh, the snakes. Dad always used to say that the house was built on a bed of snakes. And he was right. One time our eldest sister, Jean, put her hand on a snake on the railing inside the breezeway and she jumped so high that, by the time she came down again, the jolly thing had disappeared.

'I'll get that snake,' Dad vowed. So he put some poison in a saucer of milk and he took up position in his rocking chair, with a loaded shotgun, waiting for this snake to come out so he could shoot it. So us kids went off to bed, leaving him sitting there on night watch and, when we come out in the morning, all the milk had gone and Dad was contentedly snoring away, with the shotgun balanced over his shoulder.

But my father was a tough old fellow. He used to pull his own teeth and he didn't believe in doctors. One time, while he was working out on the railway track, he crushed the top knuckle of his pointer finger. I don't know exactly how it happened, but he somehow got it caught in the trike. Anyhow, as I said, he was extremely fond of his horses and he believed that what was good enough for the horses was good enough for him. Now, if a horse had anything wrong with its hoof, he'd treat it with bluestone, which was some sort of an acid that came in the form of a crystal. So he put a dab of bluestone on his crushed finger. But, instead of curing it, the finger became infected. So to counteract the effects of the bluestone, he put caustic soda on it, and the combination of the two started eating through the top of his finger. And that was one of the very rare times that Dad did end up going to see the doctor.

But oh, after that, he was sick for a good long while. Now, I'm not sure how strict he was on his fettlers, but he was so strict on us kids that we were never allowed to go out anywhere. But kids being kids we sensed that, with Dad being in so much pain, he wouldn't have the energy to worry about us. So we'd go into his room and say, 'Dad, we're just going up to Turners' or, 'Dad, we're just going off somewhere,' and it'd be all right. Then one afternoon we went into his room and we said, 'Dad, we're just going up to Turners.'

'Like bloody hell yer are,' he replied. So we knew he must've been getting better.

Then Dad's boss was his brother, and he was a railway inspector over at Bogan Gate. Because of that, Dad had quite a few privileges. Say, if he wanted to take his racehorses to Dubbo or Wellington, or he wanted to take Mum down to the Easter yearling sales in Sydney, his brother would give him the time off. So off they'd go and us kids would be left at home, in our little ganger's house, with Jean, the eldest, looking after us.

Jean was a wonderful person. At this stage, she couldn't have been any more than twelve. But, back in the late 1920s, it wasn't uncommon for someone that young to look after the other children in the family. Anyhow, this particular time, Mum and Dad had gone off down to the yearling sales in Sydney. Now, how many of us were there? There was Ted, myself, Marge and Riley – so there was five of us, including Jean. I think the baby went down to Nan's. Anyhow, that's when we got the prowler.

Now, I'm going back eighty years or so and, back then, you never locked your doors or windows. We only had one room with a door that locked and that was 'Dad's Room'. So there we were – all us kids – in our little ganger's hut, being looked after by Jean, and one night this fellow came prowling around. He might've been drunk or whatever. But oh he frightened us. Now, we always had a shotgun lying around the house, just in case of snakes. So Jean got this shotgun, then she hounded all of us kids into 'Dad's Room', and she locked the door. When we peeked through the window, we could still just make out this fellow sneaking toward our house, little by little. So Jean shouted out, 'Go away or I'll shoot!'

Of course, knowing that we were just kids, the prowler wasn't at all worried.

So he crept closer and closer.

'Go away or I'll shoot!' Jean called out again.

By now the prowler thought that this was all a great joke. Then – *Boom! Boom!* – Jean let go with both barrels. Well, I've never seen someone take off so fast. He was out of there like a shot.

Footnote – Tottenham, with its population of less than three hundred, is in the central-west wheat-growing area of New South Wales. It's known as 'The Soul of the Centre' because thirty-three kilometres to its west-north-west is a cairn that marks the geographical centre of the state. The township is at the end of a railway line from Bogan Gate that was completed in 1916. Tottenham Post Office opened in April 1907.

In 2012, Tottenham won the award for the Most Outstanding Community in New South Wales and the ACT, with a population of less than fifteen thousand. In winning the award, the judges highlighted how the townsfolk had paid for most of the sealing of the town's own airstrip, the installation of a kangaroo-proof fence around its perimeter and putting in runway lighting so that the RFDS could safely land in a medical emergency. Then, after the Heath Department declared that no suitable doctor could be found to service the town, the locals conducted a worldwide search to recruit a doctor of their own. Locals have also formed a team of volunteer ambulance officers to support its one full-time paramedic, and, on a dollar-for-dollar basis, the town constructed its own large sports centre.

Tottenham Hotel was built in 1931 and has since been 'lovingly' restored. This three-star, child-friendly, two-storey Victorian-era hotel is family owned and operated and features a beer garden, barbecue facilities, balcony and lawn areas, plus two glass-backed squash courts.

Triabunna – Tas

So you're asking me how I come to live in Triabunna, are you? Okay, well it's a bit of a story. For starters, I'd done a lot of shearing in Victoria and Queensland. Then 'She' up and left me with our three boys. They were only little fellers – between six and ten. But we got on pretty well. So then I worked on the airport in Portland, Victoria. I drove one of them scrapers and, when that work stopped, I went on to the wheat silos. I've also been a rigger and a crane driver. But see, after a couple of years, things weren't working out too good. So I thought, Well I may as well pack up me three boys 'n a suitcase 'n I'll come over to Tasmania. So I came over here with my three boys looking for a new life.

Anyway, away back in 1962, I shore in Tasmania, so I knew I'd get shearing work here, and I liked the place. Though at the time, I still didn't know what I was going to do with the three boys. But it was a new start. So we arrived in Tassie and at first we lived in an old caravan in Swansea. And oh, I'd do anything to make a crust – shearing, farm work, anything. I used to get the boys to cut their own lunches in the morning and they'd do their own washing and all that. After school, I got someone to look after them till I got home from work.

One of the first people I met when I got here was a feller, Malcolm. I remember I was with him one day when this other feller's Holden broke down. Anyhow, Malcolm's pretty cluey, so he mucked around with this feller's car and he got it going. Then he said to the feller, 'It'll be okay, but only just for today. So first thing tomorr'a, take it int'a Holden's 'n ask for part number rah,

rah, rah.' Like he rattled off this big long part number that went on forever. He said to the feller, 'Get them ter put that number part in yer car 'n you'll be as right as rain.'

Okay. So away the feller goes, scratching his head, trying to remember this big long part number that Malcolm had told him. Anyhow, I said to Malcolm, 'Malcolm,' I said, 'you amaze me. How did you know that that was the exact part the feller needed ter fix his car?' And Malcolm said, 'I didn't. I just made it up.' Then he said, 'And by the time the feller gets ter Holden's tomorr'a he would'a forgotten it anyway.' Yes, so he just made the part number up.

By then I had a nice car, an XW GTX Falcon. It'd be worth around $400,000 now, and old Mick Fermor kept on and on at me. 'I want'a have a drive of yer car. I want'a have a drive of yer car.' So one night I gave in and I said, 'Okay, Mick, yer can have a drive of it then.'

So off Mick went and on his way back he came up the lake way from Buckland. Now he reckons he wasn't going real fast, but when he drove around a corner – *Bang! Crash! Crunch!* – he ran straight into the bank. And that was a big blow because now I had no car, three kids to look after and I couldn't go anywhere. Anyhow, not long after, old Doug asked me to come in and see him. It was a Saturday. Doug was a man of very few words, but a fantastic man. When I went and seen him he said, 'Dinga, I hear yer strugglin' a bit?'

I said, 'Ter be honest, Doug, I am a little bit hamstrung at the moment. I got three little kids 'n no car 'n I need a better place ter live.'

Now, I knew old Doug had a nice little house right on the beach here. So I started dreaming along the lines of, Gee, that'd be good.

He said, 'I've just bought some property. It's a bit out'a town, between Triabunna 'n Swansea.' And you know how your heart goes down when you hear something you don't want to hear?

Well, when I heard that, my heart went down. *Boom!* He said, 'I'll take yer out ter have a look at it.' And while we were driving out there, I'm thinking, Oh shit, this doesn't look too good. Where the hell is he taking me?

Anyhow, we came to this real rocky hill. The road was so bad that we just about rattled all the way up to the top of it. And when I saw what I saw, my heart shot up so high, it just about blew me apart. *Phwoar!* It was the most beautiful sight. Mitchell Reef was right there, and the beach, and Doug said, 'Well you 'n the boys can live here if yer like 'n when yer not shearin' yer can work on the property.'

And that was fantastic, you know. And even though it rained every second bloody day, because I knew I could make a few dollars out of shearing, I bought another car. So me and the three boys lived in the old house there. It was a sheep and cattle place – mainly cattle – and I did a lot of fencing for Doug. He also had a bulldozer and so I also did a lot of land clearing. But he was a fantastic bloke, old Doug. He actually saved me, he did.

Anyhow, after a while I'd built up me kitty and so I bought this place, here in Triabunna. Then one day after I did, I was out shearing. I was grinding my gear and the cutter fell out, and the other part shot up and busted my eye so bad that it was hanging outside its socket. So I got out my hanky and I pushed it back in and I went to the hospital. They tried to do the best they could with it, but it'd been a long time blacked out and so that was it. Anyhow, by then the other two boys were at school in Hobart, so they were okay. But while I was still in hospital in Hobart, Justine come and stayed at my place to look after my youngest son. I already knew her like, but I've now forgotten how the order of things happened. But, the thing was, when I came home from hospital, Justine didn't seem like she wanted to go anywhere. She seemed sort'a keen on staying on for a bit longer. And that bit longer turned into another bit longer. I don't know why because, just between you and me, she was far too good for me. But anyway, after she'd stuck around for a fair while longer, I said to her, 'You know, how about it then?'

She said, 'How about what?'

I said, 'You know, you 'n me getting hitched? Like in getting married.'

And she said, 'Yeah, okay then,' and so we did. And now we've been married near on fifty years and it's all been good. So I'm very thankful to everyone who helped me along the way: people like Malcolm and old Doug. Because I've got a real life now and the boys have turned out real good and Justine's turned out to be the best wife in the whole wide world, or any other big place for that matter. And so that's how I got to Triabunna.

Footnote – Triabunna is in the Glamorgan–Spring Bay region of south-eastern Tasmania, near on ninety kilometres north-east of Hobart, with a population of around eight hundred. The word 'Triabunna' is an Aboriginal term for the Tasmanian native hen. In the early 1800s a sealing industry was established in the bay and, during the 1820s, shore-based whaling took over until its demise in the 1840s. The town, originally known as Tenby, was founded in the 1830s as a garrison for the Darlington convict settlement, out on nearby Maria Island. The first Spring Bay Post Office opened in February 1832 but closed later that year. It reopened in 1836 and in 1881 was renamed Triabunna and was gazetted as such in 1960.

Many historic buildings from Tasmania's colonial past remain and Maria Island is just a ferry ride away. Triabunna's Tasmanian Seafarers Memorial is a foreshore memorial to all Tasmanian seafarers – regardless of occupation and/or nationality – who have lost their lives in its waters. The town is a water-sports haven and bushwalking in the nearby forests is popular.

As far as pubs go, as well as a wide selection of beverages, Spring Bay Hotel offers a number of gourmet specialities. The Tandara is a three-star hotel-motel serving top quality steaks plus pub favourites. The Colonial Accommodation and Modern Art has a bar, garden and barbecue facilities and the breakfasts are apparently 'awesome'.

Uluru – NT

My husband and I were high school teachers back in the 1960s, when our South Australia Education Department administered the Northern Territory education system. In late November of 1966 we got a call from the director general saying how Alice Springs High School needed a new senior master and would we like to go up and teach there. The tenure was for two years and we were given twenty-four hours to make up our minds.

This would mean a big promotion for my husband. Other than being senior master, he was to teach humanities subjects such as English, History and Geography. Obviously, I was going along as well: to teach English and French. On my part, they were particularly keen to have someone who could teach French because, especially with a language, once someone leaves there's no continuity in the subject. Oh, and everybody had to teach sport! In my case it was hockey, although I'd never held a hockey stick in my life and didn't even know the rules.

After giving it a quick thought, we said, 'Yes. We'd love to.' But then the director general emphasised, 'Mrs Hutchins, but you must teach for at least one year.' That seemed to be an odd request seeing how the contract was for two years, so I said, 'Yes, that's fine with me. No problem with that.'

Then he got more pointed. 'Are you taking precautions?'

Apparently, a number of the single female teachers who'd gone up there had either met someone, got pregnant and so had to leave, or had just plain left. In fact, not long after we arrived, the senior mistress left, leaving them without a senior female. When I saw that the principal was quite upset over the situation,

I asked him, 'So what are the minimum requirements for a senior mistress' position?'

He said, 'Well, you have to have taught for three years.'

I said, 'Well, I've taught for three years and one term.'

'Oh okay,' he said, but still sounded doubtful.

Then I added, 'Plus I have a degree.'

'Oh,' he said, very much relieved, 'you're it then. You've got the job.'

So I got the job – sort of. By 'sort of' I mean, back in those days, married women were only allowed to be an 'acting senior'. So that's how it happened and, in the end, we loved it up there so much that we stayed on for four years. During that time, we travelled the area extensively. It was great. Every Friday lunchtime someone in the staffroom would say, 'Who's coming out bush? Let's go to Trephina Gorge.' Or, 'Let's go to Ormiston Gorge.' Or I'd suggest, 'It's the Harts Range races this weekend. How about we go there.' The Aileron Rodeo was another highlight. So there'd always be three or four families who'd be willing to come along, most with kids and babies – the whole works. That's how I got the idea, later on when we did have children of our own, as we'd be driving along, I'd hang their nappies out the car windows to dry and sterilise or warm bottles in billies, held out on sticks over the campfire coals.

Anyhow, we'd only been in Alice Springs for a few months when we decided to travel out to Uluru, which back then was known as Ayers Rock. This was in 1967, before we had children and we just went on our own, my husband and I. The road out there was dirt, but still quite suitable for an ordinary car. It was autumn and still quite hot. Probably Easter.

The first time we pulled over to have a drink a man in a ute, who was coming in the opposite direction, stopped for a chat. Probably a station hand I'd say. I expect we stood out like a sore thumb as newlywed rookies, with our neat clothes and shiny blue '64 Holden, so he started questioning us. 'Did we have plenty of food, extra water?' 'Yes.' 'A spare tyre?' 'Yes.' 'And what about a spade?' At that, we looked at him blankly. 'So what do you do when you get bogged?' he asked. I looked up at the cloudless sky and thought, what *is* he on about? The thing was, we didn't know back then that the dry creek beds could fill up just days after rain had fallen further north. And so, my husband replied smugly, 'Well, we'll just let down our tyres a bit, then we'll rev up and plough through.' We'd been told that.

'An' if that doesn't work?'

Light dawned. 'Um, I guess we'd have to dig ourself out.'

'Tell you what,' he said, 'I'll give you this spade.' And that's what the locals were like up there – real genuine, kind human beings.

In the old measurements, it's only a bit under three hundred miles from The Alice to The Rock – though, plenty of bulldust and luckily no boggy creek beds – so we were there in good time for the famous sunset. The thing was, when we arrived, there was nobody else about. Not even a tourist bus in sight. No one, and no other buildings apart from the ranger's small cottage. Just us, and so we decided to set up camp in the camping area and sleep on the lay-back seats of our Holden.

Soon after we'd set ourselves up, the ranger came across for a chat. He said, 'Do you want to come over to my place for supper? I'll show you some of my slides.' Which we did, and he had some of the most wonderful pictures, among them some very rare shots of the rock during rain – shiny and grey like some massive sleeping animal. The ranger also told us quite a bit about The Rock itself: such as its dimensions and about all the natural springs, the waterfalls that gushed when it rained and the various caves and so on. As far as Indigenous history went, as a white man he only knew a certain amount, but that was all. In those days, to all our shame, Indigenous history wasn't such a big topic. And of course, we were just white people who'd barged in without having any knowledge of it even being a sacred spot. That didn't come about until a long time afterwards. Nowadays, in respect, you're not even allowed to climb The Rock. But, of course, we didn't know all that back then.

The next day my husband and I felt quite off-colour. A rope only went so far up The Rock, so we just climbed a little way before coming back down. Then, being such a beautiful day, we decided to drive out to the Olgas–Kata Tjuta. The Olgas were about an hour's drive out of Uluru. They're a bunch of domelike rock-hills and, in the same way as The Rock, they'd be a sacred site. As I said, we weren't feeling too well so, when we got to the Olgas, we laid back and stretched out on a big flat sheet of rock at the base of one of the hillocks to take in the sunshine. By then it was the middle of the day and we'd soon dropped off to sleep. When I woke, I squinted up into the sky and there, circling directly above us, was a mob of 'expectant' crows, thinking we might make for a nice tasty dinner.

Oh, and another thing I remember was the dingoes. They showed some interest in us, and our camping site. They weren't aggressive, but we didn't encourage them either. Whether we knew instinctively not to feed them, or whether others had warned us not to, I can't remember. They just wandered around the place like dogs, so we didn't think too much about them really. Although on a later trip, we were travelling with the school's headmaster, his wife and their three children. One morning their twelve-year-old came up to me and said, 'Have you seen my sneakers?'

I said, 'What would I want with your sneakers?' When we searched around our campsite, we came across a dingo's paw-prints and, when we traced them, we found one of his sneakers – and we never found the other one. Actually, it wasn't much later that Lindy Chamberlain's little baby, Azaria, disappeared from the same spot where we'd camped at Uluru. And I always believed that baby Azaria was taken by a dingo. Though, for many years, nobody believed the poor mother, Lindy, so she was falsely jailed in Darwin for murdering the child. It wasn't until much later that the decision was reversed.

But oh, the stars. The stars out that way were just amazing. They shone like a carpet in the sky, only to be streaked by the occasional shooting star. And with us camping out in that vast area by ourselves, I often thought that, unless there were some Aboriginal people around, we'd be the only human beings within hundreds of miles. It was such a wonderful experience. But because of what's since happened out there, with all its up-market tourist spots and flashy hotels, I don't want to go back to Uluru. I just want to keep hold of the memory of how it was back in 1967, when just my husband and I visited.

Footnote – Uluru–Kata Tjuta is a World Heritage listed national park and sacred site for Indigenous people, particularly for its traditional owners the Anangu. The Rock, as it's colloquially known, is a sandstone monolith in the heart of the Northern Territory's arid 'Red Centre', four hundred and fifty kilometres south-west of Alice Springs. Its formation is thought to have begun around 550 million years ago. Dreamtime legend has it that two tribes had a battle over a tantalising lizard woman and Uluru rose from the site in response to the Earth's grief over the bloodshed.

The Rock is an estimated three hundred and fifty metres above the desert plain, making it taller than Paris' Eiffel Tower and, at just over eight hundred and fifty metres above sea level, it's two and a half times higher than the Sydney Harbour Bridge. It measures 3.6 kilometres in length, 2.4 kilometres in width, has a circumference of 9.4 kilometres and harbours plentiful springs, waterholes, rock caves and ancient paintings. It's estimated that some 2.5 kilometres of its total bulk lies underground.

In July 1873, surveyor William Gosse named Ayers Rock after the then Chief Secretary of South Australia, Sir Henry Ayers. In 1993, it was renamed Ayers Rock–Uluru and in 2002, the naming was reversed to Uluru–Ayers Rock. Sixty kilometres from The Rock lie the thirty-six red-rock domes of Kata Tjuta – known as the Olgas.

To support the estimated 250,000 annual visitors to the area, these days the nearby Ayers Rock Resort complex comprises numerous hotels, camping grounds, art galleries, cafes, a post office, a tourist information centre, souvenir shops, a supermarket, petrol station et cetera. More than a hundred different activities, tours and experiences are available. Nearby Yulara, with its population of just over a thousand, is a community that's emerged to help support tourism around Uluru–Kata Tjuta.

Weipa – Qld

I grew up in Brisbane, so you could say I was a city girl. Although, due to my father's occupation, we were fortunate enough to own a small property outside of the city where I'd spend weekends and school holidays. Perhaps that's why I wanted to be a jillaroo. But no, my parents were keen that I have something solid behind me. So, not wanting to have a job where I'd end up sitting behind a desk, putting on weight, I decided to try nursing. And as soon as I started my training, that was it: nursing was all I wanted to do.

I did my three years of general in Maryborough, up on the Fraser Coast of Queensland, followed by twelve months of midwifery at Nambour, just north of Brisbane. I then did a stint in the ICU at Alice Springs Hospital, in the Northern Territory. That was in the late '80s and it was a huge cultural learning curve because, up till then, I'd had very little to do with Aboriginal people.

After Alice Springs, I began doing three to six-month stints of remote relief at various places like Weipa, in the Gulf of Carpentaria and Moree, in far northern New South Wales. I also did a stint as an emergency flight nurse with the RFDS, at both their Broken Hill and Dubbo bases. So I've been around a bit. Mind you, Weipa was another huge learning curve. That was in the '90s and it got to be a pretty wild town at times. Apart from our smallish state government-run hospital and the huge Scherger air base, the rest of the place was pretty much all run by Comalco.

Back then, Weipa had a population of around two thousand and I arrived at the end of the wet season. It was still incredibly humid and the downpours were amazing. People were walking around the supermarket absolutely saturated, doing their shopping. It was a twenty-bed hospital, and we had a few long-term patients. There was just the one doctor in town and he'd only visit if we really needed him. That's because he was employed by Comalco and they had their own medical rooms, separate from us, and so all the miners would go to him on site. So there'd just be two of us on duty: a registered nurse and an enrolled nurse, and we managed to do most things ourselves. We even delivered quite a few babies and, if there was anything major, we sent them to Cairns, which was a bumpy six-hundred-and-fifty-kilometre flight away.

But overall, you were either dead bored or dead scared in Weipa. We'd even get the occasional request to patch up a wounded pig dog. Pig hunting was a big thing in Weipa, particularly among the white population ... and it was dangerous. The pig dogs came in all shapes and sizes. There were the Border collie–cattle dog crosses, then you'd get the big-chested, solid-headed Bullmastiff–Great Dane crosses. And oh, they were massive. Some were up to a metre tall. But with wild pigs' meat not being fit for human consumption, if the dogs chased one down, the pigs were either shot or they'd have their throats cut and they were left out in the bush, or they might just chop off a leg and take it home for the dogs to eat.

Mind you, some of the pigs were pretty massive as well – and with huge tusks – which is why the dogs got so badly gored. So we'd get a call and, if things were quiet, we'd let them bring in the dog. When they arrived, we'd open up the morgue, pop the dog on the slab, sedate it and off we'd go, practising our surgical skills. Most of them were gored around the abdomen or had been gashed around the throat. A lot of them survived. Some didn't.

Sometimes they'd been ripped open from head to toe and were already too far gone.

As for other memories: the council used to run outdoor movies, down on the beachfront. They were fun. We'd grab a chair and a few beers, and set up in the sand, out in the open air, under the stars. A big screen was mounted on the back of a truck and the movie was projected onto that. One night we were watching a movie with Demi Moore and Patrick Swayze in it – *Ghosts* I think it was. It was the one where Patrick Swayze died in a car accident and he kept coming back to visit Demi Moore as a ghost. Anyhow, just as it got to the exciting part, we were interrupted by an announcement, 'Please evacuate the area. A crocodile has been seen coming up the beach.'

So we all packed up and we went home, and I never got to see the end of *Ghosts* – well, not till years later when I got it out on video. Although, for some strange reason, it just didn't seem to live up to the impact it'd had when we were on the beach that night, in Weipa. So Weipa was a pretty full-on, interesting place.

Another night we got a call from the ambulance people, 'There's been a family dispute and we're bringing in a female who's received head injuries.'

When the ambos arrived at casualty, they opened up the back doors to pull out the trolley and, to my shock and horror, there, staring back at me, was this woman with an axe stuck in the middle of her skull, handle and all. Oh my God. Anyhow, her boyfriend was with her, and looking pretty sheepish. The story unfolded that they'd had a lot to drink, and they'd got into this huge argument; which, mind you, was still continuing on in the back of the ambulance. And I can tell you, this lady certainly wasn't going to be compromised, even by having an axe stuck in her head. No way. She was still letting go, full-tilt, calling her boyfriend all the names under the sun.

With it being a major injury, we decided to call in a retrieval plane from Cairns. But then, when we got the woman out to the airport, we couldn't fit her into the plane with the axe still sticking out of her head. So after we sedated her some more, we got to it and we sawed the axe handle off. That done, we bandaged down the axe head so it wouldn't move about during the bumpy flight and off she went to Cairns. And believe it or not, a week or so later she was back in Weipa, and all was well. She'd apparently reunited with her boyfriend and it was now 'happily ever after' ... Maybe ... Hopefully.

Footnote – Weipa is a mining town on the western coast of Cape York Peninsula, 2500 kilometres north-west of Brisbane. It's administered by Comalco – now known as Rio Tinto – and is a major worldwide exporter of bauxite. Weipa is known to have the largest bauxite mine in the world, with deposits likely to last for another two centuries.

The first European to visit the area was the Dutch explorer Willem Janszoon, in 1606, and, in the skirmish that followed, the Aboriginals speared one of his crew. The traditional owners are the Anathangayth, Alngith, Peppan, Thanakwithi and Wathyn people, and the name Weipa is thought to have come from an Anathangayth word meaning 'fighting ground'. Later on, in 1802, while circumnavigating Australia, Matthew Flinders noted that the cliffs around nearby Albatross Bay had a distinctive reddish hue.

Moravian missionaries arrived in 1891 and established a mission at Mapoon. By 1895, a Presbyterian mission – Weipa Mission – was established at the junction of Embley River and Spring Creek. In 1896, John Thomas Embley surveyed the land where Weipa now stands, and five years later geologist C.F.V Jackson noted the bauxite.

In 1911, the Queensland Government legislated an act that made the Protector of Aborigines the legal guardian of every Aboriginal and/or part Aboriginal in the state. This gave the authorities the power to confine Aboriginal people to reserves. In 1932, due to an outbreak of malaria, Weipa Mission was relocated just south of the town's present site, to Jessica Point. Soon after, other tribes and clans were also relocated, including those from Old Mapoon.

By 1941, an airstrip was built. In 1955 geologist Henry Evans found that Matthew Flinders' description of the cliffs around Albatross Bay having 'a distinctive reddish hue' was true – they were virtually pure bauxite, the ore from which aluminium is made – and so an exploration camp was established. *The Comalco Act of 1957* gave the company the right to remove the Aboriginal people from near on six thousand square kilometres of their reserve land. Weipa township was planned and built in the early 1960s as a joint Comalco–Queensland Government project. The first shipment of bauxite occurred in 1961 and the Port of Weipa was officially opened in 1962.

Also in 1962, the original owners accepted Comalco's offer to rebuild the Jessica Point village and, to prevent further spread of malaria, the Old Mapoon settlement was razed to the ground a year later. But by the time building began at Jessica Point, the previously offered funding was inadequate and so the Presbyterian Church handed over responsibility for the mission to the Queensland Government. The first real compensation for Comalco's uptake of the original owners' land wasn't granted until the early 1990s.

Being a mining town, Weipa is run, these days, under the administration of Rio Tinto. It has a number of hotel-motels for the traveller, although permission of entry, including prior notification of arrival and departure, plus contact details, may be required.

Widgiemooltha – WA

A while back, the wife and I were doing the old grey nomad bit through Western Australia, when we came across a place called Widgiemooltha. Widgie, as it's more commonly known, is a bit over six hundred kilometres inland from Perth. It's an interesting little town with a lot of history. Back in its day, it was a big gold-mining place. In fact, the largest nugget of gold ever found in WA was found at Widgiemooltha. And that caused such a rush of miners that, virtually overnight, the population shot up from under a hundred, to over a thousand. And it remained a bustling sort of community, right up till the gold started to run out, and that just about signalled the end of it really.

Anyhow, on this trip, we decided to overnight, around the back of the roadhouse-tavern, in their caravan park. And that's where we went for dinner – at the roadhouse. Now, just as an aside, if you ever get to go there, you've got to try one of their famous Widgie chipotle-jalapeño burgers. Oh, mate, they're just about guaranteed to burn the bum off a camel. What's more, if you can withstand the heat, your name goes up on the tavern's Wall of Flame board.

Then it was while we were having a few after-dinner ales to douse the heat from the burgers, we started chatting to another couple of grey nomads. As it turned out, the bloke's wife and my wife had both been schoolteachers. And, as old schoolteachers do, they got yarning. Of course, as my wife so often does, she started to trot out some of her old favourites. There was the one from when she'd just got out of teachers college and, as part of her penance, she'd been posted to a remote single-teacher school, somewhere out in the Pilbara. It was a dry, dusty forsaken place, but the kids were real characters; a bit on the wild side, but each and every one of them an individual in their own right.

Anyhow, as the wife's story goes, first thing each school morning, she'd get the kids to sit quietly at their desks and she'd do the rollcall: 'Alfred Arnold?' ... 'Present Miss.' ... 'Bessy Jones?' ... 'Present Miss.' ... 'Tommy Smith?' ... 'Present Miss.' And she'd go through the rollcall till she came to the last young feller, Robert Young. 'Robert Young?' ... 'Present Miss.'

As I said, it was only a small single-teacher school and so she soon got to know all the kids, not only by their real names, but also by their nicknames. And she could relate to most of them: like 'Snow' was for the blond Alfred Arnold and 'Bluey' was for the red-haired Bessy Jones and 'Smithy' was for Tommy Smith and so forth. But one nickname had her stumped. Whenever the kids ever talked to a lad who was down on the roll as Robert Young, they called him 'Johnny'.

Now, this started to niggle at my wife; you know, as to why someone called Robert was known to all and sundry as Johnny. She just couldn't make the connection, like. So one day she pulled aside one of the more senior kids, Thomas Moore; better known as 'Windy'. I'll leave the explanation of that one up to your own imagination. Anyhow, she said, 'Thomas, can you please explain why everyone calls Robert Young, Johnny?'

'Well, Miss,' replied Windy, 'we call him Johnny because he's such a liar that we're not even sure that his real name's Robert.'

Well, didn't that get this feller's wife going. In fact, as it turned out, the feller's wife had also received her first posting, out into the back blocks of WA. The only difference was that it was to a two-teacher school. But being fresh out of teachers college, she was having the Devil's own trouble connecting with the littlies; like they weren't communicating as well as she would've liked. And so she went to have a chat to the headmistress – as they were called back then – who'd been around for yonks.

Anyhow, after she'd expressed her concerns about her non-connection with the littlies, the headmistress told her a story about her first posting out of teachers college which, as it happened, was at Widgiemooltha – which, in part, was why the couple had come out here. Anyhow, this was back in the early '50s and by then Widgie only had a handful of students. It was the middle of winter and, I don't know if you know or not but, as we found out, around June–July it gets pretty chilly out that way. Anyhow, it was the end of the school day and one of the littlies was struggling to put his boots on.

As the story goes, the now headmistress decided to do her best to connect with the little feller and help him out. So she got down on the floor with this little kid and started pulling and pushing, writhing and wriggling these boots around, trying to get them on his feet. Anyhow, after a real struggle, she managed to do it. 'There you go,' she said. 'All done.'

'But, Miss,' the little feller said, looking down at his boots, 'them's on the wrong foot.'

And he was right. She'd mistakenly put the boots on the wrong foot. 'Oh, sorry,' she said, embarrassed by her mistake. So she got to it and she pushed, shoved, wriggled and wrangled the little boy's boots back off. She then swapped them over and, again, after a lot of pushing, shoving, wriggling and wrangling, she managed to get them on to the little feller's correct feet.

'There you go,' she said. 'All done.' Pleased with her efforts.

'Oh,' said the little boy, taking a closer look at the boots.

'What's wrong?' she asked.

'Sorry, Miss,' came the reply, 'but them's not my boots. Them's me bruvver's boots.'

So taking a deep breath to calm her mounting frustration, she struggled to help him pull the ill-fitting boots off. Then, under the little feller's instruction, they went over to the boot rack where he pointed out the right boots. 'Them's mine, there, Miss,' he said.

But even then, she had the Devil's own job to get his boots on; you know, pushing and shoving and wriggling and wrangling. 'Are you sure they're your boots?' she asked. 'They seem to be very tight.'

'Yes, Miss,' came the reply. 'Mum said she'd get me a new pair next year.'

Anyhow, it was only through great perseverance that she finally managed to get them on – and on the right feet.

'There you go,' she said. 'All done.' And so she helped the little feller up off the floor and, when they got over to the coat rack, she even offered to help him into his winter coat.

'Thanks, Miss,' he said, and started fishing around in his coat pockets.

'What's up?' she asked.

'Just lookin' fer me gloves,' he said.

'Do you know where you put them?' she asked.

And the little kid looked up at her. 'Miss,' he said, sheepishly, 'I think I stuffed 'em down int'a the toes of me boots.'

Footnote – Widgiemooltha is six hundred and thirty kilometres east of Perth, on the southern shoreline of Lake Lefroy. The town's name is thought to have come from the Aboriginal word for a nearby hill and rock hole, which resembles the beak of an emu.

With small discoveries of gold in the area, by 1898 Widgiemooltha's population consisted of a hundred males and just twelve females. But in 1931, when the largest nugget in the history of Western Australia – the 32.2-kilogram Golden Eagle – was found nearby, over a thousand prospectors rushed to the site. The town then flourished with merchandise stores, smithies, a school, a church, a town hall and a couple of pubs.

But by 1956, with the gold rush well and truly over, Widgie's population consisted of just four railway fettlers and their families, plus the employees of a local salt works, a shopkeeper, a schoolteacher and a few hotel staff. Today, the population of Widgiemooltha is less than twenty and a monument to the Golden Eagle nugget is located near the town's park.

William Creek – SA

In memory of Ted Gade.

Back in the early days of the old Ghan train, there were all these little remote railway sidings where, say, a ganger and his five or so fettlers would live in tents or makeshift huts. It was then their responsibility to maintain approximately thirty mile of track: fifteen mile to the south and fifteen mile to the north of their location. Now, the particular bloke who told me this story was the ganger – the boss of the fettlers – at a little siding called Beresford, which is about thirty mile south of William Creek, in the far north of South Australia.

To give you a better idea, William Creek's out along the Oodnadatta Track, just over a couple of hundred kilometres east-ish of Marla and around one-fifty k's north-ish of Coober Pedy. So it's a pretty remote sort of place, which makes Beresford even 'remoter' – if I can put it that way – meaning that these fellers had an even more isolated existence. Added to that, the roads out there were either non-existent or in such bad nick that hardly anyone owned a car. And so, these fettlers only mode of transport was a government railway's section car cum trike, which was a little motor-driven maintenance vehicle that ran along the railway track.

To compound these fellers' isolation, trains came by so rarely that all their supplies – including their grog, in this particular case – used to run out pretty darn quick. And without a regular supply of grog, the fettlers would get a bit uppity – if you catch my drift – and so things in the camp could turn crook. Now, what you have to realise here is that, this was back in the early days after World War Two when there was a lot of immigration to Australia from war-torn places in Europe like Poland, Italy and Czechoslovakia.

Now, to repay the Commonwealth Government for their free passage over here, these immigrants were made to work for the government for a couple of years. And so, quite a few of them were dispatched out along the various railway lines across Australia, to work as fettlers. As it happened, in amongst these immigrant workers were some extremely well educated people, the likes of doctors, lawyers, professors and so on. So while many of them couldn't speak a word of English, they were pretty smart cookies, as in characters.

Now to demonstrate the depth and brilliance of this particular small gang of outback fettlers from Beresford Siding, I'll relate to you the plan that was hatched.

Now this gang's only communications with the outside world were through Commonwealth Rail's Main Control, three hundred miles away, down at Port Augusta. Of course, the railway hierarchy would've taken an extremely dim view of things if they'd found out just how much grog these fettlers were consuming. To that end, these fettlers devised a secret code that they'd send to their trusted mates in Main Control who, in turn, would forward it on to the publican at William Creek. This secret code informed the publican of the exact date and time he should be prepared for the arrival of the fettlers' unmanned section car.

By this stage, these fettlers would've already sat down and calculated the exact quantity of fuel an unmanned section car would use on its thirty-mile journey from Beresford Siding to William Creek. In doing so, they had to take into account such things as wind direction and velocity, track conditions, the weather forecast and so on. That done, they'd put that exact amount of fuel in their section car. Then they'd put a little more than an equal amount into a separate fuel can, which they'd place on the section car, along with an envelope containing the required amount of cash to pay for the grog. They'd then start up their section car and wave it off, up the railway track, on its thirty-mile trip to William Creek.

As to why these fettlers sent the section car unmanned, was – or so my mate told me – based on the fact that, if one of the fettlers had gone with the section car, they would've a) taken up a hell of a lot of precious grog-space on its homeward journey, and b) if one of their mates had gone up to William Creek in the section car, upon his arrival, he would've most likely spent all the grog-money on himself and forgot to come back. So that's why the section car went unmanned.

Of course, things didn't always go exactly to plan. Due to the ever-changing weather conditions and so forth, sometimes the section car would run out of fuel a couple of hundred yards short of William Creek; other times it'd chug to a halt a couple of hundred yards a bit further on. Though, such was the genius of these fettlers that, nine times out of ten, the section car would come to a halt pretty much on the spot, right outside William Creek. So, when it'd arrive, the publican would grab a couple of his mates and they'd go over and turn the section car around. Then they'd load it up with the grog order, refill the tank from the spare fuel can, take the money, start it up again and away she'd go, back to Beresford Siding, where the fettlers would be eagerly awaiting its arrival – personal delivery. Brilliant. I mean, something like that could only happen in Australia, ay?

Footnote – William Creek is approximately nine hundred kilometres north-north-west of Adelaide. It has a population of ten and is said to be 'the gateway to Lake Eyre, in the Tirari Desert'. John McDouall Stuart named William Creek during his 1859 exploration: William being a son of a pioneer South Australian pastoralist friend and co-sponsor of Stuart's many exhibitions. Due to the expansion of the Great Northern Railway – now known as The Ghan – a small settlement rose out of the dust and a boarding house, along with James Jagoe's Eating House, was established in 1886. As larger railway work parties arrived, Henry Lane was granted a 'wine licence' for the site in 1890.

In 1896, William Creek became a repeater station on the Overland Telegraph line. In 1925 an extension was built onto the hotel to include a post and telegraph office and by 1935 the hotel provided accommodation. During the 1940s, the Old Telegraph Line was upgraded, linking William Creek Hotel to the national telephone network. During the 1960s, railways maintenance was centralised at William Creek and, in 1970, a town water supply installed. William Creek is on the traditional home of the Arabana people who, in 2012, were granted native title to more than 68,000 square kilometres of land in the region.

The world's largest cattle station, Anna Creek, is nearby, as is the prohibited-entry Woomera Rocket Range. A warning to all outback travellers can be found in William Creek's Memorial Park where there's a commemorative to a young Austrian woman who lost her life in 1998 trying to walk back to William Creek from a four-wheel-drive vehicle that had been bogged beside Lake Eyre. William Creek is serviced twice weekly by the Coober Pedy–Oodnadatta One Day Mail Run. The Run also carries some general freight and some passengers. The town has never been larger than a few cottages, a small school and a hotel-store.

William Creek Hotel is one of the world's most remote pubs and is on the South Australian Heritage Register. It serves a welcoming cold beer and good pub-grub. For the more adventurous, author Bill 'Swampy' Marsh suggests a crack at their famous Rogan Josh Goat Curry.

Wyalkatchem – WA

In memory of Bernard Arrantash.

One of the things I most enjoy about small towns is their characters. During research into my father, Anglican Parish Rector, Reverend Reginald 'Reg' Arrantash, I interviewed a woman from Wyalkatchem, in the central Wheatbelt region of Western Australia. As it turned out, my father had saved her life. The woman's name was Mrs Phil Hutchinson. Now, I'm not sure if the Phil came from Philomena or whatever but, when I interviewed her back in December 2012, she'd just celebrated her ninety-ninth birthday.

Phil was born in the United Kingdom. When she was a young girl she migrated with her family to Korrelocking, which is fifteen kilometres east of Wyalkatchem, where her father got work on a farm. She remembered how her family was met at Wyalkatchem Railway Station by someone carrying two buckets of water. When asked what the water was for, the reply went along the lines of, 'God only knows when we'll get more rain out here.' Apparently, conditions were so dry that bulk water was delivered to the district by train, then transported to homes via horse and cart/buggy and, in some cases, by hand.

Phil's family then camped on the farm at Korrelocking before taking up their own property, Wyalla Farm, which was six miles south of Wyalkatchem. She remembered the tough life they experienced during the Depression years of the 1930s. Her father, in particular, suffered physically through the hard manual farm labour and she remembered him having to lift heavy sacks of wheat up onto wagons and trucks and stacking them. But whatever the cause, her father died at the age of fifty-one. This left Phil's mother to run the farm and, although her mother supported the church on social occasions and for fundraising, this was the days before cars, and, along with working the farm, the distance into town on rough dirt roads meant church attendance was irregular.

Distance and farm work were also the reasons why Phil rarely attended school. If she walked, she'd hardly ever come across anyone else on the road and, because of her home chores and the distance to school, she'd usually arrive an hour or so late and would also be late getting home – often missing out on dinnertime. If the farm horse and buggy was ever available, she remembered the horse having to be tethered and fed at a tree in the schoolyard, along with the other students' horses. She also recalled how Sid Baster, the town butcher, had about eight horses, which he let roam free around the town. Phil told me how Sid's horses had the habit of arriving at school just in time to score a free feed of hay.

With distance and transport being such a restriction, Phil didn't get to see the ocean until she was twelve. That was when she was sent to Perth, where she had her only two years of continuous schooling. Although, unfortunately, because she'd missed most of her elementary education, the city students continually teased, threatened and bullied her. She said, 'They made me feel such a dunce that I cried and cried.' On one occasion they pushed her over the back of Crawley Baths into Matilda Bay and, with Phil never having learnt to swim, she almost drowned.

After her return to Wyalkatchem, Phil married a Scotsman named Tom Hutchison. That was in December 1940. So she would've been around eighteen. Their wedding was held in St Saviour's Anglican Church, an old timber structure that had earlier been brought by rail to Wyalkatchem from Kanowna.

My father, Reverend Reg Arrantash, conducted the wedding ceremony. Phil remembered their wedding day as being extremely hot, with a huge dust storm, and that Tom was dressed in his army uniform. From what I can piece together, their wedding must've occurred during Tom's pre-embarkation leave because, to Phil's mind, he almost immediately went off to war. Tom then served overseas, in the Middle East, then later in New Guinea, during the Kokoda campaign. Phil recalls a very worrying time when she received news that Tom was posted as 'missing' – which later proved incorrect.

During the war years, Phil proved herself to be a capable, self-taught seamstress who helped local families when war rationing restricted the availability of clothes. She also remembered how tea, biscuits and other foods were rationed and that the farm was only allocated two gallons – less than ten litres – of petrol per month. Thankfully, they had cows on the farm and she sold whatever extra milk and cream they had, which provided a little extra income. For many years, Phil was a member of Red Cross and, during the war years, she cooked for and packaged food parcels to send to the soldiers. She also donated items that she'd made to raise funds in support of the church and Wyalkatchem Hospital. For entertainment during those war years, films were shown in the town's hotel gardens and there were occasional dances.

When there was fear of Japanese air attacks on Perth, people were evacuated by train, out into many country areas of Western Australia, including Wyalkatchem, where they were taken in by locals. Some of these city folk later chose to stay in the bush and carve out their own rural lives. There was no telephone connected to Phil's farm and, to preserve fresh meat, she used to hang it in a bag on the clothesline overnight, where it'd catch a cooler breeze. She fondly remembered when the farm got its first Coolgardie safe, which made food preservation and storage a little better.

When Phil's husband, Tom, returned from war, like many, he suffered from health problems. While he'd been overseas, he'd contracted malaria and he'd also got some sort of skin rash. Phil told me how he'd sometimes apply methylated spirits to the rash, in an attempt to reduce the tormenting itch. It also appears that, due to the horrors of those war years, Tom became a bit too fond of a tipple and he later died. After Tom's death, with family support, Phil continued on at the farm. However, when the land went salty, the family decided it should be sold. As she confided in me. 'When they did, they sold a bit of me with it.'

Previous to all this, at the time of the birth of one of her sons, Phil fell seriously ill in the old Wyalkatchem Hospital. The doctor was Dr Orton. Anyhow, a call went out to the town that blood for a life-saving transfusion was urgently needed. From those who responded, only one, my father, Reverend Reg Arrantash, had the blood group required. So blood was transferred from my father to Phil, and, at this point in our conversation, she looked me straight in the eye and, with quivering lips, said, 'Your father saved my life.'

And so, after all these decades, the paths of us two Wyalkatchem folk – Phil Hutchinson and myself, Bernard Arrantash, the son of Rector Reverend Reginald 'Reg' Arrantash – crossed, and I've been able to tell this story.

Footnote – Wyalkatchem is a hundred and ninety kilometres east-north-east of Perth, with a population of less than five hundred. The town's name is a mystery. One story goes that it was named after an Aboriginal trooper called 'Wylie' and, because he was wily and good at catching criminals, the town's name was adapted from 'Wylie-catch-'em'. A second, and more plausible story, goes that it's an adaptation of an Aboriginal name for a waterhole, spelt *walkatching*. The change of spelling to Walcatching was used in 1881, when the Toodyay Road Board referred to a tank – dam – to be built there. Then, in 1892, when the road from Northam to Yilgarn Goldfield was surveyed, the spelling Wyalcatchem – with a 'c' in 'catchem' – was used. The switch from Wyalcatchem – with the 'c' – to Wyalkatchem – with a 'k'

– was made in 1911 when the town began to develop. The Shire Council of Wyalkatchem was founded in 1920.

In the early 1930s, for a more efficient removal of the abundant grain crop, a pair of engine-driven grain elevators were installed at the Wyalkatchem railway siding. The town won the state tidy town award in 2000 and again in 2002, then won the national award in 2003. In 2012, a bio-blitz was held in a bush reserve between Korrelocking and Wyalkatchem where fifty-four people collected samples of scorpions, pseudoscorpions, isopods, spiders and centipedes, including some new species.

The Wyalkatchem Hotel is described as being a 'simple honest pub' providing cold beer, good 'grub' and company.

Zanthus – WA

In memory of Elsie Jackson, Alfred 'Alf' Harris and Nancy 'Madge' Harris.

Elsie Jackson's Story: My husband, Mick, was a fettler on the railways. So I think it was around 1956 when we went out on the Transcontinental Line. At that time, Parkeston, which is just out of Kalgoorlie, in Western Australia, and Port Augusta, South Australia, were the two main Commonwealth Railways centres. So they both had big stores where you could do all your shopping. First, we travelled by train from Perth to Parkeston. Then, because they'd lost all our furniture on the journey up from Perth, we had to stay out at Karonie with my husband's sister. We were then stranded at Karonie for a week while they searched for our furniture. Once that'd been sorted, we got on a goods train and headed out to Zanthus. And oh, I remember arriving at Zanthus at about three in the morning and only seeing six little houses, sitting out in the middle of nowhere. And I can tell you, coming from a big city like Perth, that was a real shock.

As it turned out, Zanthus wasn't the most barren or isolated place out along the Nullarbor. At least there were peppercorn trees along the railway line and there was a small rest house for the crews for when they were changing trains. The railway houses were constructed of weatherboard. But there were no floor coverings or anything and we had an old thunderbox toilet down the backyard. They're the ones where you did your business in a can and, when the can was full, it was taken out bush and emptied. As for our water supply, once a week the Tea and Sugar train brought in water-gins, which were big tankers that they'd drop off in the railway yard, and we'd get our water from there. That water was used for bathing and cleaning, and so forth. We also had rainwater tanks but, because it rarely rained, we only used the rainwater for making tea and so forth.

There was also a small, one-teacher school in Zanthus and I remember how the government issued the school with liquid Ideal Milk. Ideal Milk was an unsweetened milk that came in tins and, at ten o'clock each school morning, the teacher would dish it out to the pupils. And because Zanthus didn't have a hotel, if there was a party or something, the men had to send in an order to Kalgoorlie and the beer would come out in huge crates. I can't remember how many beer bottles were in each crate, but every bottle was individually wrapped in straw to protect it from being broken. That's how precious the beer was. I mean, some of the other gangs, like at Coonana and places like that, brewed their own beer. And, my oh my, it was powerful stuff. When they got stuck into it, you'd be certain of a disastrous weekend. I remember one story that went around how, after one of their dogs had got stuck into their homemade beer, it crawled off into a corner, laid down, placed its paws over its snout ... and that's where it stayed for a week, suffering through a devil of a hangover.

Anyhow, all that aside: of a morning, when the men went out to work on the track, us women – the wives and partners of the fettlers – would get together and have a cup of coffee or a cup of tea and a cigarette. Those days I was a smoker. Most of us were, and we'd meet at someone's house or just out in the yard. Our houses had big front yards, large enough for a dusty old playground. And also, some of the women might get together to sew or mend their families' clothes. Then, just before the men knocked off at about four, we'd go home and get a cup of tea ready for them, for as soon as they walked in. Then we'd cook dinner and, with Zanthus not having any electricity, it was quite a ritual how, every night, we'd light up all our tilly lamps.

For cooking, we had a wood stove and, because the Tea and Sugar train came on a Thursday, we'd always have a big cook-up on the Friday. See, each week we'd give our supply order to the ganger, who'd ring it through to the railway stores at either Parkeston or Port Augusta. And most times too, on the Wednesday, the day before the Tea and Sugar train arrived, us women would get together and share what we had left. You know, somebody might have some flour, another one might have an egg, so we'd make pancakes. Things like that. It was very communal.

Oh, and another thing – talking about food – we had a family of German fettlers who'd go out spotlighting and sometimes shoot a camel. Anyhow, attached to all our houses was a big long sleep-out, covered in with fly-wire. So they'd skin this camel and hang it up in the sleep-out. And oh, the blowflies. I don't know how they found their way into the sleep-out but, oh, you've never seen so many blowies in your entire life. And they'd hang this blessed camel up till it got a greenish film on it, then they'd skin the green film off and cut the animal up and put it in their kerosene fridge.

Anyhow, the only music we had was a wireless and an old wind-up gramophone. We only had a few records, the likes of Bing Crosby, Louis Armstrong and all those real oldies. I've still got a couple of them, though, believe me, they're pretty worn out. And on the weekends all us ladies would do a bit of cooking and all the families would get together and share the food. And if anyone had musical instruments, we'd have a bit of a dance or maybe a sing-along. I still remember the time we had an Aboriginal family come in from Cundeelee Mission with a guitar and, oh, they had beautiful voices. Just beautiful.

Cundeelee Mission was quite near Zanthus and so we'd occasionally go up there in the back of a truck to visit the people who were running the mission and go to church. They accepted any denomination. It was all pretty casual. You'd see the Aboriginal mums sitting in church feeding their babies. And oh, when our kids first saw the babies suckling on their mothers' breasts, their eyes just about popped out of their heads. It was hilarious. But conditions out that way were quite unchanged. We'd often see Aboriginal people walking about out bush with their spears and that, hunting for food.

Our school kids also used to visit the other railway camp-schools along the track, for sports days. A train would bring in a special carriage with water and a kitchen, and we'd go and live in that while the kids did their running and jumps, bike riding and all those sorts of things. The kids really enjoyed it. Nursing sisters would also come out on the Tea and Sugar to check the children and any of us adults over. Even Father Christmas came out on the Tea and Sugar train. Oh, the Tea and Sugar train, it was a very special train. It stopped at all the sidings across the Nullarbor with supplies and that. I mean, we didn't go without too much. The Tea and Sugar was our lifeline, really; the thing that linked us all together.

But I must say, the Commonwealth Railways were very good in emergencies. They always made sure something was done. I was in charge of the Flying Doctor medical kit so, if a child got sick or if anybody got hurt, they'd first come to me and I'd try to patch them up. Then, if they were too bad, they'd catch a train into Kalgoorlie to see a doctor. I didn't have any of the proper certificates or anything. The only nursing I'd done was maternity nursing: which reminds me, one time the office in Port Augusta rang and asked if I'd join the next goods train coming through because there was a woman on it who was having a miscarriage. So I did that, and I accompanied her into Kalgoorlie. She was the wife of one of the fettlers, back down the line. However, she unfortunately lost the baby, which was very sad. Then after she came home, she wrote me a very nice note, thanking me for all my help. The railway people were good like that. So there you go, we were at Zanthus for two or three years, sharing all those sorts of experiences with the other six families and their children.

* * *

Alf Harris' Story: I'm coming up to seventy-six and I'm determined to continue to make everyone's life as miserable as possible for at least another twenty-four years. That's my goal. Anyway, I was born in Adelaide and, virtually straight away, we went to live out on the east–west railway line. My father was the ganger, in charge of a railway maintenance gang. To start with we were just out from Tarcoola, at what they called the old 298 Mile. We were there for a few years, then we went out to Zanthus. That's where I went to school – Zanthus. A lot of people say to me, 'Hey, Alf, where did yer go to school?'

And I puff out me chest and I say, 'Zanthus Tech.'

'Oh, geez,' they say, 'you must'a had a good education, then.'

'Too right I did,' I say, and leave it at that.

See, they don't realise that Zanthus was a bloody little tin-pot place, out in the middle of nowhere, a hundred and thirty-seven mile east of Kalgoorlie. Although, I might add, it's the prettiest little railway siding on the east–west line, with big gum trees, the lot.

Now, I'm not sure how many people were living there back in the early '40s. But I do know there were seventeen of us school kids. Although, in saying that, you've got to remember that some of the families had half a dozen kids. And the whole time we were there, apart from your usual sorts of scraps, there was never any real big arguments – neither between families or us kids. Us kids mucked about amongst ourselves very happily. We even went out, twenty-five mile north, and played with the Aboriginal kids from Cundeelee Mission. And occasionally they'd come in and join in with us, and there were never any problems.

But from as far back as I can remember, I always loved trains. Always. And at Zanthus, when they used to do shunting, the crews would give us kids a ride on the train around the triangle. And like, they'd show us how to stoke the fire and all that. Oh, they were wonderful. Although there was one incident when 'the fit hit the shan'. Now, you know how there's always a 'Dennis the Menace' in every place. Well, out of the seventeen of us school kids, that was me. And then there was a particular mate of mine, Donny Mitchell. Donny was a bit of a Dennis the Menace too. We were both about eight and, if anything happened in the camp, we'd be the first suspects. What's more, more often than not, we were usually guilty as charged.

Anyhow, this particular day, a bullion train stopped at Zanthus on its way through. Back then, old Kiwi Walters was the stationmaster. Of course, every train that came through was a big occasion. Although, with this being a bullion train, it was an even bigger occasion than usual. Of course, all us kids went down to see this train arrive. Anyhow, three or four armed guards had got out of a carriage and they were hanging about on the platform. So me and Donny, we started asking them about what sort of guns they had and how much bullion was on the train, and if they'd ever been robbed and how many robbers they'd shot dead and all that stuff. So they're sitting there with their guns, very relaxed, chatting away to us, when I had a thought. I said to Donny, 'Hey, Donny, come with me.'

'Okay,' he said, and so we went down to what's called the trolley shed. The trolley shed was where my father kept his section car and all the maintenance gear. And also, it was where all the detonators were kept; you know, those explosive things they use to put on the railway tracks as a warning device. So Donny and me, we got four detonators and we went back to the train. But instead of going up the platform side, we crept along the other side of the train – the blind side – where nobody could see us. Then we placed these detonators under the wheels of the bullion train. Next thing, old Kiwi Walters blows his whistle and gives the right-of-way and, as the train starts to move – *Bang! Bang! Bang! Bang!* off goes these detonators.

Holy Mackerel! The bloody train screeched to a halt. Next thing all these armed guards were crawling out of windows and jumping out of doors. We didn't know there were so many of them guarding this bullion train. But there were. Guns were aimed left, right and centre, all over the bloody place. And poor old Kiwi Walters, the stationmaster, he'd ducked so fast back into his office that he'd banged hisself on the door and nearly broke his arm.

'Bloody hell,' I said to Donny. 'We'd better get out'a here.'

See, I just thought it'd be a bit of a joke and that these armed guard fellers would know the difference between an exploding detonator and a hold-up gun. But apparently not. So Donny and me, we took off out bush. Then after the train had finally left, they did a round up of all the kids. And of course, when they done the count there was two missing, wasn't there? Me and Donny. And that's how they found out who the culprits were. Anyhow, with my father being a very strict man, I got a hell of a hiding and I was sent to bed without me dinner. But then, later that night, I heard all the men yarning over a few beers in our kitchen and, oh, they were laughing and going on about it all. Oh, they thought it was a hell of a joke.

Footnote – Zanthus is a remote, uninhabited siding on the Trans-Australian Railway line, approximately two hundred kilometres east of Kalgoorlie and eight hundred and fifty kilometres from Perth. The name Zanthus comes from the Latin name for Western Australia's floral state emblem, the kangaroo paw flower. Due to its name, Zanthus also has notoriety as being last on the list of Western Australian placenames.

In 1915, when the Trans-Australian Railway was being built, a depot was set up at Zanthus, where trains unloaded materials from Kalgoorlie. The line opened in 1917 and Zanthus had a triangle for shunting and a crossing loop: a crossing loop being a separate section of rail track where one train pulls off the main line to allow another, that's coming from the opposite direction, to pass.

During World War Two, Trans-Australian Railway was the main east–west route for Australian troops. Zanthus has not been without incident. In 1948, due to flooding, the train got stranded there and several passengers were flown to Kalgoorlie. A derailment occurred in 1953, when five coaches of the eastbound express left the tracks and tore up a section of the line. The 1975 aftermath of Cyclone Trixie also caused a line closure. In 1999, the Indian Pacific passenger train accidentally collided head-on with a stationary steel train, when both were mistakenly diverted through the cross loop. On that occasion, the RFDS airlifted twenty-one injured passengers to Kalgoorlie. One carriage was a write-off and remains on site at Zanthus. The original stationmaster's cabin is now on display at Bassendean Rail Museum in Perth.

MORE GREAT AUSTRALIAN STORIES FROM BILL 'SWAMPY' MARSH

*The term 'Bible bashing' took on new meaning in our household.
Not so much for its reading, though God certainly remained
high on Mum's spiritual priorities, but more for its treatment
of bunions, chilblains, corns, etc. Mum suffered from bunions
until she started bashing them with the heavy family Bible,
believing the Lord's weight behind the Lord's word could
move anything from mountains to bunions.*

More Great Australian Outback Yarns includes many of the
most memorable tales from Swampy's collections. The colourful
characters in these pages capture the generosity, humour and
laconic quality that bring to life the heart and soul
of outback Australia.

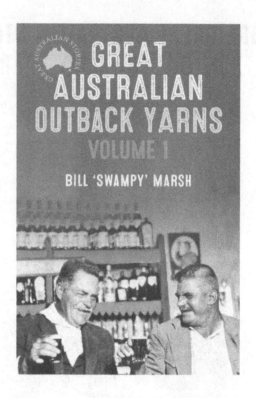

GREAT AUSTRALIAN OUTBACK YARNS
VOLUME 1

BILL 'SWAMPY' MARSH

The Australian Outback can be harsh, but it's the kind of place where you either learn to laugh off your troubles or fold under the pressure.

Bill 'Swampy' Marsh has a deep affection and respect for people living in the Australian Bush, and he's spent more than twenty years travelling to every corner of our wide brown land, talking to people from all walks of life, collecting their memories and stories.

Great Australian Outback Yarns captures the funniest tales from Swampy's many books in one volume. The colourful characters in these pages are full of generosity, humour and a larrikin Aussie spirit. These true stories of life in remote and regional Australia from Australia's master storyteller will leave you grinning from ear to ear.

GREAT AUSTRALIAN AMBOS STORIES

BILL 'SWAMPY' MARSH

Yeah, while some of my stories are quite gory, others can be very enlightening. Though, in hindsight, the best outcomes are when the patient pulls through. It's then that you know you've done your job, and you get a bit of a buzz out of that.

Put the sirens on and get ready to hit the road, because fact is stranger than fiction in this fabulous Australia-wide collection of ambos stories from bestselling author Bill 'Swampy' Marsh.

Rural and remote ambulance drivers and paramedics are a dedicated and gutsy bunch who work tirelessly to care for their communities, often in isolated and inhospitable conditions, with few resources.

This memorable and eye-opening collection of real-life accounts of professionals and volunteers alike racing by road, air and water to save people in strife is by turns poignant, bizarre, heartbreaking and hilarious.

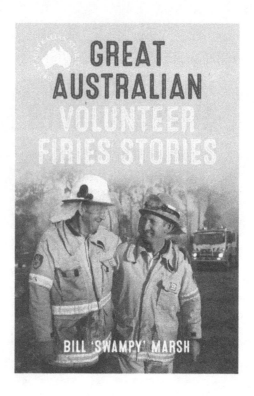

GREAT AUSTRALIAN VOLUNTEER FIRIES STORIES

BILL 'SWAMPY' MARSH

The devastating 2019–2020 Black Summer bushfires threw the importance of our volunteer firefighters into sharp focus. But these brave men and women don't just step up to protect life and property in fires; they are also there to help in road accidents, plane crashes, natural disasters like cyclones and floods – and, yes, they even rescue pets that have got themselves into strife.

In this collection of first-hand stories, ranging from the 1880s to 2020, our courageous volunteer firies take us right up to the frontlines and reveal the stark realities of the dangers they face to keep our communities safe.

This book serves as a tribute to the thousands of volunteer firies across Australia who roll up their sleeves and selflessly put their lives on the line to assist their fellow human beings.

GREAT
AUSTRALIAN
OUTBACK
TRUCKING STORIES
BILL 'SWAMPY' MARSH

Whether they're carting produce, stock, fuel, or even (unbeknown to them) dead bodies, there's one thing that can be said about outback truckies – they're a colourful bunch.

Meet the outback truckies who brave interminable distances, searing heat, raging floodwaters and foot-deep bulldust to transport goods all across this vast land, serving as lifelines not just to those in the bush but those in cities as well.

From the truckie who found a creative means of transporting penguins, to the one who refused to 'abandon ship' as his truck sank into a river, these real-life accounts show the lengths to which these enterprising and resourceful men and women will go to ensure their load arrives safely at their destination.

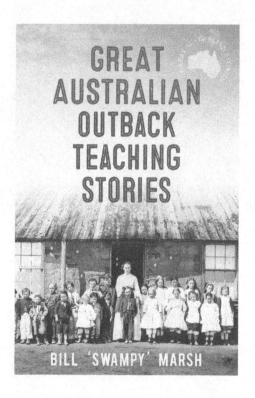

GREAT AUSTRALIAN OUTBACK TEACHING STORIES

BILL 'SWAMPY' MARSH

From beyond the black stump to the Australian Alps; in schools on stations, missions, mines and over the air, it takes a special kind of person to be an outback teacher.

Back then, not only did we have to teach the three Rs but also sewing, arts and craft, music, physical education - you name it. Plus there were the duties of gardener, cleaner, nurse, registrar, office administrator, free milk dispenser, librarian and, on occasions, school bus driver. Oh, and in one school I was even responsible for 'mother craft'. And being male and just nineteen, as I was at the time, you might imagine my surprise when a young girl asked me, 'Sir, what's the best milk for babies?'

Master storyteller Bill 'Swampy' Marsh has travelled the width and breadth of Australia to meet with many of our extraordinary outback teachers and their students whose recollections so perfectly capture those special days of growing up in the bush.